EVE

DAVID W. ROBERTS

Published in Australia by Sid Harta Books & Print Pty Ltd,
ABN: 34632585293
23 Stirling Crescent, Glen Waverley, Victoria 3150 Australia
Telephone: +61 3 9560 9920 E-mail: author@sidharta.com.au

First published in Australia 2021
This edition published 2022
Copyright © David W. Roberts 2021

Cover design, typesetting: WorkingType (www.workingtype.com.au)
Typeset in Alegreya 11/18

The right of David W. Roberts to be identified as the Author of the Work has been asserted in accordance with the Copyright, Designs and Patents Act 1988.

All rights reserved. No part of this publication may be reproduced, stored in a retrieval system, or transmitted, in any form or by any means without the prior written permission of the publisher, nor be otherwise circulated in any form of binding or cover other than that in which it is published and without a similar condition being imposed on the subsequent purchaser.

Roberts, David W.
Eve
ISBN: 978-1-925707-60-1
pp444

ABOUT THE AUTHOR

David Roberts migrated as a qualified teacher from the United Kingdom. After seventeen years working as a teacher, deputy principal and principal in country New South Wales, he became a university academic. University appointments and consultancies enabled David to travel widely and broaden his horizons. Now retired, he lives with his wife in Adelaide. This is the author's fourth book. Earlier books include *One Thing Leads to Another*, *Easytimes* and *Graham's Story*.

*In memory of Mary Evelyn Dillon
(nee Chadwick) known as Eve (1908-1987)*

FOREWORD

This is the story of Eve, an English woman, who lived during the turbulent years of the twentieth century. Born into a working-class family, Eve determined early in life to do whatever was necessary to lift herself out of her working-class origins by marrying well and above her station. Blessed with good looks and a vivacious personality, she was largely successful, but along the way endured a number of crises, some of which were of her own making.

Upwardly mobile girls, like Eve, were not uncommon in twentieth century Britain. What makes this story special, however, is that it is largely true. Wherever possible, the author has carefully researched Eve's story. Eve never achieved fame;

she was just one of the many enterprising, ambitious young women of her time seeking a better life through marriage.

Born in 1908, Eve's life was seriously impacted by the two World Wars and the Great Depression. These catastrophic events provided an unsettling backdrop to her personal story.

Some parts of Eve's story are well-documented in newspapers, journals, photographs, books and historical records. Sadly, there are also major gaps in Eve's story, and where these exist, I have attempted to imagine what she was experiencing. The book is, therefore, partly authentic and partly fiction. It could be described as a historical novel.

I hope you enjoy travelling with Eve on her journey.

LIST OF ILLUSTRATIONS

Front Cover: Eve, aged 18. (Photo donated by Ted Knights)

1. Holland Villas, Bilsborough, Eve's birthplace in 1908. (Photo taken by the author in 2012)
2. John Cross School, Bilsborough, Eve's first school. (Photo taken by the author in 2012)
3. Saint Lawrence Anglican Church, Barton, where Eve was christened. (Photo taken by the author in 2012)
4. Tulketh Cotton Mill, Preston. (Photo taken by the author in 2012)
5. Street of typical tenements in Preston. (Photo taken by the author in 2012)
6. 195 Tulketh Brow, Eve's family home in Preston. (Photo taken by the author in 2012)

7. The marriage of Captain Thomas Dillon to Mary Evelyn Chadwick, November 24th, 1926. (Photo taken by the Lancashire Daily Post)
8. Michael Dillon, aged 11. (Photo donated by Michael Dillon)
9. Captain 'Freddy' Drummond circa 1939. (Photo donated by Ted Knights)
10. 'Freddy' as the Transport Officer at Marsabit in 1939. (Photo donated by Army Personnel Centre)
11. KAR Askaris commanded by 'Freddy' in Kenya. (Photo donated by Army Personnel Centre)
12. The environs of Moyale in July 1940. (Map taken from Colonel Moyse-Bartlett's book)
13. 'Freddy's' temporary grave at Moyale July 10th, 1940. (Photo taken from *The Green Tiger*)

CHAPTER ONE

Bilsborough, February 1911

Mrs Annie Beatrice Chadwick was the only one in the family to hear the ringing of the 'wake-up' bell from across the way. Unsurprisingly, having given birth to three children in five years, she was acutely attuned to any sounds that demanded her attention, both in and out of the house. During the night it was usually one of the children calling out, but early in the morning, six days a week, it was the 'wake-up' bell clanging imperiously from nearby Bilsborough Hall Farm that penetrated her sleep.

It had been a bitterly cold night but eerily quiet. The children had slept peacefully throughout and her husband's snoring had been pleasantly muted. Now she dug him in the ribs with her elbow hard enough to produce a muffled groan followed by an incoherent grumble.

'Gotta get up love, bell's gone.'

George Brady Chadwick, head of the household, stuck his whiskered visage cautiously out from under the blankets and squinted reluctantly at his wife who was already out of bed and placed a grey woollen shawl around her shoulders. Padding over to the window, Annie pulled back the thin curtains to peer outside at the insipid pre-dawn gloom.

'Snowed last night George, backyards covered. Rug up well.'

Clambering out of his snug bed, George reflected on the one advantage of being a farm labourer in wintertime: the days were blessedly short. Daylight was insufficient for any outside work until around eight in the morning and by four in the afternoon it was virtually dark again. An eight-hour working day was all his boss could expect at this time of year. Today the 'wake-up' bell had woken the Bilsborough Hall farm labourers, scattered about the neighbourhood at seven in the morning, and they were expected to report for duty punctually by eight.

George was barely thirteen when first employed at Bilsborough Hall Farm and over fifteen years had become one of their most trusted, reliable and knowledgeable labourers. So much so, that when he and Annie married in February 1905, he was offered one of the four flats available in Holland Villas especially erected in 1900 for selected married labourers working at Bilsborough Hall farm. Their two-storey apartment consisted of four rooms: a kitchen and living room downstairs and two good-sized bedrooms above. The toilet was in the backyard. George and Annie and their two children, Annie Isabel (known as Bell) and Mary Evelyn (known as Eve, but pronounced *'Evee'*) slept together in the larger bedroom and the other bedroom was occupied by Annie's sister-in-law, Alice Houghton, and her nine-year-old son, William.

Holland Villas, Bilsborough, Eve's birthplace in 1908. (Photo taken by the author in 2012)

George dressed hurriedly, trotted downstairs, and with some difficulty shoved open the backdoor that led out to the toilet. The heavy snow overnight had drifted up against the back wall of Holland Villas and covered the ground to a depth of six inches to a foot. An icy blast of a northerly wind smacked him in the face as he shivered his way down to the small wooden building in the backyard. It was going to be a brute of a day!

Returning to the relative warmth of the kitchen, George was pleased to see Alice had risen earlier, stoked the fire and was already well into making the porridge. Annie squatted close to the fire holding the three-pronged toaster with a hefty chunk of rye bread attached. A slab of creamy butter together with a large pot of thick honey waited expectantly on the kitchen table.

'Won't be long, love. Better go wake the children. There's school today. Bring Eve down here, I've got her clothes warming.'

George headed back up the stairs to wake William first with a firm warning to put on his warmest gear. Bell and Eve, who shared a single bed, were predictably, not happy about leaving their snug nest. Bell was five and had started school only two months earlier. It was William's special responsibility each school day to safely escort Bell to John Cross School located in the village less than half a mile away. There was only one teacher at John Cross and on a good weather day about sixty children attended. Today, being bitterly cold and snowy, the numbers would be well down. Children who had to walk two or three miles or more to school, or rode their ponies in from the many small farms scattered about the district, would have difficulties making the journey.

After breakfast, on hearing the 'ten-minute bell' clanging across the snow-covered landscape, George reluctantly exited via the front door. He was soon joined by the three other farm labourers who resided at Holland Villas and together they

Chapter One Bilsborough, February 1911

trudged along Bilsborough Lane towards the farm. It was snowing heavily again and large goose-feathered flakes floated and fell steadily around them. George was always intrigued at how heavy snow, like a thick fog, dampened all sound. From above, the four men looked like dark blobs moving slowly and silently to their destination through a plane of whiteness. The gate leading into the farmyard at Bilsborough Hall was a mere four hundred yards from Holland Villas, normally a five-minute walk, but twice that time was needed today as they negotiated drifts and high-stepped their way through the deepening snow.

John Cross School, Bilsborough, Eve's first school.
(Photo taken by the author in 2012)

The four labourers were pleased to assemble at the blacksmith's forge where, for a short time, they could enjoy the warmth from the fiery coals. The stern-faced farm manager awaited them there, puffing quietly on his pipe. There were twelve farm labourers on the manager's books, but it was soon apparent that only ten had fronted up that day. Arriving late meant a day without pay, unless you could convince the manager of mitigating circumstances. Heavy snow had never been deemed an acceptable excuse for absence from work in the fifteen years George had laboured at Bilsborough Hall.

The likelihood of the snow lasting all day had necessitated a revision of the day's tasks. Two men were assigned to mucking out the stables, and the two most recent additions to the workforce were to clear the snow drifts from the paths and main tracks surrounding the buildings and to do whatever they could to rescue plants in the kitchen gardens groaning under the weight of the snow. The manager took pity on the two oldest workers, now in their fifties, and assigned them special duties indoors. George and the remaining three labourers were sent out into the fields to continue work on the construction of a drystone wall that would eventually encircle a new piggery planned for spring. George, as the most experienced of the four, was placed in charge.

An hour after George had left for work, nine-year-old William Houghton took hold of Bell's bare hand as they emerged from Holland Villas and headed for John Cross School. The snowstorm had eased and visibility had improved. A few villagers had already tramped along the lane towards the village so the children were able to use their footprints to make the walking a little easier, especially for Bell, who at times seemed to almost disappear in the snowdrifts.

Chapter One   Bilsborough, February 1911

Both children were coping surprisingly well at school, despite the extraordinarily difficult educational circumstances. With the best will in the world, one woman teaching up to sixty children between the ages of five and twelve is an almost impossible task. Understandably, Miss Bolton ruled with an iron hand and poor behaviour resulted in the frequent use of the cane. The twelve-year-old children acted as assistant teachers and worked with small groups of the younger children. Amazingly, most of the school's graduates left with rudimentary reading and writing skills, and a few even qualified to go to the Grammar School in Preston.

Annie and her sister-in-law Alice dressed and fed little Eve and settled her down with the set of small peg dolls bedecked in clothes sewn by Alice, who perchance, was a dressmaker by trade. With big sister Bell away at school, Eve had quickly learnt this meant she could enjoy the peg dolls undisturbed, for as long as she wanted.

The daily grind of domestic chores soon pervaded the house. Alice unpacked the Singer treadle sewing machine and resumed her work on the wedding dress she was fashioning for the second daughter of the manager up at the farm. It was to be a springtime wedding in early May, and Alice had promised to have the dress ready for a first fitting by the end of March. The work was progressing well.

Annie was preparing rabbit stew for the night's dinner. The night before, when George arrived home, he had come armed with a decent sized rabbit he'd heard squealing in one of his traps out the back. Breaking the rabbit's neck before bringing it indoors, George had proudly slapped the animal down on the kitchen table with a thud and announced, 'dinner tomorrow night.' Annie had already skinned the rabbit and assessed it as being a rather ancient specimen requiring a long, slow cook in the pot. She wouldn't have to go out in the weather for vegetables as she had turnips, potatoes, onions and swedes safely stored indoors. She had no red wine to add to the stew but an assortment of her own dried herbs would add some richness to the flavour.

* * *

On the drystone wall, the men were working in pairs. Two were scouring the fields hunting for suitably sized stones. It was a thankless task, especially with the ground snow-covered. Every five minutes one of them would come struggling over to George at the wall face with their latest find and drop it clumsily nearby. George was the acknowledged expert in the precise placement of the stones to deliver both a durable and aesthetically pleasing result. Nobody else was given this responsibility, although George was now training James, the man who lived next door to him in Holland Villas.

George had for some years been fascinated by stone structures of all kinds. Stone was used everywhere: in the construction of houses, bridges over canals, bridges along railway lines and roads, in cemeteries and even as paving stones. His creative work with drystone walls had further developed this interest and he enjoyed a heightened sense of

Chapter One   Bilsborough, February 1911

satisfaction from slotting the right stone into the right place and later standing back to admire his handiwork. George took great care to select the best large base rocks and paid close attention to the neat finishing of the slanted rocks across the top of his structures. He dreamt of one day earning his ticket to become a properly qualified stone mason.

It was not just the patterning of the stones that appealed to George, there were other attributes of the building material as well. Although he had not been fortunate to travel widely, he realised there were many different kinds of rock and stone, each with its distinctive qualities. Dark basalts were cold and hard to the touch, whereas the lighter sandstones he used in his walls were softer with a greater range of colours. He also loved the grainy feel of the sandstones and siltstones. Then there were the flaky shales and slates that had totally different qualities again.

Dry stone wall building afforded George time to daydream and think of a brighter future for his family. Life as a farm labourer was tough. He was exposed to the elements all year round and was constantly undertaking heavy physical work. His wages were meagre and a proportion of his weekly wage always had to be returned as rental for his lodgings at Holland Villas. He did not want to suffer the maladies of the older men he met about the place who had remained labourers their entire working lives. These men were riddled with arthritis and rheumatism, chilblains and backaches, hacking coughs and, more often than not, had suffered a debilitating accident at some time.

More important than George's future, however, was that of his children. He and Annie had been blessed with two gorgeous, bright girls who might one day wish to seek a life away from the rural parts and live amongst the bright lights of the towns and cities. To give them this opportunity two things had to happen: the family must move into town and the girls must benefit from a grammar school education. George and Annie were also acutely aware that if their girls were to enjoy a better life, they must marry well and that meant marrying above their station.

Annie and George had often spoken together about the future. They were not unhappy as such, but both were ambitious for their offspring. Whereas in the past, if you were born a farm labourer you accepted your lot in life and remained a farm labourer. Some parents dared to think differently nowadays. Undoubtedly, the key to a brighter future for their girls was education. If Bell and Eve could make it to a grammar school at the age of twelve, a whole new world might open up for them.

George and Annie were also realists. They knew how grammar school education systems worked. Each year grammar schools accepted new students into first year who had been successful in the entrance examinations. Places were competitive and highly sought after, with the majority of children never making the grade. Bell and Eve would have hardly had a promising start to their education attending the one-teacher, over-crowded John Cross village school in Bilsborough!

Annie and George were a determined couple, however, and had already decided there were two positive steps they could take to help their daughters with their education. The first

Chapter One Bilsborough, February 1911

was to devote time in the evenings to assist with their reading, writing and arithmetic. Annie, in particular, had done well at school and was smart, so she was sure she could tutor the girls for several years and maybe up to the time they were ready to sit for their grammar school examinations. Annie declared 'practice makes perfect,' was to be the family motto, and they already had chalk and slate boards in readiness together with a few old books to help with reading.

The second part of the plan was far more ambitious. Each week George and Annie put aside a small sum of money which they were saving in order to hire a tutor when the girls were in the last two years of schooling at John Cross. George conscientiously put aside a tenth of his weekly wages and Annie grew bountiful vegetables in the backyard which she sold at Thursday afternoon's market in Bilsborough. Occasionally, when the hens or ducks were being particularly cooperative, Annie added some of their eggs to the market produce as well.

The two sisters, Bell and Eve, got along well enough. As soon as Eve appeared on the scene, Bell assumed the role of the 'senior' sister and never quite let Eve forget it. Bell became the responsible, older sister, serious but caring, well-behaved and polite. Eve, on the other hand, soon developed into a rather different personality. Most of the time she tolerated Bell's slightly bossy attitude towards her, but nevertheless, was quick to rebel if she felt her older sister was going too far. Eve was the cute, pretty one with a mischievous twinkle in her eye. She was more adventurous in spirit, vivacious and possessing a great sense of fun.

During the afternoon it stopped snowing, the icy wind moderated and visibility improved significantly. Glimpses of a weak sun brightened the day and the mood of the workers on the dry wall lifted. For the first time the men began to thaw out. A cheeky robin red breast flitted and twitched about around their wall and the crows in the stand of pine trees nearby began to argue. Way above them all, a sparrow hawk hovered in search of a tasty morsel. The wall had been progressing; slowly but surely.

Not all George's thoughts were about the future, however; at times he became despondent when he recalled a tragedy that had befallen Annie and himself nigh on a year ago. Annie had fallen pregnant a third time, not many months after Eve was born. They had managed to bring two beautiful girls into the world but George, like most men, yearned for a son. It was only natural for a father to long for at least one male offspring.

They had named their first-born Annie Isabel, after her mother, and when a boy came along, he would be called George, after his father. The happy event was in February, a normal birth according to the elderly and experienced midwife. The arrival of little George was a great thrill for the young family and George Senior was said to have grown a foot taller overnight. Now that Annie and George had one of both genders, they intended to stop having any more children so they could give their three young ones the best education and upbringing they possibly could.

Things did not go quite to plan, however. There was a massive storm one night in March: the wind howled mercilessly,

Chapter One Bilsborough, February 1911

trees that had stood a hundred years or more were uprooted and some roofs in the village were damaged. The terrified girls climbed into bed with their parents leaving a much-reduced space for Annie who was downstairs nursing five-week-old baby George. The family stayed together until the storm blew itself out in the early hours of the morning and then returned to their beds. Annie fed and burped George and put him down. He looked sweet and contented.

When she went to him in the morning, he was dead.

George and Annie were not a superstitious couple, but many in the village nodded knowingly. Clearly, they said, it was the devil who had visited them during that horrendous storm!

CHAPTER TWO

Bilsborough 1911–1915

The tragic loss of George Junior was a hard blow for the Chadwick family to bear. The wee baby was perfectly healthy and happy when Annie placed him back in his crib shortly after the storm had passed, and yet, scarcely five hours later, he was cruelly taken from them. Two days later, George was laid to rest in the churchyard of the Anglican Church of Saint Lawrence in the nearby village of Barton. Hundreds of villagers made the journey by foot, horse or cart.

It was not unheard of for seemingly healthy babies to die suddenly in their sleep. Kindly Doctor Stevens, who confirmed the death and signed the death certificate, did his best to console the grieving family but could offer no explanation as to why apparently healthy babies occasionally died unexpectedly overnight. Medical science knew of the phenomenon, he assured them, but Doctor Stevens regretted that, as yet, science had no answers.

Saint Lawrence Anglican Church, Barton, where Eve was christened. (Photo taken by the author in 2012)

Early in 1912, twelve months after the loss of George, Annie fell pregnant again. She had carefully put away George's few belongings in a drawer hoping that she might be able to use them again. Naturally, there was much speculation about the village as to the gender of the child-to-be. Annie was sensible enough to tell everyone she would be more than happy whether it was a boy or a girl, as long as it was healthy, but secretly, and for George's sake, she longed for a boy. More than anything, she wanted to present her husband with a beautiful bonnie lad. There was no doubt which way the father was leaning: a boy was essential to continue the male family line. Bell and Eve both sensed that a brother was what was needed to better balance the family, but to be honest they just wanted a baby to fuss over and play with.

The pregnancy was normal again and the same dependable midwife officiated. There were huge celebrations about the village when it was announced that it was another healthy boy. George and Annie hadn't dared to discuss possible names before the happy event, and even now, they were in two minds. Annie wanted the child to be named George again to honour her loving husband but George Senior was unsure. At the back of his mind, a fear lurked that it might be unlucky to name another child George. The traumatic loss of their first George, only a year ago, still haunted him.

Annie's wishes prevailed, however, and George was the name selected. The new George, like his siblings, was baptised at Saint Lawrence's Anglican Church in Barton.

Throughout 1912 to 1914 George Senior laboured on at the Bilsborough Hall farm. It took another four months to finish the drystone wall project in readiness for the piggery. George was enormously proud of his achievement and was now recognised around the village and its environs as 'the expert'. His boss was so pleased with the final result that he awarded George a small increase in his wages. Even the pigs appreciated their splendid enclosure!

Annie and George never wavered in their ambitious plans for their children. Now that they had *three* extra mouths to feed, they worked even harder to put away ten percent of their earnings for the children's future education. George's excellent reputation as a dry stone waller resulted in him being offered a lucrative contract on the property adjoining Bilsborough Hall farm. He was employed there to construct a wall around the kitchen garden that the new owners had planned. During the long summer days, when he could work until ten o'clock in the evening, George would finish his normal day job, go home for a hot meal and then set off again to work on the kitchen garden wall. The long days were exhausting but the extra income made it worthwhile.

Behind their home at Holland Villas, Annie had steadily extended her vegetable garden. They were blessed with excellent soil to which they added any horse droppings from along the lane. Annie kept an old shovel at the ready and would check every morning to see if any horses had obliged. Two of the farmers along their lane now owned automobiles and the talk in the village was that soon cars would take over, and horses as a mode of transport, would disappear. Annie though, still used the services of old Norman, who lived down their lane with his horse and cart, to take her produce into Bilsborough's market on Thursday afternoons. In return, she let Norman take what vegetables he wanted for the week. Norman, his cart, and the horse were all ancient and rickety and Annie expected one of the three to expire at any time. While Norman kept coming past Annie's house on Thursdays her market sales steadily increased and she too was able to save more money for the children's future education.

The three young Chadwick children got along well most of the time. They had their fights occasionally, like any family group, however, it soon became apparent that all three had inherited their parents' resilience and determination to achieve. At times these energies were not easy to control but George and Annie were thankful that some of their own ambitious ideas and work ethic had rubbed off on their offspring. The children were bright, motivated and competitive, all excellent qualities needed for success in later life. The two girls doted over their young brother and were pleasingly protective of him.

In 1913, when Eve turned five, she joined her big sister attending John Cross School in the village. Eve was way ahead of most of the other pupils that started their education that year because she had benefited from the homework that her mother had been conscientiously doing with Bell over the last three years. The hour or so that Annie had devoted to Bell's studies almost every night was certainly paying off. Bell was perhaps the best reader and speller in her year and already knew her times tables inside out. Simple addition and subtraction were a breeze for her and she was moving on to multiplication sums.

Little Eve had been longing to go to school for a long time and often would sit next to her big sister when she was doing her homework. By some process of osmosis Eve had learnt how to read, a skill that highly intelligent children, given adequate opportunities, will acquire naturally.

When the two girls arrived at school mid-July for the start of the new school year, they were surprised to discover that the elderly teacher who had reigned supreme there for the last fifteen years had suddenly, and without warning, retired, and had been replaced by a much younger lady. The new teacher was more energetic and had different ways of teaching too. The pupils responded well to Miss Taylor and the attendance improved. Singing was introduced and Physical Training (called PT) was conducted twice a week. Most of the parents welcomed Miss Taylor's innovations, although some of the old timers in the village snorted derisively at the introduction of 'silly' subjects like singing and PT.

Both girls thrived under Miss Taylor's tutelage so that in the evenings Annie had two highly motivated children eager to learn as much as she could give them. Annie had only stayed at school herself until she was twelve but she had been a gifted scholar and had made the most of her short education. Passing on her limited knowledge was a joy for her but she knew Bell, in another year or so, would need someone better qualified. If Bell was to make it to high school in Preston, the nearest big town, she would need to be challenged with work that was beyond what Annie could provide.

* * *

Britain declared war on Germany on August 4th, 1914 and the 'war to end all wars' commenced. Volunteers throughout the British Empire answered the call to arms and enlisted. George was deemed to be undertaking work of national importance helping to supply the nation with vital food supplies so was not required to sign up. Many believed the war would be over by Christmas anyway.

Over the years George had developed a trusted, friendly, but respectful relationship, with the farm manager at Bilsborough Hall Farm. Mr James had always been supportive of George and his young family and occasionally went out of his way to do something special to assist. It might be a few spare vegetables from his kitchen garden, a basket of Cox's Pippins from the orchard or the loan of a particular tool. If there was serious illness in the Chadwick household, Mr James paid for the local doctor to call, and he had been known to even help cover the cost of any prescribed medicines.

Sometimes, after work during the long summer evenings, Mr James would invite George to stay back and share an ale. They would sit outside somewhere and enjoy each other's company. As a result of these informal conversations, the manager became increasingly aware of George and Annie's ambitions for their children and came to realise that at some point in time George would most likely resign and depart for Preston where far greater educational opportunities were available. He certainly didn't want to lose the services of George who was almost his longest-serving and perhaps most effective hard-working labourer.

Mr James was a confirmed bachelor nudging sixty and occupied the extensive old farm house on the property, together with Daisy Ashton, the elderly housekeeper. Daisy was beginning to find the house's upkeep too demanding for her arthritic limbs and had gradually retreated more and more to the kitchen where she concentrated her remaining energies on providing rather too much food for Mr James both in quantity and richness. Consequently, the farm manager had grown seriously rotund in recent years and waddled rather than walked about the property.

Mr James, ever conscious of his station, always dressed as a gentleman farmer replete with tweeds, waistcoat and plus fours. He insisted his footwear be thoroughly cleaned by Daisy each evening. A shooting stick, pipe and tobacco pouch were his constant companions wherever he travelled. The twelve permanent labourers liked their boss — they regarded him as fair and considerate.

Many years spent out of doors had left Mr James with a well wrinkled ruddy face and a mop of hair that resembled an untidy thatch, which he endeavoured to restrain, with only partial success, beneath his ancient cap. His responsibilities outdoors were only supervisory so that his fingers were red and sausage-like, and certainly not the digits of a labourer. Sociably inclined, he spent much of the working day hobnobbing with his employees, although it must be said, he knew what was happening about the place and what needed doing on the property. Mr James 'knew' farming.

One evening, late in the summer of 1915, Mr James and George were enjoying a warm beer in the kitchen garden where they occupied two knobbly old wooden benches situated opposite each other. George had finally decided it was time to broach a highly sensitive topic with his stout boss.

'Mr James, you remember me mentioning that one day I

want to move me family into Preston so's the children 'ave a better chance of gettin' a high school education?'

'Aye, George, I do. I remember the conversation all too well.'

'Well, with this 'ere war raging on and on, Annie and I think it's time to make the big move. Bell, me eldest, 'as just turned ten. If she passes them examinations to get 'er a place at a high school, she'll need to be livin' in town, not 'ere in Bilsborough.'

Mr James remained silent and puffed quietly on his pipe for a moment or two before responding. With his legs crossed he was the epitome of an impassive English gentleman. Clearing his throat, he looked directly at his faithful labourer.

'To be perfectly honest George, I have been expecting to have this conversation with you for some months now. You are my best worker and it will be almost impossible to replace you with the war continuing and young fellows going away to the war all the time. As you know, four of our young lads are already serving their country over in France and I suspect I will lose others soon if this war goes on. If you go too, I will have to ask for help from the Women's Land Army.'

'Mr James, I've always respected the way you've run this 'ere farm and enjoyed workin' for yer and I certainly don't wanna sound ungrateful for all yer many kindnesses to me family over the years. We've prospered in them married quarters you built at Holland Villas which we've enjoyed ever since me misses and I married way back in 1905.'

Mr James smiled to acknowledge George's compliments, took another pull on his pipe, exhaled and moved into a more comfortable position.

'Tell me George, have you found work in Preston?'

'No, Mr James, and that's really worryin' me. I wanna move the family as soon as possible but if there's no work we could end up in the bloody poor house. I gotta find suitable employment afore I take the risk of movin' the wife and kids.'

'I think I may be able to help you there, George.'

George put down his beer and observed his boss keenly.

'I have an elderly aunt who lives in Preston. She's about seventy years old and lost her husband to pneumonia last winter. She has a huge garden that is quite beyond her now, so she's looking to employ a gardener/handyman. You have heaps of experience growing vegetables and looking after the gardens around this place. Would you be interested?'

'If the pay and conditions be right, I'd be very interested.'

'Well, it so happens that I have just written a draft advertisement to place in the Preston Evening Standard, so I know all the details. The dear lady really didn't know how to go about finding a gardener so she asked me to help. She's still very much in command of her faculties and is a kindly soul. I think you would get along fine. The wage is a little more than you are currently earning here and you would be required to work from eight in the morning until five in the evening during summer and an hour less during the winter months. How does that sound?'

'How long is the job for?'

'My aunt is still in pretty good health so the job will be there until she dies or goes into a nursing home. Be warned though, she is hard of hearing.'

'I'm very interested then, Mr James. May I 'ave tonight to talk with me misses about this position please? Then I'll let you know, one way or t'other, first thing in the mornin'.'

'Take a couple of days, George. You need to be absolutely sure this is what you want. If you do decide to leave us, I will want a month's notice please.'

George gulped down the last of his pint and wiped the froth away with the back of his hand; he was desperate to get back home and break the news of this exciting opportunity to Annie.

* * *

Annie was less than impressed when George hurried in late for dinner. The family were finishing off their bubble and squeak with poached eggs when he arrived breathless at the front door.

'Sorry I'm late luv, 'ad to talk with the boss.'

'Having a beer more like,' Annie retorted in an annoyed tone while wagging her finger at her husband.

'Yes, I was 'aving a beer, but it were the best beer I've ever 'ad!'

Something in George's excited demeanour registered with Annie and she looked again at her husband but rather more carefully this time.

'What is it, George?'

'I've been offered a super gardening job in Preston!'

Before Annie had time to dish up his dinner, all the news had poured out of him. Everything Mr James had said was repeated for the whole family to hear. George's enthusiasm was infectious and the children sat there with their forks in the air transfixed and hanging on his every word.

Ever the practical one, Annie's first comment was, 'and, pray, where are we all going to live?'

'Ah,' said George, 'I 'aven't worked that one out yet. But don't you see, this's the opportunity we've been waitin' for? Findin' a job in Preston were ne'er goin' to be easy.'

Annie placed a plate loaded with a substantial pile of crispy bubble and squeak, two freshly poached eggs and a chunk of brown rye bread an inch thick in front of her still effusive husband.

'What do you think, children?' inquired George, looking at each of his three youngsters in turn.

Bell, the eldest, who had just turned ten, was the first to react. 'Dad, does this mean we might be able to go to high school?'

'Yes, of course Bell, if yer can pass the bloody entrance exam.'

'Wow, that's super then.'

Bell had continued to work hard at John Cross School and also with her mother in the evenings. She had assumed the role befitting of the eldest child and developed into the most responsible of the three children. Quiet and modest, she set what she believed was a good example to the others. As a result of what the teacher described as 'an above average brain' and sheer hard work, her parents now had high hopes she would qualify for high school. She was a rather plain, solid girl but had many fine qualities of character such as honesty, reliability, industriousness and excellent manners.

'What do *you* think, Eve?' George asked, through a large mouthful of crusty brown bread.

'Terrific Dad. There are so many things to do in Preston, like go to lots of parties.'

George smiled to himself, this was exactly the kind of reaction he had expected from Eve, the most social, extroverted, party-going member of his family. Eve was a ball of energy, lots of fun and as bright as a button. Her teacher said she was likely to go off the rails at the drop of a hat but had a terrific brain. As long as she could keep Eve concentrating on her work and not chatting and joking with the other pupils, she excelled. Annie had the same experience with homework: Eve's lively imagination was likely to take her flying off anywhere. Highly active, Eve stayed slim and had looks to kill even at this tender age.

George poured himself a glass of water and looked quizzically at his youngest child, George Junior, for his reaction.

Young George was already smiling at his dad. A cheeky five-and-a-half-year-old, he was loving school. Like his eldest sister he was on the podgy side, but his parents felt it was just puppy fat and would come off in a year or two. George Junior worshipped his dad and trailed along behind him whenever and wherever he could. He had a naturally inquisitive mind and was fascinated by anything vaguely scientific or to do with nature. Creepy crawlies, animals, the sky at night, crops and farming, the weather, diseases; everything intrigued him. George Junior was forever asking questions, and every answer seemed to provoke even more questions. His thirst for knowledge was insatiable. Through it all was a mischievous, dry sense of humour. The parents felt truly blessed to have brought three bright children into the world, each capable of benefitting from a high school education.

Young George, for once in his lifetime, said nothing but left his chair and ran around to his father and gave him a massive hug.

The children were clearly thrilled at the idea of moving to Preston; it was only Annie who was somewhat restrained as she tried to come to terms with the many challenges that lay ahead. Later that evening, when the children were asleep, she and George thrashed out a few ideas about how they might find some accommodation in Preston which was walking distance from Mr James' aunt's garden.

Next morning George boldly asked Mr James to see if his aunt would accept him as her new gardener. If she was happy to proceed with the arrangement, then George would tender his resignation by giving a month's notice. Mr James remarked that the timing was excellent, because tomorrow he had accepted a lift in a neighbour's car to visit his aunt in Preston. Mr James promised to bring back the latest copy of the Preston Chronicle for George and Annie to look at which would list all the houses for rent in town.

Everything went beautifully to plan. The elderly aunt, Mrs Moriarty, was delighted to accept George Chadwick as her new full-time gardener on the strong recommendation of her nephew. The starting date was settled for Monday, October 18th, 1915. True to his word, Mr James returned with a copy of the latest Preston Chronicle containing some thirty rental properties available for immediate occupation.

Preston in 1915 was still a cotton town with no less than forty massive red brick cotton mills dominating the skyline. To accommodate the thousands of workers, who had poured in many years ago from surrounding towns and villages, street after street of tenements had been constructed radiating out in all directions from the 'dark satanic mills.' These tenements were small, red brick and all looked identical, with the front doors opening directly onto the footpath with only small pocket-sized walled gardens at the back.

Tulketh Cotton Mill, Preston. (Photo taken by the author in 2012)

A Street of typical tenements in Preston. (Photo taken by the author in 2012)

Mrs Moriarty lived on the edge of town away from all the cotton mills and tenements and overlooking the banks of the pretty River Ribble. Her husband had been a medical practitioner, thereby allowing them to enjoy a more genteel lifestyle in a large stately house surrounded by a substantial and professionally landscaped garden. Since her husband's death, the condition of the garden had steadily deteriorated. In the space of a few months the garden looked overgrown and uncared for. There was certainly plenty of work for George. The Chadwick family found a tenement for rental not too far from Mrs Moriarty's and handy to the shops and schools.

195 Tulketh Brow ended up becoming the Chadwick's home for many years. However, moving there in October 1915 created enormous tensions between George and Annie. While the house was similar in size to their home in Holland Villas, it was in a far less desirable location. They now lived cheek by jowl with scores of other families struggling to manage in these frighteningly uncertain times. The cotton industry was showing signs of collapse and two mills had already switched off their machines and dismissed their workers. Young men had left their homes to join the armed forces and some of them had already lost their lives or returned maimed for life. This was a time of great stress, sadness, increasing poverty and petty crime.

Annie's greatest regret in moving to 195 Tulketh Brow was the loss of her magnificent garden where she grew plentiful supplies of fresh vegetables for the family, friends and sale at the weekly Bilsborough markets. The miserable damp patch at the back of her new home surrounded by a six-foot-high brick wall, where the sun rarely penetrated, was virtually useless. She desperately missed her garden and took out her frustration on George. Before Christmas George had taken steps to try and pacify his wife. He arranged with a more than sympathetic Mrs Moriarty that Annie could come with him a couple of times a week and grow vegetables in a part of her extensive garden.

This was a master stroke for the two ladies hit it off instantly, and whilst he laboured in the garden, the ladies kept each other company and Annie once again had the satisfaction of growing her own vegetables. Before long, George would return home most days carrying a bundle of freshly picked produce.

The three children were enrolled at the nearest elementary school where they settled in reasonably easily. It was daunting at first, used to as they were to one teacher for almost sixty children. Here, at their new school, the classes were smaller, around fifty in each room, but they found themselves sharing a classroom with only children of the same age. This made it so much easier for the teachers. Bell was surprised to find she had a male teacher. Thanks to all the help Annie had given the three children and their own innate abilities they soon discovered they were up near the top of their classes in almost every subject.

As the war dragged on through 1915 and into 1916, it became clear that on the western front there was a virtual stalemate and no end seemed in sight. Casualties were horrific. In January 1916, the British Government passed the Military Service Act that introduced conscription. All able-bodied single men between the ages of 18 and 40 were called up for active service. Desperate for yet more servicemen, the Act was revised in June 1916 to include married men across the same age bracket. By early August 1916 George, aged thirty-three, reported for duty at the Fulwood Barracks in Preston and after six weeks of basic training was assigned to the Lancashire Fusiliers. Early in February 1917, Private George Chadwick's regiment set sail for Le Havre en route to the western front.

Chapter Two Bilsborough 1911-1915

Mrs Moriarty was saddened to see George leave because in the ten months he had worked for her he had restored her garden to its earlier splendour and even built a couple of low drystone walls to house new compost bins and to hide the ugly garden sheds. Knowing how knowledgeable Annie was with gardening, Mrs Moriarty offered to pay her a wage slightly less than George was receiving to maintain the garden until George was able to return. Annie leapt at this opportunity for it meant that the Chadwicks now had two incomes to support their children's high school education.

CHAPTER THREE

Growing Up

Shortly before George departed for war service, Bell sat her high school entrance examination and passed. It was estimated that only approximately 15% of children who completed an elementary school education graduated to high school, so the Chadwick family were justifiably proud of Bell's achievement. Bell had worked extremely hard both at school and at home to make the high grade required.

The fee-paying schools (confusingly known as public schools) were financially out of the question for the Chadwick family which left two other state-run high schools in Preston, the fourteenth century Preston Grammar and more recently established, Golden Hill High. Annie and George discussed the advantages and disadvantages of both schools and made inquiries with neighbours before George left for overseas. Preston Grammar was supported by the government but still charged low-level fees, although nothing as expensive as the Public Boarding Schools. Golden Hill High was a smaller school and less prestigious, established by Richard Balshaw in 1782 specifically to provide a high school education for the poor. There was a means test that took into account the parents' combined income and the number of children that had to be educated. The Chadwicks were, at the time of their means test, still a single wage-earning family and so narrowly qualified. Consequently, Bell began her high school education at Golden Hill High in August 1916.

The high school was largely supported by generous benefactors from the wider community, although parents were asked to contribute what they could. The school motto was 'Non Sibi Sed Aliis' ('not for oneself, but for others'). There were nearly 200 boys and girls enrolled when Bell started her education there in 1916 and the founder, Richard Balshaw, remained there as the long-serving headmaster.

Late in 1918, a battle-hardened Lance-Corporal George Chadwick returned safely to his family in Preston. Although he had written regularly from the trenches, he had studiously avoided describing the horrors of war and remained equally tight-lipped on his return. Annie and the children never knew what he had endured; they were just hugely relieved he was home

Chapter Three Growing Up

and apparently well. George's return, however, understandably signalled a time of re-adjustment within the family.

Dear old Mrs Moriarty's health was failing and she was now being cared for in a nursing home. Her house and garden were up for sale and Annie was no longer on the payroll as her gardener. George, fortuitously, had met up with a Preston stonemason while serving overseas who had offered George a job in his headstone business on his return. George had always longed to work in stone, so this was his great opportunity. For a time, he would not be paid much more than an apprentice's wages, but as he developed his skills this would increase steadily to eventually end up a better wage than that commanded by a farm labourer or gardener. His prospects were promising.

When George returned, he was thrilled to find the children were doing so well. Bell had started her third year at Golden Hill High and was showing a strong interest in pursuing a nursing career. The lively Eve was in her final year at elementary school and working hard to sit her exams in a few months' time, with her mother helping her with extra tuition. George Junior had lost none of his natural inquisitiveness and at the age of eight was a member of a small gang of like-minded boys who roamed the highways and byways looking for interesting things to do and observe.

The end of the war brought harrowing repercussions for Preston. During 1918 the cotton industry, which had been struggling for years, finally collapsed. All except two of the forty cotton mills in town closed their doors and thousands of men and women lost their jobs. The dark satanic mills had finally ground to a halt. Unhealthy places as they were, they had at least provided massive employment. Widespread poverty and social unrest ensued. Some families were able to return to the farms and small villages where they had lived previously, and some found work in other nearby cities such as Liverpool and Manchester. The population of Preston declined steadily and many tenements became vacant.

A constant stream of returning serviceman further complicated matters. Many bore physical or psychological scars and did not take kindly to returning to a hometown where unemployment, poverty and misery were so prevalent. These young men had not spent years of their young lives suffering during the war to finally return home to such deprivation. Domestic violence flared up across the town.

The Chadwicks, although doing it tough, were not nearly as bad off as most of their neighbours. George began work at *Johnson and Sons, Stonemasons* within a couple of days of returning to Preston. He loved the work but had much to learn. In times of hardship the death rate inevitably increased so the demand for gravestones was strong. The catastrophic Spanish flu also ravaged Preston during 1918/19 to further increase the need for gravestones. In addition, surrounding towns and villages wished to commemorate their fallen and those that had served in the Great War by erecting stone monuments and memorials. There was a steady stream of local dignitaries, charged with the planning of these monuments, calling at *Johnson and Sons* for advice, quotations and to place their orders. George's wage may have been lower, but his job satisfaction

Chapter Three Growing Up

was high and he knew his wage would improve with time and experience.

Annie regularly visited the ailing Mrs Moriarty at Saint Agnes Nursing Home where the good lady had her own private room. Mrs Moriarty felt guilty she had let her lady gardener of the last two years down by entering the nursing home so, by way of atonement, she urged Annie to keep using the extensive vegetable garden for her family's benefit. Annie didn't need asking a second time and spent many pleasant hours every week cultivating an extensive range of vegetables. With careful planning and management, Annie kept her family in healthy vegetables most of the year and was able to provide apples, plums, gooseberries and pears in season. Whenever there were surpluses, she took one of the children with her to help carry back the heavily-laden baskets and sell the produce at reasonable rates around the neighbourhood. Mrs Moriartys' garden proved a godsend and helped the Chadwicks survive during a financially challenging time.

All was not doom and gloom in Preston however. As the cotton mills closed down, emerging industries arrived to make use of the available labour. Electrical goods and engineering factories opened up first and then the Preston based company, Leyland Motors, which had first produced petrol driven cars in 1904, was so busy it was unable to keep up with demand. The Preston Dock on the River Ribble was also an ongoing concern handling international trade.

* * *

Eve remained focused on her studies and romped home with an excellent mark in the high school entrance examinations. The Chadwicks, however, were no longer deemed to be sufficiently poor to be allowed to enrol Eve at Golden Hill High School so Eve began her high school education in 1920 at the historic Preston Grammar. This was a large school with a tradition ranging back some five hundred years. The gregarious Eve fitted in easily and was soon popular amongst her peers. The vivacious twelve-year-old was instantly in demand for social occasions and parties in private homes and adored these events. Being an observant child, and to some degree prompted by her parents, Eve soon realised she was blessed with good looks and that boys swarmed about seeking her attention. Desire for her company quickly became a powerful tool that Eve learnt to skilfully manipulate to her advantage.

In July 1920, fifteen-year-old Bell graduated from Golden Hill High School and was accepted to start as a pupil nurse. Three years of conscientious high school studies had paid off: her friends had for some time recognised her caring nature and felt she was well-suited for a nursing career. Her greatest challenge now was to withstand the over-bearing and demanding expectations of the Matrons who ran the hospitals with iron fists. Bell was, however, a resourceful lass; intelligent, determined to succeed in her chosen profession and above all, tolerant. Her family were immensely proud of her achievements to date.

The only hospital in Preston in 1920 was the Whittingham Mental Hospital that catered for nearly 3,000 patients drawn from all over Lancashire. Severely over-crowded and a dangerous and unpredictable environment, it was no place for a young person to commence their training as a nurse. Consequently, Bell was obliged to move to Manchester to commence training at Saint Mary's Hospital in the suburb of Chorlton-on-Medlock. This part of the hospital had opened in 1911 and provided gynaecological and paediatric services. Most importantly for Bell, there was a School of Nursing based there that certified midwives.

Rules were strict. Together with the other trainees, Bell had to report for duty by 6.00am every day and be in bed by 10.00pm. The trainee nurses all resided in the nurses' quarters provided. She was entitled to one day off every three weeks and one Sunday per month. By the end of 1923 she was a fully qualified midwife and free to apply to move elsewhere. Bell's three years as a trainee at Saint Mary's had been challenging because she had been terribly homesick. Preston was too far away to visit when she had her occasional days off so she scarcely saw her family during the three years. Bell worked for a number of years as a midwife in and around Manchester and eventually married and had her own family.

Young George continued to do well at his elementary school but his interests had changed. Arriving in Preston had opened his eyes to several new and exciting worlds. He began to spend more and more time pottering around building sites, the Preston Docks and various factories. He considered the monstrous cotton mills the dinosaurs of the past and imagined a future in engineering or manufacturing. He was fascinated by Leyland Motors and the mass production line they had developed, but was even more enamoured with the huge hangars being erected on the edge of town for the manufacture of aeroplanes. Talking to some of the workers, he soon realised if he was ever to become an engineer working on exciting new production lines, be it cars or aircraft, he needed to go to university to acquire an engineering degree. At the age of ten he set his sights on this goal.

At the end of elementary school, George sailed through his high school entrance examinations and followed Eve into Preston Grammar School. Here he studied the subjects he required for university entrance to read engineering (Mathematics, Physics, Latin, English and Chemistry). He realised his dream and graduated from the University of Manchester with a strong degree in Engineering in 1929. This led to ten successful years as an aircraft engineer until the outbreak of the second world war when he served with the Royal Airforce as a senior engineer working on Spitfires. George never married. After the war he continued working as an aircraft engineer and lived with his mother until her death in 1960.

Eve Chadwick was possibly the brightest of the three children but was becoming quite the party girl. The 1920s was a time of much promiscuity amongst the English upper classes and this filtered down to some extent to the upwardly mobile middle classes. Divorce was totally unacceptable amongst the upper class, but affairs and liaisons were common and, in many cases, happily tolerated, provided some discretion was exercised.

The Chadwick parents certainly could not rate themselves

as members of the middle classes but through hard work, determination, innate intelligence and some good fortune, were able to lift their three children out of the working classes. Bell and George achieved upward mobility through education to become a midwife and an aircraft engineer respectively. Eve, however, managed to climb the social ladder, not through education alone but also by the application of her feminine charms. Early in her teenage years, Eve came to understand that if she could develop the polite finesse of the ladies in high society then she would appeal to their gentlemen. Throughout Eve's time at Preston Grammar School, she sought to educate herself, not just academically, but strongly in the mores of polite upper-class society. She was encouraged in this by her parents who also recognised the potential opportunities opening up for their attractive daughter.

Coming as she did from a working-class background, Eve did not find it easy to find appropriate role models to meet, or observe. Socially, her family had few opportunities to mix with the upper-classes, so Eve took it upon herself to discreetly seek out her role models and imitate their behaviours.

Every Sunday the Chadwicks would attend Matins at their nearest Anglican Church. Eve was not particularly drawn to the order of service, or the hymns, or the religious ceremonies that were an integral part of Matins, but she was fascinated by some members of the congregation. Certain rows of pews at the front of the church were 'reserved' for notable families in the community. Every time she attended Matins, Eve noted that the sidesmen on duty would quietly and modestly show these families to their pews. It was little more than a nicety, since the families knew perfectly well which pews were theirs. It was a form of polite recognition shown towards each upper-class family, in return for which it was hoped that a generous offering would be placed in the offertory plate when it was quietly passed along the pew later in the service. A small rope stretching across the end of the pew informed any visitors that these particular pews were not for common use. Eve was intrigued with the genteel folk who occupied these special pews.

The families usually consisted of the head of the family, a gentleman dressed in a smart dark suit with waistcoat, shiny black shoes, and carrying a rolled-up umbrella in case of inclement weather, always accompanied by his wife and possibly their children and a nanny. Eve took particular note of how the wives dressed and conducted themselves, for she intended to become one of them in the future. A smart hat was mandatory; one that might draw compliments. The ladies of the wealthiest families would never wear the same hat twice and must have kept their milliners frantically busy. The not quite so classy ladies had a rotation system going whereby their entire range of hats began a repeat cycle after a few weeks and just occasionally they would surprise everyone by introducing a brand-new piece of millinery.

Eve carefully observed how the ladies were tastefully attired so that vulgar loud colours were never seen and great care was taken to wear clothing that matched colour-wise. Shoes, handbags, hats and dresses were carefully selected to please. Whenever she could, Eve would edge close to the female members of these families after the service was over, when they stood about for a few minutes chatting outside the church. This was her chance to look more closely at jewellery, brooches and necklaces. Again, she began to develop her own sense of what was tasteful and what was not. Dress sense became almost an obsession.

The wives always attracted Eve's attention but even more interesting were the teenage daughters and the young women in these families. The airs and graces exhibited by these younger females were a revelation. Eve was intrigued by how the younger females of marriageable age flirted with eligible men. Their skilful use of makeup, attractive hair styles, brighter clothing and general deportment were all designed to appeal. Best of all, Eve would try to guess the current liaisons within the church. Often, she would spot flirtatious glances being exchanged between young men in the choir and attractive females sitting in front of her. It was all so exciting. Eve couldn't wait to be involved herself one day in this intriguing world of flirtation and desire.

Dear old Mrs Moriarty, rather surprisingly, turned out to be another source of role modelling for Eve. Occasionally Eve accompanied her mother when she went to work for Mrs Moriarty in her garden and this gave the eager young lass another opportunity to observe how a real lady behaved and carried herself. It was here that Eve learnt how to speak 'proper' English whenever she spent time chatting with the elderly lady. She also learnt how to serve afternoon tea with a full tea set. The finer points of hosting tea were not lost on Eve as she watched, fascinated, when visitors arrived to enjoy tea with Mrs Moriarty. There was a teapot in a cosy and pretty cups and saucers with teaspoons. A tea strainer was essential as well as plates that matched the cups and saucers. There were matching jugs for the milk and sugar bowls for the white sugar lumps and tongs to serve with. Of course, there were always attractive tablecloths and napkins and a plate of delicately prepared sandwiches with ugly crusts removed. Finally, a three-tiered cake stand would arrive with an assortment of small cakes and gateaux.

A few times, before the kindly Mrs Moriarty was obliged to retire to a nursing home, she allowed Eve to help pass around the cups of tea, sandwiches and cakes. Eve was always warned about these special days in advance, so would arrive dressed in her very best dress, polished shoes and a pretty bow in her hair. It was a wonderful chance to listen to 'polite conversation' and practice her own speaking voice when spoken to.

When Mrs Moriarty moved into Saint Agnes Nursing Home for Gentlefolk, Eve always asked to go with her mother whenever she was planning to visit the good lady. She would spend some of this time walking the corridors observing the interplay between male doctors and young nurses. Once again, she witnessed flirtatious behaviours between the sexes and sometimes even between the elderly male patients and the pretty young nurses. Everything she witnessed heightened Eve's desire to somehow become an accepted member of the upper echelons of society.

For Eve, blessed with her winsome looks and engaging

personality, the way to the 'good life' was, quite simply, to marry well. For this to happen, however, she must learn to conduct herself convincingly as a 'lady' in order to attract acceptable suitors.

CHAPTER FOUR

Learning the Game

Eve adored her time at Preston High School and was up early every morning, itching to walk through those hallowed gates. She relished the fact that the school, as a place of learning, was nearly five hundred years old and some of the buildings nobly reflected its distinguished past.

Academically, Eve was gifted: she found her lessons challenging but not overwhelming. She would be the first to admit that she took a rather relaxed approach to her studies and never overexerted herself. She was content to just drift along, achieving reasonable grades, but never having any ambitions to enter a university. A good marriage was the way of the future for her.

Eve made up for her less than outstanding academic results with her bright personality. Naturally friendly, cheerful and engaging, she quickly became popular. There was an attractive innocence about her that some might think was naivety, but most found to be charming. Eve was certainly gregarious and great fun to be with and soon developed a reputation for being a party girl. If anyone in her class was having a birthday, or some other celebration, Eve would always be there in the midst of all the frivolity and be one of the last to leave. She adored bright clothes and was one of the first in her class to tentatively apply a little makeup when attending special events.

Eve was well-liked by her teachers since her cheerful sense of humour and lively contributions to classroom discussions helped to keep the classroom climate positive and enjoyable for everyone present. Occasionally she had to be pulled into line for chattering too much or getting overexcited about some remark from a friend, but on the whole, she was well-behaved and cooperative. Homework was always satisfactorily completed and on time. When Eve's school reports came home, she was usually assigned a B or B+ grade; it was rare for her to perform higher or lower than a B-grade performance. The teachers' comments often suggested, however, that Eve could achieve even better results if she was more highly motivated and applied herself.

Eve's parents were proud she had made it to high school and not unduly concerned that some of the teachers felt she was capable of achieving higher grades. George had settled down now as an accomplished stonemason and was steadily building a reputation for the quality of his inscriptions on gravestones and war memorials. Now that he was fully qualified, his wage had increased, but it was never enough. To bring much-needed additional money to the family, Annie had turned her hand to dressmaking. Alice Houghton, Annie's oldest sister who had lived with them in Bilsborough, had more work than she could handle and increasingly turned to Annie to assist with work from her Preston customers. Annie worked from home and in her own time so it suited her well.

Eve, being of a fine-boned delicate build, did not enter puberty until she was fourteen. As she became shapelier, she found her interest in boys intensified. Preston High School was unusual in that it was co-educational and there was no shortage of boys in her various classes, or in senior classes, who showed an interest in her. Intelligence, a bright happy disposition, combined with exceptional good looks made her a magnet for many of the male teenagers. *'Bees around a honeypot'* was an apt description one of her friends coined.

Eve quickly learnt there were simple, but vitally important rules to this game of boy meets girl, that were essential to apply if she was to survive this testosterone-charged environment, and it all began, or ended, with eye contact. She had observed for years at church and elsewhere, how couples made or avoided eye contact. Now, at the age of fourteen, she had graduated into the ranks of those seeking or rejecting the attentions of certain males through the use of this strategy.

Wherever she looked around in her classroom, in the playground, at church, shopping, or even in the streets of Preston, there seemed to be a boy or a man trying to catch her eye. The golden rule was never to look back at the ogler because to hold a male's gaze for just a fleeting second was tantamount to inviting them to come and have a conversation. Eve rapidly developed a range of avoidance techniques such as keeping her eyes fixated on her books when in the classroom, looking only at her girlfriends in the playground and staring vacantly straight ahead anywhere else. These techniques proved highly successful until Eve realised that she was cutting off all male attention and that she was not encouraging the few males about the place that she found interesting and wished to befriend.

Following animated discussions with her girlfriends, Eve began to apply rule two. Rule two was to surreptitiously identify a boy who *she* liked the look of, then, once a likely looking prospect was identified, to do some research. How old was he? Was he handsome? What were his future prospects like? Was he intelligent? Was he fun to be around? What did his parents do? And, most importantly, could he elevate her into the society lifestyle she craved? The answer to these questions, more often than not, had to be gleaned from her girlfriends who regularly held 'huddles' at which the merits and demerits of a succession of potential male partners were analysed in depth.

There were other rules that also needed to be followed, such as 'don't steal another girl's boyfriend', although this rule seemed to be observed more in the breaking than in the keeping. Another rule was to totally ignore all wolf whistles, cat calls or suggestive remarks or signs from rude men. The rules of initial engagement or avoidance were quite simple if you followed them meticulously and didn't let your guard down. Later, Eve was to discover there was a whole plethora of additional rules that applied once you were actually in a relationship.

At Preston High School, Eve was introduced to some of the great English novelists. Her studies included Shakespeare's *Hamlet* and *Macbeth*, Charles Dickens' *Oliver Twist* and *Hard Times*, Thomas Hardy's *Tess of the D'Urbervilles* and *The Return of the Native* and Emily Bronte's *Wuthering Heights*. These works ignited a love of great literature for Eve that would stay with her for life and helped shape her maturing attitudes towards tragedy, violence, class distinctions, love and romance. The impressionable young Eve was acutely aware that an appreciation of literature, to the extent that she could discourse meaningfully with others, was an essential part of her ticket to the upper classes.

Likewise, Eve relished every opportunity the school offered in the fields of poetry (Coleridge, Wordsworth, Pope and Keats), opera and classical music. If she was one day to become somebody's 'lady', she needed to know something of these exciting worlds that were only now starting to open up to her. From the few musical concerts the school provided for its pupils, Eve discovered an appreciation for the works of Beethoven, Mozart, Tchaikovsky, JS Bach and Handel. It was enough to whet her appetite for more should she be invited to accompany an eligible young gentleman to concerts in the future.

Preston High School was progressive in that it provided basic ballroom dancing for those who wished to take this option. Eve jumped at the opportunity and quickly became proficient at the waltz, foxtrot and quickstep. She realised that these were the three most common dances that would stand her in good stead at balls, but that there were others out there such as the thrilling Charleston that she needed to add to her repertoire if she was to be at least minimally accomplished on the dance floor.

Ballroom dancing lessons were available at weekends in Preston at Gwen Doveton's Dancing Academy but the fees were way beyond what the Chadwicks could afford. Help came from an unexpected direction. Mrs Moriarty, who had a particularly soft spot for Eve, heard that she was longing to learn more than the basic ballroom dances and generously offered to pay for a course of fifteen weekly lessons at the academy.

It was at the academy that Eve first fell in love. At the tender age of fourteen, she met an attractive young man named Michael Knowles-Smith. Michael was her senior by two years, tall, slim and athletic and his accomplishments on the dance floor had her spellbound. He moved with such grace and poise that he seemed to glide effortlessly around the room. Not only was he a superb dancer but he was good-looking too. Michael attended one of the private fee-paying schools in Preston and had all the airs and graces of a pupil from such elitist schools. Many of Eve's girlfriends at Preston High sneered derisively at the 'snobs' from the public schools and would have nothing to do with them; but Eve felt differently.

She had no qualms about mixing and hopefully marrying into money and class.

Eve's 'crush' on Michael Knowles-Smith was not reciprocated. Gwen Doveton required a demonstration pair for her young dancing class and had selected Michael and his dancing partner, Josephine Bagshot, to fulfill this role. Nobody knew for sure, although everyone suspected that Michael and Josephine were more than just dancing demonstrators. They combined beautifully on the dance floor and basked in the attention they received from their young neophytes. Eve was light on her feet and a quick learner but scarcely merited a smile or a kind comment from her heartthrob on the few occasions she danced with him. So, Eve learnt a painful lesson: despite her attractive appearance and engaging personality — not all males wanted anything to do with her!

The climax to the fifteen weeks of dancing lessons at Gwen Doveton's Dance Academy was traditionally 'The Dancing Exhibition'. On such occasions the successful young graduating dancers would be given opportunities to demonstrate their newly acquired skills, and at the end of the evening receive a Certificate of Commendation from none other than the Worshipful Mayor of Preston. Sadly, not all the young boys and girls graduated. Gwen Doveton had high standards to maintain and declined to pass any of her young charges that did not meet her exacting expectations. Two of Eve's class failed.

Gwen Doveton's Dancing Exhibitions were well-known in Preston and the surrounding towns. Through many years of hard work and dedication, the academy had earned its reputation as the best in the district. If you graduated from Gwen Doveton's Dance Academy you were likely to be invited to partner a member of the opposite sex to one or more of the local dances, balls and even debutante balls. In short, it was considered a prestigious accomplishment and therefore, a ticket to a brighter social life.

A new dress for Eve was crucial. The Dancing Exhibitions were always staged in Preston's Town Hall before a large and exuberant audience of families, friends, other dancing enthusiasts, VIPs and the simply curious. Several hundred could be expected to attend. Once again, Mrs Moriarty's generosity came to the fore: she arranged for Eve to have private fittings for a brand-new dress with all the accessories at June Doyer's fashionable dress shop in the High Street. Miss Doyer was up on all the latest styles from London and Paris and produced a gorgeous bottle green dress that was quite breathtaking. Mrs Moriarty even paid for Eve to have a special hairdo. The dear lady had successfully raised two sons but had always regretted never having a daughter. Eve, it seemed, had become her surrogate daughter.

The Saturday in August chosen for the Dance Exhibition was a balmy evening with soft sunlight lasting until almost ten o'clock. Eve's entourage of supporters was substantial. Pride of place was given to Mrs Moriarty who had arrived in a wheelchair together with her own nurse from the nursing home. Eve's parents were there of course and barely able to contain their pride and excitement. George, Eve's younger brother, had been dragged along against his wishes: he didn't

Chapter Four   Learning the Game

have much time for all this fuss. Bell, unfortunately, failed to persuade the matron that she should be permitted to have an extra day off to attend. Also present at the function was Eve's dancing teacher from school and four of her closest girlfriends.

The evening was an enormous success and proceeded without any major hitches. Gwen Doveton had seen to it that any of her students likely to falter on the big night had been excluded beforehand. Eve's partner for the evening was a pimply lad called Norman Castle. Eve and Norman had been dancing partners for several weeks and had learnt to combine well. Norman was dreadfully nervous on the night, however, and on a couple of occasions, when it looked as though he was getting into difficulties, Eve had to rescue him. After only one full dress rehearsal, the graduates performed to music provided by a real live orchestra that sat below the stage in the pit; a great improvement on a solo piano.

Eve's benefactor, the gracious Mrs Moriarty, was thrilled with the evening and praised Eve effusively at the end of the evening.

'My dear, you were fabulous! You have beauty and talent and must make good use of your attributes.'

'Thank you, Mrs Moriarty, but it was your generosity that made it all possible.'

'Don't mention it dear. I'm pleased to have been able to help. I always longed for a daughter of my own, so you are helping to fill in a gaping hole in my long life. I do have a granddaughter, but she is at the Sorbonne in Paris and I rarely see her these days.'

'Would you like to see my dancing certificate?'

'Oh yes, please dear. Now where are my spectacles?'

The nurse came to Mrs Moriarty's aid, recovered the spectacles from somewhere and then the two of them made all the appropriate complimentary comments.

'Thank you dear, most impressive. Now, with your fine looks and happy disposition, you are going to be very popular with all the young men about town. You do know that, don't you?'

Eve blushed prettily. 'Yes, I suppose so,' she admitted.

'Whatever you do Eve, dear, don't throw yourself at the first nice-looking young man that asks you out. Men can be very persuasive! There are a lot of fish in the sea and you must ensure that you catch a worthwhile one. Do you understand me, dear?'

'Yes, I think so, Mrs Moriarty.'

'So, you must come and visit me up at Saint Agnes and tell me all about any young man who wants to be your suitor. Is that a deal?'

'Yes, of course. I'd be happy to.'

'I may be ancient, but I'm still in contact with most of the respected families around Preston and might be able to offer you a few tips.' Mrs Moriarty surprised Eve with a mischievous wink and a knowing smile.

'Thank you, Mrs Moriarty.'

'Now run along dear and get some beauty sleep. Nurse, please take me home before I collapse from exhaustion. I've had more than enough excitement for one day.'

Eve stole one last amorous glance at Michael Knowles-Smith, who was laughing heartily with Josephine about something or other, before re-joining young brother George and her parents.

CHAPTER FIVE
Preston 1923

1923 was an exciting year in England for those fortunate enough to enjoy the events. It was the time of the 'Roaring Twenties' but also a period of massive unemployment. Over two million people were out of work, mainly in the north which included Preston. Some towns recorded up to 70% unemployment!

This was the year the British Broadcasting Company was launched, and Howard Carter unsealed the extraordinary burial chamber of Tutankhamun, a pharaoh of the eighteenth Egyptian dynasty. In the world of sport, London's Wembley Stadium was completed, a modern marvel, and the first FA Cup final was staged there. The third visiting cricket team from the West Indies toured the country and played twenty-eight matches.

There was a general election in November and for the first time, at the age of fifteen, Eve was mature enough to be interested. Stanley Baldwin was elected Prime Minister representing the Conservative Party. Eve was, of course, too young to vote but had already at this young age developed a preference for the Conservative Party, the political persuasion she stayed with for the rest of her life. Even at this tender age, Eve realised that if she was to try to become a part of the 'upper classes' then this was the political persuasion for her.

The Chadwick family still resided at 195 Tulketh Brow. Eve's father, now forty, continued to enjoy full employment as a stonemason but was starting to feel a few aches and pains from the tough physical life he had endured since leaving school at age twelve. Twenty-eight years toiling outside in England's severe climate eventually invited rheumatism and arthritis. Annie still managed to contribute to the family's income through her dressmaking, although with so much unemployment about, the work had declined considerably.

1923 was an important year of decision-making for Eve and her family. In August, Eve would turn fifteen and she needed to decide whether or not to remain at Preston High School. If she stayed at school, and concentrated intensely on her studies, her teachers predicted she could win a place at university. The alternative was to leave school in July and try to find work during a time of unprecedented high unemployment. George

Chapter Five Preston 1923

and Annie strongly favoured the former. Apart from their enormous pride in having one of their own enter a university, they considered a university degree to be a guaranteed ticket to a better life. Few females went to university in the 1920s. However, there was still a belief among many women that being 'smart' did you no favours in the marriage market. Men, it was feared, did not want to marry a woman who was cleverer than they were. Mrs Moriarty was of this view too, and Mrs Moriarty was a powerful influence on Eve's thinking.

Despite the hard times in Preston and throughout the north of England, Eve had been enjoying a merry social life. She remained a popular girl at school and her newfound prowess on the dance floor had made her a favourite with some of the local boys at the dances and balls that had bravely struggled to keep going during these difficult times.

Eve had also fallen in love again, this time with a fine-looking young man who suddenly appeared at their church one Sunday morning together with his family. Since moving to Preston, the Chadwicks had been worshipping at a new, modern building called Saint Cuthbert's Anglican Church.

Eve's new beau was Anthony Cavanagh, the eldest son of Dr and Mrs Cavanagh who had recently moved to Preston so that Dr Cavanagh could take up a position as the senior engineer at the rapidly expanding Leyland Motors factory. Anthony was sixteen and a pupil at Stowe Public School where he was a boarder. The family had arrived at the start of the six-week-long school summer holidays which gave Eve an opportunity to get to know Anthony before he had to go back to his school for the next term.

195 Tulketh Brow, Eve's family home in Preston.
(Photo taken by the author in 2012)

Eve couldn't keep her eyes off Anthony. He was tall and solidly built for his age being a rower and an all-round athlete. A firm jaw, that already needed shaving on a regular basis, added to Anthony's strong appearance. A crop of unruly hair gave the impression that, despite his impressive build, he was still a bit of a mischievous scallywag. But it was his eyes that Eve

Chapter Five Preston 1923

adored most. They were at once friendly and kind and she felt like melting every time he looked at her, which was not often enough. Anthony had immediately identified Eve as the most appealing girl in this new church congregation, and had taken steps to introduce himself on only the second Sunday he had attended church. Eve was smitten. Subconsciously, it was her crush on Anthony that also encouraged her to leave school and stay in Preston.

What finally sealed it for Eve though, was an offer too good to miss, thanks once again to the redoubtable Mrs Moriarty. Having moved in all the best circles throughout her long life, Mrs Moriarty maintained and cultivated some valuable contacts and one of these was Miss June Doyer, proprietor of the best dress shop in town. Work as a junior assistant at June Doyer's upmarket establishment was considered a plum job. She always employed the smartest and best-looking girls who at times were called upon to model some of her latest fashions.

June Doyer had no vacancies for junior assistants when Mrs Moriarty first approached her, indeed, her fashionable dress shop had suffered a significant reduction in sales as a result of the lean times. But Mrs Moriarty was a persuasive lady and persisted.

'June, dear, this is no ordinary lass I'm advising you to employ. She is so pretty with a superb little figure, very intelligent and a most attractive personality.'

'I'm sure you're right Mrs Moriarty, however, I'm struggling at present to keep all my girls usefully employed. Business is hardly booming. As you know, I have eight young girls in my employ already and I really cannot take on yet another one.'

'Well, let me make a little proposal to you June, dear. If you give me an appropriate time, I will send Eve Chadwick to your shop to meet you. I'm absolutely certain when you meet her you will recognise what an asset she would be to your business. If you like her, as I'm sure you will, I will personally pay her wages for the rest of the year, by which time I'm sure one of your eight girls will have moved on. Now, there's an offer too good to miss my dear? What's more, I'll frequent your establishment shortly to purchase my winter apparel if you agree to take on this lass.'

'Well, Mrs Moriarty, that is indeed a most generous offer, one that is hard to resist. I'll ask my secretary to book Eve in for an appointment with me here at five-thirty on Friday afternoon. Did you say, Eve Chadforth?'

'No, dear, it's Chadwick. C-H-A-D-W-I-C-K.'

'Thank you. I must stress, however, Mrs Moriarty, that I cannot guarantee that Eve Chadwick will be able to stay with me next year if business does not improve. I have a strict policy of last one to be employed is the first to leave if things get really tight. You must understand that?'

'Of course, my dear, I quite understand. I'm sure you will be delighted with Eve and find her to be a first-rate employee. She has excellent manners and is a fast learner.'

'Well, that's settled then. By the way, Mrs Moriarty, the selection of London's latest winter garments for mature ladies arrived only last week if you would care to make an appointment to come and visit us?'

'Splendid! How about three o'clock Wednesday next week?'

So it was that Eve Chadwick commenced work as the most

Chapter Five Preston 1923

junior assistant at Miss June Doyer's highly esteemed dress shop in Preston's High Street shortly before her fifteenth birthday.

* * *

As the most junior assistant, Eve had a series of mundane daily tasks to perform. She had to arrive first every morning and leave last to ensure that the shop was fully opened on time and locked up correctly at the end of the day. If there was a high-spending customer present at the official closing time, she had to stay later until all transactions were completed necessitating her having to remain sometimes until after six o'clock. Eve was also responsible for the kitchenette and spent much of her day making cups of tea for Miss Doyer and her fellow employees and washing up afterwards. Should a customer remain in the dress shop for any length of time Eve had to politely offer them a cup of tea, too. In addition, the general tidiness of the shop was Eve's responsibility. If she was not dusting or sweeping floors, she was running around picking up and returning discarded clothing to their rightful places.

Boring as these tasks often were, Eve took the time to carefully observe the sales techniques of her colleagues and was soon picking up little tips. Winning the initial trust of a customer was paramount, and then continuing with a friendly, relaxed, but professional approach. Some of the girls, she noted, were more successful than others and Eve tried to model herself on the high flyers. Initially, Eve experienced some resentment from the girls, who were all too aware that sales were down and saw no reason for additional staff to be appointed when they were becoming nervous about holding their own positions. Miss Doyer soon sensed the disquiet and took steps to explain that Eve was being sponsored by a benefactor and may even leave after Christmas.

As it turned out, two of the girls left Miss Doyer's employ at Christmas time; one had gotten married and moved to Liverpool, and the second had fallen pregnant and since disappeared, much to everyone's shame and embarrassment. With the loss of two staff, Miss Doyer decided to offer Eve a position but insisted she would have to continue her duties as the most junior assistant. Eve grabbed the chance and a few months into 1924 another young lady left to be married so Eve finally joined the sales staff and relinquished the position of general dogsbody with the arrival of a new girl.

CHAPTER SIX
A Serious Prospect?

Eve's crush on Anthony Cavanagh was short-lived. At the end of the long summer holidays, he returned to his boarding school for the next fourteen-week term. For a few weeks they corresponded but this 'love at a distance' had no appeal for Eve and she steadily lost interest. Besides, there was another young man she was increasingly falling for in Preston who had come, unwillingly, to June Doyer's with his mother one day. Acutely embarrassed to have been dragged into such a feminine establishment, Eve had taken pity on him and offered him a cup of tea. He was soon to become one of a succession of young men that Eve counted as boyfriends over the next eighteen months or so. It became a regular pattern for Eve. She would fall for a young man, think she was passionately in love with him, and then, almost as quickly, lose interest as a new paramour appeared on the scene. Her parents and Mrs Moriarty were not overly concerned for they saw this behaviour as typical of a young woman seeking the right man with whom to eventually settle down.

There was no way Eve could afford to attend the expensive public balls held annually in Preston. However, her dancing attributes, good looks and lively companionship meant that there was no shortage of young men prepared to purchase two tickets to a ball and then invite Eve to be their partner. Being one of the most desirable 'catches' in town enabled Eve to usually attend the prestigious Catholic Ball, the Anglican Ball, the Debutante Ball, the Mayoral Ball and even the Military Ball. Although she didn't have to purchase the tickets or buy the drinks for these social occasions, she did have the considerable expense of dressing to look the part. Most of her modest salary seemed to disappear into buying new dresses, shoes, makeup, handbags, gloves and any other accessories. Mrs Moriarty continued to support Eve financially sometimes and working at Miss June Doyer's dress shop proved a bonus too. Not only did Eve have first viewing of new dresses arriving at the establishment but she could reserve items and, just occasionally, Miss Doyer would give her a special deal.

In addition to the annual balls there were a number of smaller private dances. A formal invitation would arrive through the mail complete with an RSVP date. These private gatherings were, of course, free and usually held in large country estates or mansions in town with a room large enough to be converted into a ballroom. Nearly always these private functions were smaller, more intimate and friendlier affairs since most people present already knew each other. It was at one of these private functions that Eve had her first kiss. Several young men had asked to kiss her before this particular occasion, but Eve had always laughed it off, firmly declined, or found some other way to avoid the situation. Next morning Eve realised she had let her guard down as a result of having one too many alcoholic drinks. She craved male company but, like nearly all girls raised with a strong Christian religious background, had every intention of remaining a virgin until marriage.

Boyfriends came and went like seasonal changes. The youths were usually a year or two older than Eve and always from families that were somewhat superior to Eve's with regard to class, status, father's occupation and definitely wealth. Eve loved her parents dearly but recognised they had not had her opportunities in life so were doomed to a more pedestrian sort of life where they would always struggle. They had done everything they could to launch her on her way, but in the end the challenge to achieve a better life was hers. Eve totally comprehended the situation she was in and realised her future depended on marrying well. All the young lads she had had as boyfriends so far had been fun, and she remained good friends with several, but at the age of seventeen and a half she now felt experienced and mature enough to start looking for a serious life partner.

Early in December, the army officers at Fulwood Barracks, based in the centre of Preston, traditionally held their Christmas ball. Known by the locals as the 'Military Ball' it was a rather different affair to the other balls held each year. Fulwood Barracks dated back to 1842 and remained a significant entity in Preston. Erected on the side of Watling Road, and built so long ago by the Romans, it was the pre-eminent military establishment in Lancashire. In 1925 Fulwood Barracks was the home of the Loyal North Lancashire Infantry Regiment as well as the East Lancashire Regiment.

The army always did things differently. Attendance at the ball was restricted to commissioned officer ranks plus the two regimental sergeant majors. A joint invitation was despatched by the commanding officers of the two regiments who were usually at the rank of brigadier general or major general. Every officer based at the barracks was expected to be present and needed an extraordinarily good reason to be excused. Around two-thirds of the serving officers were married and these were accommodated in the married quarters on site. This left the single, and generally younger and more junior officers, needing partners for the event. Nobody seemed to quite know how it was that the two commanding officers chose which young eligible Preston ladies they wished to invite, but they did take great care to invite the right number. If there were forty single officers in the barracks at the time, then forty young damsels from town would be invited. A free army bus was made available for young ladies requiring transport to and from the ball.

The Military Balls had been staged for as long as anyone

could remember. The army viewed the balls as an important way to promote good relationships between the military and the community and went to an enormous amount of trouble to decorate the Drill Hall, where the event was held, according to the particular theme selected for that year. Needless to say, it was the lower ranks who did all the preparation work but were not permitted to attend.

The young ladies about town had mixed feelings about attending the Annual Military Ball. Some longed to be invited as it was an opportunity to meet a group of highly desirable young men and perhaps find the love of their life. Others were more cautious. Stories circulated around town of lusty young men, normally confined to barracks, who were unable to contain their urges when a bus-load of gorgeous young wenches suddenly materialised in the Drill Hall. It was true that a handful of the Preston ladies had fallen for officers at Fulwood Barracks and ended up getting married. However, being married to an army officer was not every young lady's choice of a partner, because it inevitably resulted in extensive travel and moving house across the country or even overseas. This life did not appeal to the stay-homers.

Early in November 1925, Eve was pleasantly surprised to discover an envelope addressed to her embossed on the back with the regimental arms of the East Lancashire Regiment. She guessed correctly that it was an invitation to attend the 1925 Military Christmas Ball. Being of an adventurous nature, Eve had no hesitation in deciding to accept and the same day penned her formal reply. Later that week, she was intrigued to discover that the indomitable Mrs Moriarty had twice been invited to the Military Ball as far back as 1864 and 1865. The esteemed old lady was all in favour of Eve presenting herself at the Military Ball.

'They are well-paid young men, Eve dear, and would be an excellent catch if you find a young man to your liking. I had a boyfriend at the barracks once by the name of Lieutenant Roger Thompson, but he was suddenly sent off to India, so that was the end of that! As you know, in the end I married a doctor. If you want to travel and see the world, and can put up with the strange hours that soldiers keep, it's a good life. A man in uniform is quite something to behold.'

Mrs Moriarty gave a little chuckle and a couple of knowing nods.

'Are they in uniform at the ball, Mrs Moriarty?'

'Oh no, my dear. They are all impeccably dressed in their penguin suits, bow ties, tails and shoes so shiny you can see your face reflected.'

For a moment Eve visualised rows of penguin officers standing at attention in long rows motionless, but Mrs Moriarty was speaking again.

'How about we get you a new dress for the occasion, my dear? I'm sure with something glamorous, and just a little revealing, you'll have the young officers chasing you about everywhere.'

'I'm not sure that's what I want, Mrs Moriarty.'

'Well dear, a whole bunch of you are going to be dumped up there in a bus so you need to stand out in the crowd. Ask Miss Doyer to fix you up a new outfit and to put it on my account.

There's one condition only: I want you to come and see me afterwards and tell me all the scandal and lurid details. Is that a deal?'

'Oh yes, please. Thank you so much, Mrs Moriarty. I promise to tell you everything. Let's make a time and a date right now.'

So, a time and date were arranged for Eve to visit Mrs Moriarty in her nursing home to impart the 'lurid details'.

* * *

The officers' mess at Fulwood Barracks was, more often than not, a hive of activity. To promote collegiality, the two regiments shared the one large area and on the whole this worked well. A long shiny bar ran along one end of the mess, behind which, three or four men, well-versed in the mixing of cocktails and concocting whatever particular alcoholic delights were requested, provided a prompt and professional service. Windows were minimal along the long side walls since wall space was essential for the proper display of regimental honours and awards, flags and citations as well as portraits of distinguished commanding officers from yesteryear. The regimental regalia of the East Lancashire Regiment adorned one of these long walls and the regalia of the Loyal North Lancashire Regiment filled the opposite wall. At the other end of the mess and away from the bar, was a large framed colour picture of the popular reigning monarch, King George V, resplendent in his beard and the uniform of a vice admiral. Tables and chairs were scattered about the room sufficient in number to seat the eighty or so officers entitled to make use of the building. An internal door led to a second room which was about the same size as the mess and served as the officers' dining room.

One evening dinner had been served, and a group of five young single officers from the East Lancashire Regiment retired next door to the mess where they were enjoying a quiet smoke and an after-dinner port. A game of billiards was underway nearby and four more officers were playing darts on the other side of the mess. Two or three waiters, clad in smart white jackets and black trousers, circulated slowly dispensing drinks and snacks. The young men's conversation turned to the upcoming Christmas Military Ball now only ten days away.

The youngest, and the junior of the group, was second-lieutenant Sam Mills, fresh out of the Royal Military Academy, Sandhurst and enjoying Fulwood Barracks as his first posting.

'So, what happens at this Military Ball, gentlemen?'

Lieutenant John Ainsley was first to respond. 'Well Sam, if you don't have a current girlfriend, this is your best chance. The commanding officer buses in about forty young lasses from all around Preston for us single blokes and there are just about the right number to go round.'

'And there are some rippers too,' added Lieutenant Robbie Johns nodding enthusiastically.

'You can say that again,' chimed in Lieutenant Charles Smythe. 'It was last year's ball when I first met Jane. She and I have been going steady ever since. What about you, Captain Dillon? You've been based here for a few years now, so you must have seen a few Military Balls go by?'

Chapter Six   A Serious Prospect?

Captain Thomas Anton Dillon was by far the most experienced officer of this small group having joined the regiment back in 1911 at the age of nineteen. His first posting had been overseas in Kashmir, North-East India, for three years, from whence he, along with nearly all the other officers serving there, were rushed back to England after the outbreak of war in 1914. He had served with distinction in the trenches until badly injured at the battle of the Somme in 1916. Proudly Captain Dillon had witnessed the first use of tanks in warfare at this battle, however he had to be invalided home to undertake a long and painful recovery at a military hospital just outside of Bolton in Lancashire. The army had sent him there because Bolton was his family's home and the family could provide additional support.

Thomas's slow convalescence dragged on for almost eighteen months by which time the war was virtually over. Finally, he was deemed fit to re-join his regiment and was stationed at Fulwood Barracks early in 1919. His leg still gave him grief, particularly in the cold wet weather, but he made light of it. Military Balls were suspended during the war years but resumed in 1920 so Captain Thomas Dillon was about to attend his sixth Military Ball in a row. No wonder the junior officers sitting around him now regarded him as the sage on such matters.

The Captain took another sip of his port, moved his aching leg into a more comfortable position and looked across at his questioner.

'Aye Charles, this will be my sixth Military Ball. I think I might be the only officer here to have endured six in succession.'

There was a titter of laughter.

'Surely, they're not that bad, are they?' queried Sam.

'No, of course not. They're great fun really if you stay reasonably sober and behave yourself.'

'You'll need to watch your behaviour young Sam. Last year two blokes were put on a charge for being drunk and disorderly. The CO told them it was their one and only chance. Do it again and they would lose their commissions,' added John.

'Tell me Thomas, how many girl friends have you picked up at the balls over the six years?'

'Only a couple,' the Captain, replied. 'Pleasant enough girls, but certainly not marriage prospects.'

'You're getting too fussy Thomas. You must be about the only officer in the whole barracks in his thirties and not yet hitched,' remarked Robbie, good-naturedly.

'Just haven't found the right one yet Robbie, but you never know, the girl of my dreams may turn up at this year's Military Ball.'

* * *

When Captain Thomas Dillon returned to his lonely single officer's digs that evening, he opened the book he was reading but found it difficult to concentrate. Robbie's comment, 'you're getting too fussy Thomas' was worrying him. He was thirty-three years old and still single. When he looked around at his fellow officers of the same age, most had been married for years and had families by now, it was only the young lieutenants and subalterns who remained single. They must regard him as a bit of an oddity, a captain, likely to be promoted to major soon, receiving an excellent salary, but still stubbornly single. There was only one officer in the entire barracks who was older than Thomas and still not married, rather disrespectfully referred to as 'Old Soppy'. Rumour had it that Major Sopworth was homosexual although this remained unsubstantiated. Now in his forties, and podgy, the major stood out as an embarrassing anomaly. Captain Thomas Dillon certainly didn't wish to become an object of derision like the unfortunate 'Old Soppy'.

Captain Thomas Dillon was a man of high principles with a deeply held moral code based on his strong Roman Catholic faith. Coming from a family steeped in religious observance, his faith was central to all he did and how he behaved. His older brother had even entered the church and was a priest currently serving in a rural parish in Cumberland. Thomas would never swear, or smoke, or take advantage of a young lady, although a quiet alcoholic drink was considered perfectly acceptable. Thomas would never miss Sunday Mass and prayed or read his Bible every day.

Thomas was aware that some people considered he was a bit too strait-laced. Naturally reserved, he was never the life and soul at a party but still managed to enjoy himself quietly and respectfully. Captain Dillon possessed a number of personal attributes that made him an excellent officer and these he had displayed with distinction during the war and in the aftermath. There was no doubting his courage when leading his men in the trenches, together with his humility and intense concern for the welfare of his men. At the height of battle, he had displayed calm, rational leadership that had earnt the greatest respect from his men. In addition, he had built up an enviable reputation during his fourteen years as an officer for total honesty, devotion to duty, reliability and decency as a human being. He was well-liked and respected by all who met him.

Over the years Thomas had had a number of girlfriends, a few he had become very fond of, but there had never been a girl he wanted to marry and with whom he might wish to spend the rest of his life. Perhaps they were right, and he was too fussy? Maybe he was looking for the perfect girl and no such person existed?

The captain had a general impression of the person he hoped to marry. Ideally, she should be a good Catholic girl, intelligent enough to engage in lively conversation and enjoy aesthetic pursuits such as concerts, opera, theatre, ballet, art galleries, literature and museums. He hoped to find someone who was more outgoing than he, who, in a few years' time, would be gifted at frequently entertaining important visitors as he climbed the promotion ladder. Thomas was ambitious and his CO had already hinted that he anticipated he would make full Colonel in a few years' time. In fact, Thomas's name had already been put up to the War Office Selection Board for consideration of a promotion to the rank of major. Captain Dillon hoped the person he married was a more relaxed sort of person and could bring a sense of fun to formal occasions. Good looks would be a bonus, but not essential, since it was what was inside a person that mattered most.

Chapter Six   A Serious Prospect?

With his sixth Military Ball to be staged in ten days' time, Thomas retired to bed, after praying earnestly that this time the right young lady would miraculously appear.

CHAPTER SEVEN

The Military Ball

Eve Chadwick was particularly excited about going to the Military Ball. Several friends had also been invited for the first time so there was much giggling and silly chatter about the chances of becoming romantically involved with a handsome young officer in uniform as they awaited the bus to take them to the ball. It was a cold crisp night as the young ladies climbed aboard the special green army bus sent from the barracks which was to transport them to their destination in time for the grand opening at eight o'clock. Climbing up the steep steps of the bus in their lovely long dresses and high-heeled shoes was no easy business and it took a good deal longer than anticipated. Finally, after much nervous twittering, everyone was seated, and the two corporals, entrusted with the task of safely conveying the young women to the barracks, announced they were leaving.

They made for a colourful coterie, bubbling with excitement with some surreptitiously checking their appearance in the bus's windows. A cacophony of intriguing and contrasting perfumes filled the interior and the lively hubbub of conversation was punctuated by the occasional squeal when a handbag was mislaid or some other minor mishap occurred. On arrival, ten minutes late, the process of disembarking seemed to take even longer until at last they were led, like a long multi-coloured snake, into the Drill Hall.

Most were heard to gasp as they entered the brilliantly lit Drill Hall accompanied by the music of a tall bagpiper resplendent in full military regalia. They were ushered to two rows of empty chairs behind the married officers sitting with their wives who stood politely as the young ladies entered and found their seats. At the very back of the Drill Hall stood the single officers busily assessing the qualities of the young ladies as they paraded past them to find their seats. Once the guests were comfortably seated the formal proceedings began.

At the front of the hall stood a temporary stage onto which a number of dignitaries now filed. Eve recognised the Mayor of Preston and his wife, Gertrude, but had to wait to discover who the other five distinguished people were. One was the regimental chaplain who duly blessed the proceedings and the others were the two commanding officers and their wives. Both COs spoke briefly and then thanked the band in advance, those who had decorated the hall and the chefs and stewards who had prepared the food and would be waiting on the guests throughout the evening. The formalities ended with a rousing rendition of 'God Save the King'.

As if by magic, the chairs were relocated to the sides of the ballroom and the full extent of the decorations became apparent. The theme this year was King Neptune and his watery realm. The walls were festooned with underwater scenes of sunken ships and gleaming treasure, strange deep-sea creatures of all shapes and colours and seaweed forests replete with an occasional mermaid peeping out. King Neptune sat majestically upon his throne holding his trident aloft and surrounded by gymnastic water nymphs and benign-looking seals. The Loch Ness monster lurked menacingly in the backwaters. It was a sight to behold.

An eight-piece band was busy tuning up at one end of the hall and some of the married officers were already frequenting the bar at the other. In front of the band was a microphone behind which stood the compere for the night, rather strangely dressed as a penguin, but with his face clear so he could communicate. While the girls were taking all this in, the single officers were moving in, perhaps indecently quickly, to engage them in conversation. As always seemed to happen at these events, two or three men would select the same attractive girl and arrive concurrently, thereby leaving a few of the plainer, less attractive lasses without a partner at all. A few minutes of embarrassing jockeying for positions ensued before the penguin welcomed everybody again and called on the gentlemen to please select their partners for the first dance of the night, a Barn Dance.

Eve, being one of the most beautiful girls to grace the ballroom, found herself unexpectedly confronted by three young men, two of whom were so busy talking at her at the same time that she couldn't work out what on earth they were saying. Standing between them was a tall good-looking man who was just smiling pleasantly at her. He had the most fabulous eyes, she noted, and they were fixed on her in a kindly way. Without hesitation she extended her hands to the officer in the middle, thereby accepting his invitation to join him for the Barn Dance. The music began and they quickly found a place in the elliptical circle of dancers that had already formed and were off and away for the first dance of the evening.

Eve was relieved to find her partner was an excellent dancer being light on his feet while at the same time providing her with a firm lead. He was well built, extremely smartly dressed and a good deal older than the men she normally danced with. She wasn't sure what to make of the age difference but enjoyed the dance anyway. The music soon stopped and the penguin announced in a loud voice that the Barn Dance would now become a Progressive Barn Dance. They barely had time to draw breath before the music resumed. Eve wondered if this quiet pleasant man would seek her out again when the dance ended.

Ten minutes later the dancers had progressed right round the hall and were just back with their original partner when the music abruptly stopped and the penguin was heard to compliment the band on their clever timing. So, surprisingly, Eve was back with her quiet pleasant officer.

'May I introduce myself. My name is Thomas Dillon.'

'Good evening Thomas. I'm Evelyn Chadwick, Eve for short,' and she flashed him a smile.

'I expect you'd like something to drink after all that exercise?'

'Oh, yes please, something long and cool.'

'Follow me.'

Thomas led her towards the bar but didn't join one of the lengthy queues lined up waiting to order drinks. Instead, he went to one end of the bar and caught the eye of one of the men serving who finished what he was doing and came straight over to Thomas who quietly gave him his order. Eve was impressed! The man she was with must be quite senior to be able to pull rank like this.

'Would you like to meet a few of my colleagues?' Thomas inquired.

'Yes, of course, I'd love to.'

Eve expected to be taken to meet some of the young, single officers, however, Thomas instead led her over to a group of married officers and their wives. She lost count of the number of hands she shook and names she heard and just kept smiling sweetly and saying 'glad to meet you' or 'how do you do' to each new person. These older, more senior officers, were clearly Thomas's friends rather than the young studs still scrummaging at the bar to get their drinks. She noted the respectful way they all spoke to Thomas and how pleased they were to welcome him into their circle. This was certainly a more mature gathering than she had ever joined before but everyone seemed welcoming. The married ladies were particularly interested to meet her. For a fleeting moment, Eve wondered whether she had learnt enough socially correct etiquette and polite behaviour for the wives to accept her as a lady. She was worried she might accidentally drop an 'h' or do something else to reveal her true working-class origins. The folk she was mixing with at this Military Ball had most likely been through private schools and hailed from upper or middle-class backgrounds. Eve was exchanging small talk with a couple of the ladies when the penguin invited the gentlemen to find their partners for a waltz. Thomas caught her eye and the next moment she was back on the dance floor.

'This is a beautiful dress you are wearing, Eve.'

'Thank you, Thomas, I'm so pleased you like it.'

'Is it one of the latest fashions?'

'Yes, this dress is from the London winter collection. I work at Miss June Doyer's Dress Shop which is undoubtedly the best in Preston.'

Thomas laughed easily. 'I have to admit I don't frequent the Preston dress shops very often so I'm sure you're right.'

It was Eve's turn to laugh. 'I must say you look very smartly turned out too,' she said with a mischievous smile.

And so, they spent the evening together. They danced energetically until the last waltz was called at around two in the morning. Captain Thomas Dillon was fascinated with Eve. He couldn't decide what it was that intrigued him so, but there was something refreshingly different about this young woman. She had a delightfully engaging personality and was stunningly attractive to look at. There would hardly be another woman at the Ball to match her beauty. Many of his fellow officers cast envious eyes in his direction as he swirled around the dance floor leading this excellent, natural dancer. They chatted pleasantly whenever possible, but he didn't discover much about Eve's background, apart from where she worked. The fact that she found it necessary to work at all was revealing in itself.

Eve, on the other hand, was quietly smitten. She admired this strong, quiet, good-looking man who seemed to be almost too nice to be true. Thomas was a fine dancer and she formed the impression that anything he did he would work at assiduously until he reached near perfection. He was reticent to speak about his age or previous army service but a couple of times she noticed him flexing his right leg as though it was paining him. When she inquired if his leg was hurting, he dismissed it as an old war wound that still flared up from time to time. She enjoyed his maturity, his 'man of the world' persona. When she was with Thomas, she felt more grown-up, lady-like, no longer an immature seventeen-year-old teenager. Eve knew he was interested in her by the way he treated her and looked at her but at the same time she sensed a certain reservedness in his behaviour. He came across as the perfect gentleman.

As they took to the floor for the last waltz, and fell easily into the correct dance hold, she could feel his strong body up against hers. She allowed herself to be gently serenaded as the two of them seemed to move to the music as one. Never before had she experienced such closeness with a man and she found it excited her. If Thomas was to kiss her now, she realised she would be helpless to resist. These feelings of desire were powerful and disturbing.

'Eve?'

'Yes, Thomas.'

'This has been a beautiful evening. I've loved dancing with you. You're an exceptional dancer.'

'Only because you know how to lead.'

'I wonder if I might see you again?'

'Yes, I'd like that.'

'I have a car, so we can go anywhere we want.'

'Wow, do you? That's marvellous.'

'Before you get back on that bus perhaps you could give me your telephone number?'

'Of course. We don't have a telephone at home yet, but you can ring me at work between eight in the morning and five in the evening. It would be best if you ring during my lunchtime though.'

'When's that?'

'Twelve to twelve-thirty.'

'Okay, I'll organise something and ring you next week.'

'That would be lovely.' And she felt him give her a slight squeeze.

As soon as the dance finished the spell was broken. Thomas escorted her to the bus and saw her safely aboard. He gave her hand a gentle squeeze but there was no attempt at a kiss. She slipped him a piece of paper with her telephone number. All around them were couples embracing and snogging and it took the two corporals several minutes to disengage the numerous amorous pairs and herd the girls back on the bus.

CHAPTER EIGHT

Early Issues

It was three o'clock in the morning when the army bus dropped Eve off at 195 Tulketh Brow. She had endured her fair share of ribbing on the journey home and one drunken lass had rudely referred to Thomas as a 'cradle-snatcher'. However, Eve could give back as well as she received, and didn't hesitate to remind Thomas's detractor that she was too drunk to even know whether the officer she was with had kissed her or not. Eve tiptoed to her bedroom and was soon sound asleep.

Not unexpectedly, Eve slept in on Sunday morning and

didn't attend matins with the rest of her family. When they returned from church around midday, she was slowly surfacing. There was no hangover since Thomas had told her two alcoholic drinks for the night was enough. Eve had been mildly surprised by this drinks embargo since she had preconceived ideas that all soldiers drank heavily, if not to excess. Certainly, many had over-imbibed but not Thomas. Her parents dragged her downstairs for lunch where her brother George, now fifteen, was also sitting and interested to hear about what had happened at the Military Ball.

Eve spent ten minutes outlining the proceedings, describing in some detail the watery King Neptune decorations and singing the praises of the eight-piece band. Her mother's antennae were twitching furiously, however, for she had sensed that her daughter had met someone special at the ball, and, like all mothers, she wanted details. It was a situation Eve couldn't avoid; she might as well tell them now.

'So darling, did you meet any nice young officers?'

'I bet she did,' chimed in George junior, with a grin plastered all over his face.

They looked at Eve expectantly and waited.

'Well, yes, I did meet a nice man.'

'How nice?' challenged her brother, cheekily.

'Okay, lay off son,' interjected George Senior.

Again, they stared at Eve, hungrily awaiting further clarification.

'I danced with the same man the whole evening. His name's Thomas Dillon. He's a great dancer so we got on well.'

'Thomas Dillon? I don't think there's any Dillons around these parts?' Eve's mother pondered out loud.

'Ain't ever done a gravestone for a Dillon.'

'Well, what's he like then? Are you going to be stepping out together?'

'Possibly.'

'That's nice dear. What's he like then?'

Eve knew she had to feed them some crumbs otherwise her mother would pester her for days.

'He's a captain, Captain Thomas Dillon, and he was in the war.'

'In the war?' exclaimed her father. 'Ow old's this geezer then?'

'I don't know father.'

'Well, if he were fightin' in the war 'e must be at least twenty-five cos the war ended seven years ago.'

'He told me he was wounded because his leg was hurting sometimes when we danced.'

'A captain you said, Eve?'

'Yes, Father.'

'Well, I be blowed! A captain's getting up the ranks a bit. When I did all them war memorials, I had to inscribe the names of the dead accordin' to their seniority. Didn't get too many dead'uns up above a captain.'

'So, is he all hoity-toity then, dear?'

'No Mother, he's not at all. I think you'll like him.'

There was an uneasy quiet. The family was unconvinced.

'And when are you stepping out with this captain, Eve?'

'I don't know mother. He's going to ring me at work next week and arrange something. He owns a car!'

This last piece of information was met with astonishment. 'A car!' they exclaimed in unison.

'Is it a Leyland?' George Junior asked. 'It better be,' he added.

'I don't know what it is,' Eve replied.

'Righto, wash your hands, it's time for lunch.'

* * *

Eve knew her mother would corner her sometime soon and probe for more information and probably offer some well-meaning motherly advice. Each time she had 'stepped out' with a boy previously her mother had acted as both inquisitor and mentor. Going out with a captain from the British Army had come as quite a shock and Eve knew her mother was having trouble coming to terms with this potentially more serious suitor. She was not wrong; on Sunday evening as they washed up, her mother seized her chance.

'Eve dear, I've been thinking about this army officer that wants to take you out. Are you sure his intentions are honourable?'

'Oh, come on mother, can't you trust my judgement?'

'Well dear, sometimes men can be awfully persuasive. You are still so young and this is a mature man who has seen a lot of the world. You said he had fought in the war and been injured but what else do you know about him?'

'Not much mother. That's why I'm happy to go out with him to find out more.'

'Up to now you've had a few boyfriends but they have all been around your age but this is a totally different situation. This captain fellow is a much older man. Do you think he's genuinely interested in you, or is he interested in something else?'

'What are you suggesting, mother? I have no intention of losing my virginity until I get married so please don't say things like that!'

'I'm sorry darling that comment was probably not called for. I'm just a mother worrying about her lovely daughter and not wanting her to get into trouble.'

'I'm sure Thomas is not like that, mother. Did you know he stopped me having another alcoholic drink because he was worried it might affect me? That shows how responsible he is, doesn't it?'

'All right darling, I'm looking forward to hearing all about him when you find out some more.'

And there the conversation ended. Eve realised her family were anxious and she resolved to quiz Thomas thoroughly and then, hopefully, put them at ease with the information she had gleaned.

* * *

Eve went to work as usual on Monday morning to find her colleagues abuzz to hear how the Military Ball had gone. Even June Doyer seemed interested. Eve provided a glowing report but made no mention of her dancing the night away with the captain. The girls appeared almost as interested to discover whether Eve had received complimentary remarks about her new dress since it had been one of June Doyer's latest acquisitions from London. Eve was able to truthfully report she had indeed enjoyed several positive comments. As the group broke up, Eve was able to have a quiet word with June Doyer on her own about the likelihood that a telephone call might come for her during her lunch break. Miss Doyer never encouraged the use of her business telephone, but on this occasion, she was perceptive enough to think that it might be a young man Eve had met at the ball who would be ringing.

'You may use my work telephone just this once Eve, but not again please.'

There was a small room, not much bigger than a broom cupboard at the back of the shop where the girls took their lunch breaks. Half an hour was permitted. The room was next door to Miss Doyer's office so it was easy to hear if the telephone rang. Eve was surprised to find her heart beating faster than usual as she moved to the back of the shop to start her short break anticipating a call from Thomas. Lunch for her was a sandwich and a piece of fruit. As a special treat her mother sometimes included a biscuit or a small piece of cake. Eve, and the other girl rostered to have lunch with her, squeezed into the only two rickety wooden chairs provided and began chatting and eating. Miss Doyer was in her office but there was no telephone call.

Tuesday was the same.

Things went badly wrong on Wednesday. Eve and her colleague were having their lunch when the telephone started ringing. Eve jumped up, much to the surprise of her colleague, who was unaware that Eve was expecting a call. However, Miss Doyer was not in her office so the telephone rang out. It had been made abundantly clear to the girls that Miss Doyer, and only Miss Doyer, ever answered telephone calls. If Miss Doyer was not in the office to take the calls then they went unanswered. Eve was convinced that this was the call from Thomas that she was expecting. Feeling panicky, she excused herself and ran out into the shop to find her boss but there was no sign of her. One of the girls said she had left to do a spot of shopping. Eve knew she had let Thomas down; she was sure it was him. Now he might decide not to bother with her anymore and to totally forget their night of dancing altogether.

Eve was even more anxious when she arrived at work on Thursday. Would Thomas try again? Would Miss Doyer remain in her office during her lunchbreak? The shop was unusually busy during the morning and ten minutes before Eve was scheduled to go to lunch a large buxom woman entered and made it abundantly clear she expected immediate service. Eve was the only one of the girls not already preoccupied with a customer so, with a forced smile, she advanced towards the rotund lady and posed the appropriate opening question she had been trained to use. 'Good morning madam, may I be of any assistance?'

Twenty minutes later Eve was still dealing with this rather disagreeable woman, when Miss Doyer approached them. It was now well into Eve's lunch break and she was at her wits' end to find a way out of her predicament. But the problem resolved itself beautifully.

'My dear Mrs Hardcastle, how delightful to see you again,' gushed Miss Doyer. 'Let me give you the benefit of *my* personal attention. Miss Chadwick, would you please answer the gentleman on the telephone for me?'

Eve needed no second bidding. Trying to remain calm and collected she headed for the office and picked up the receiver.

'Good afternoon. This is Miss June Doyer's Dress Shop. May I be of assistance?'

'Is that Miss Eve Chadwick?'

'Yes, it is Thomas. I'm so glad you have rung. Did you ring yesterday?'

'I did, but there was no answer and I was going to order three new dresses too.'

Eve laughed. 'I can take your order now if you like?'

'Well, I owe you an apology for not ringing earlier in the week. We were unexpectedly sent out on manoeuvres on Monday and Tuesday so it was impossible to telephone you. But here I am now. Now, I have booked a table for two at *The Three Nuns Hotel* in the High Street for Saturday evening. Would you care to join me?'

'Oh, yes please.'

'It will be a good opportunity to get to know each other a little better. If you give me your address, I'll call round and pick you up in the car at about seven o'clock.'

'Thank you, Thomas. That sounds wonderful. I live at 195 Tulketh Brow. Do you know where that is?'

Chapter Eight   Early Issues

'No, but we army officers know how to read maps. I look forward to seeing you at seven.'

Before Eve had time to say anything more, Thomas had rung off.

* * *

A minute before seven o'clock, in the true military tradition of being punctual, anyone moving along Tulketh Brow on Saturday evening would have witnessed a shiny bright red car, with its hood locked down, pull up outside number 195. Not many automobiles were ever seen on Tulketh Brow because the residents there were not in a wealthy enough income bracket to afford cars.

Eve was waiting anxiously at their front window with her parents hovering behind her keen to get a glimpse of this new man in Eve's life. A slight drizzle was falling and it was dark. The nearest street lamp gave off little more than a soft glow so that the arrival of a car outside number 195 appeared to light up the whole street. None of the houses in Tulketh Brow boasted outside lights.

A moment later there was a polite knock at the front door. Eve kissed her parents quickly, grabbed her evening handbag and hurried to open the door. Thomas was standing there smiling under a large umbrella. Once again she was struck by how tall and strong he looked. He opened the passenger door for her and she climbed in. Eve had only twice been in a car before so this was really exciting.

'What kind of a car is this, Thomas?'

'It's a 1922 Sunbeam 16/40 two-seater Sports Tourer.'

'Wow, does it go fast?'

He glanced at her. 'Why, do you like speed?'

'I don't know. This is only the third car I've ever been in and never in the front seat.'

'Well, it's a sports car so it's built to go fast with seats for only two people.'

Eve giggled and studied the instrument panel to try and work out what everything did.

Preston was not a large town and within a few minutes they pulled into the car park at the rear of *The Three Nuns*. Another dash under the umbrella and they were safely inside in the relative warmth of the restaurant.

Eve realised she was on dangerous ground, never before had she eaten at a high-class restaurant. She had decided beforehand that her best tactic was to carefully follow everything that Thomas did. The last thing she wanted was to expose her total ignorance of etiquette and polite manners when eating out. If she was to marry into the upper classes one day she had better learn how to behave on these occasions. Should she make a mess of things tonight, she feared Thomas would drop her like a hot plate and Eve desperately hoped it would not come to that.

'Good evening sir, good evening madam. Welcome to *The Three Nuns*. May I take your umbrella and coats?'

A young man, smartly dressed in a dinner jacket, had asked this question as they entered the dimly lit, but warm foyer.

The young man placed Thomas's umbrella in a special receptacle with a couple of others. Next, he stood behind Thomas, eased off his coat and took his scarf and gloves which he proceeded to hang up on a row of pegs. He returned to repeat the process for Eve who felt acutely embarrassed because her one and only coat was a cheap, poor quality one, and she had no gloves or scarf to give to the young man. A true professional, the young man gave no indication that he had noticed anything out of the ordinary as with a flourish he hung Eve's meagre coat on the hook next to Thomas's.

'Do you have a reservation, sir?'

'Indeed, I have. Captain Dillon.'

'Thank you, sir. If you would care to follow me, I will convey you to your table.'

The young man smiled and gestured towards a closed double door which miraculously opened as they approached. The large room they entered contained perhaps twenty tables each with a soft red light glowing in the centre. Most tables were occupied by well-to-do looking people chatting amiably. As Eve followed Thomas and the young man, winding between the tables, she was acutely aware that many pairs of eyes were assessing her, judging her and trying to place her in Preston society. She would have rated highly for her looks, poorly for her apparel and a complete blank with regard to where she fitted in with the upper echelons of Preston gentry.

The young man led them to the side of the room where there was a table for two set up ready for their meal. A waitress was already waiting for them at the table.

'Good evening sir, good evening madam. My name is Susan and I'll be your waitress this evening.'

Up to this point Eve had been able to hide behind Thomas and simply follow his lead but now it was 'ladies first'. Susan had pulled one of the chairs out and was looking directly at Eve, who correctly interpreted this as an invitation to sit on it, which she did. Susan repeated the procedure for Thomas. Next Eve was surprised to find Susan flicking open a napkin and placing it gently on her lap. The same happened to Thomas. Susan then announced that the soup du jour was French Onion and quietly left to be immediately replaced by a waiter, wearing white gloves, who presented a small booklet to Thomas together with a slight bow.

Thomas sat back, completely relaxed and at ease, whilst Eve sat with a straight back on the edge of her chair looking nervously at this man who was taking her out to dinner.

'Let's decide what we are having before I order the wine,' and he picked up his menu and began thumbing through. Eve did the same but was horrified to discover that not only was the menu presented in a peculiar fancy style of writing but she barely recognised any of the words. Half of what was set out before her was either French or Italian, so there was a plethora of strange words she was totally unfamiliar with.

'What would *you* recommend, Thomas?' Eve complimented herself on this clever move.

Matters became a little easier for Eve from hereon. She allowed Thomas to do the ordering of their meal together with an appropriate bottle of wine. Eve was surprised to find

Susan return to reorganise their cutlery. Apparently, there were specially shaped spoons for the soup and then her knife and fork were suddenly whisked away and replaced by different shaped ones to be used for her fish. Eve was still perplexed by the considerable array of eating utensils arranged on either side of her placemat but was quick to observe that you start from the outside and work inwards. All quite fascinating!

Eve was intrigued at the slow pace of the meal. At home she grabbed her chair, wolfed down her meal before jumping up again to do the washing up; a meal lasted twenty minutes at best. Here at *The Three Nuns*, after twenty minutes the soup still hadn't arrived. The long waiting between courses didn't appear to worry anybody else; they simply ordered more drinks and chatted on increasingly loudly.

Eve and Thomas were well into their second glass of wine before the French onion soup put in an appearance. She had to admit it was delicious though, as was the warm bread roll gently placed on her side plate with a set of tongs and accompanied by peculiar curly pieces of butter. Two glasses of excellent white wine, and nothing to eat since lunchtime, was making Eve light-headed and less inhibited. She was starting to relax. Thomas kept looking at her with those gorgeous eyes and she felt warm and tender towards him.

As the meal progressed, Thomas and Eve both knew they must raise issues that were worrying them. For Thomas it was his age, for Eve it was her working-class roots. While they were awaiting their main course, Thomas grasped the nettle.

'Eve, would you mind if I asked how old you are?'

Eve coloured slightly for she knew she was years younger than Thomas and if he realised her youthful age, he might regard her as little more than a girl. Nervously she replied, 'I'm seventeen.'

'Only seventeen!' Thomas immediately regretted he had reacted with such surprise in his voice, for he had wrongly guessed she was about nineteen, and this revelation of her youthfulness made his next question even more difficult.

'How old do you think I am, Eve?'

She looked at him steadily, realising he must be feeling as though he was too old for her. After a moment or two, and still holding his gaze, she decided to underestimate.

'Twenty-nine, perhaps thirty?'

Thomas gave a little laugh. 'Eve, there are quite a few years between us. Is that a problem for you?'

'I don't think so. How old are you then?'

'I'm thirty-three.'

Eve tried not to look surprised but Thomas was certainly rather older than she had suspected. She did the sums: Thomas was nearly twice her age!

He was looking earnestly at her now while this information sank in, pleading with his eyes for confirmation that his age was not going to be a barrier to their relationship.

'It's okay, Thomas. It really is.'

A look of relief relaxed his face and he smiled broadly. She loved that big smile that creased his handsome face.

'Thomas, I have something I want to tell you.'

'Fire away.'

Eve ignored the military term and pitched in.

'I don't quite know how to broach this topic with you, Thomas.'

'Well try me.' And he gave her an encouraging smile.

'I... I... you may have realised... I have had a very different background to you... I...'

Thomas placed his hand over Eve's and interrupted her.

'I think I know what you are going to tell me and it doesn't worry me one iota. I like to think I have strong Christian principles and somebody's background never worries me. In God's eyes we are all born equal whatever circumstances we are brought up in. Nobody can choose who their parents are. What is important is what you become.' And he gave her hand a little squeeze.

'So, you don't mind that I didn't go to a private school like you, or that my parents are working class people, or that we live in Tulketh Brow, the poor end of town?'

'Not in the slightest. In fact, I rather like the idea that you have come from a less fortunate background than I, because it means I can more easily spoil you and take you to see heaps of things you have probably never even heard about.'

'Oh Thomas, that's wonderful.' Bravely she placed her spare hand over his, just as Susan reappeared with their desserts.

The remainder of the evening went swimmingly for them both. Thomas ordered coffee and port to follow and Eve began to feel quite amorous as the additional alcohol took effect. The more time she spent with Thomas the more she liked him. She watched with interest the intricacies of settling the bill and tipping the waitress and then managed to walk out between the tables at the end of the evening without losing her balance.

She wondered whether her captain would try to kiss her and what she would do if he did. Only one young lad had ever managed to kiss her on the lips and it was nothing to write home about. It lasted for a fleeting second and she hardly realised it had happened.

Captain Dillon, however, proved the perfect gentleman. Polite and attentive on the way home, he jumped out of the car to open her car door and escorted her to the door of her house where he bade her good night and promised to be in contact again soon. No kisses!

CHAPTER NINE

The 'Drinks' Party

Their first date had been a resounding success. Thomas and Eve both believed their budding relationship had a promising future and wanted to keep seeing each other.

Christmas was rapidly approaching and they managed to meet three more times before the actual day. One of these occasions was when Thomas invited Eve to join him at the Officers' Mess for their Christmas party. There was much carousing and most of the officers were the worse for wear by the time the evening fizzled out in the early hours of the morning. Thomas was a modest drinker and Eve was more than happy to follow his example. Concerned that the party might get out of hand, Thomas drove Eve home just after midnight. He felt almost paternal and certainly protective towards her since she was only a seventeen-year-old.

Eve's most exhilarating date was the night Thomas took her to see Shakespeare's Macbeth. The Manchester Repertory Society staged the production in the Preston Town Hall over five nights and played to packed audiences. This was Eve's first experience of theatre and she was amazed. Thomas had warned her to dress up for the occasion which was, indeed, a glittering affair. Eve couldn't believe the dresses, hairdos and expensive jewellery on display. She sensed the thrill of anticipation before the first curtain and revelled in the performances of the leading actors. Thomas had outlined the plot to her beforehand, so she was able to follow the play reasonably well. Halfway through the third act she was surprised to discover they were holding hands.

The third time they met before Christmas was the one most fraught with danger. Eve's parents were desperate to meet Captain Thomas Dillon and Eve knew she must oblige. Never before had she brought a male friend home but this liaison was clearly becoming a serious one. It was only proper that Thomas be invited to their house to meet her parents, although, like most teenagers, Eve dreaded the prospect. There were long, and at times, fierce discussions about how best to host Thomas. Eve's father was keen to have him come for tea one night and had to be reminded that it was not 'tea' but 'dinner'. Mrs Chadwick was dead against this idea because, as she quite rightly asserted, she didn't have a proper dinner set or

Chapter Nine   The 'Drinks' Party

any decent cutlery. As a family they had always made do with a disparate collection of odd plates, cups and eating utensils.

'But you're a bloody good cook, Mother. What the man needs is a good feed after all the rubbish they serve up in the army.'

'Maybe George, but I ain't got the proper stuff to serve it up on. I can't give an officer food on old cracked plates.'

'It ain't the stuff you serve it up on that matters, it's the quality of the grub, Annie.'

'I'm still not doin' it!'

'Oh, come on Annie, your shepherd's pie is fit for a bloody king. I bet he doesn't get one 'alf as good as yours up there at bloody Fulwood Barracks!'

'I don't care 'ow good my shepherd's pie is, I'm not dishing it up on cracked and chipped plates and that's the end of the matter, George!'

'I've got an idea,' interjected Eve.

'What's that then, love?' her mother asked.

'Why don't we forget the meal altogether and invite Thomas round for Christmas drinks?'

'Hey, that's a dandy idea and then we can get him pissed.'

'No Father, it's something the snobs do. They're often going round to other people's places for drinks. I know that because Thomas has told me he has been invited out for Christmas drinks to friends' places.'

'We've never done that before,' her mother said, cautiously, 'what do you need for that?'

'Thomas says they have a few drinks, usually alcohol, and they put out plates with snacks on them.'

'What sort of snacks?'

'Just some biscuits or some cheese. Nothing special, Mother.'

'I think I could do that but we'd need four wine glasses and some wine.'

'What's wrong with beer, Annie? We've got four beer tankards, but we ain't got no wine glasses,' George chimed in.

'Well, it might be time you lifted your game then, George,' Annie remarked.

George sniffed. 'The boss 'as got wine glasses. I'll borrow 'em. I'll call in at the pub on me way home tomorrow and buy a bottle of wine too. Give us a bit out of your housekeeping money, love.'

So, it was decided that Thomas would be invited to Christmas drinks, a first for the Chadwick family.

* * *

The next day, Annie went up to Mrs Moriarty's nursing home to visit the good lady but she also had an ulterior motive: she wanted to quiz the matriarch about what was involved in having someone round for 'drinks.' An hour or so later she emerged feeling far more confident. As she walked home, she planned precisely what she would provide at her inaugural Christmas drinks party.

An evening was selected and Thomas politely accepted their invitation. As might be expected, the Chadwicks were nervous wrecks as the time for the captain's arrival drew nigh. The part of the house that might be seen by Thomas was scrubbed, dusted and polished like never before, much to George Senior's annoyance.

Chapter Nine The 'Drinks' Party

'Cleaning's a waste of time,' he claimed, 'all you're doing is moving the dirt from one place to another.'

Be that as it may, Annie was determined to make as good an impression as possible. No doubt Captain Dillon had servants at his home and Eve had told her he had a kind of a servant in the army too. Apparently, this man was called a 'batman' although Eve didn't know why he was called that, or what he was supposed to do. Annie reasoned that if Eve was serious about this captain fellow then the rest of the family must do everything possible to encourage the match.

Punctual as always, Captain Thomas Dillon's bright red sports car pulled up outside number 195 Tulketh Brow precisely one minute before seven o'clock. Conscious of the importance of the occasion, the Chadwicks had taken extra special care this year with their Christmas decorations. The sitting room boasted three separate small windows arranged in a slight curve to form a shallow bay window. Into each window Annie had placed a candle that now glowed welcomingly. Multicoloured interlocking paper chains were suspended diagonally across the sitting room ceiling and the mantlepiece displayed a small nativity scene illuminated by another candle. Small sprigs of prickly dark green holly with shiny red berries sat atop the three old pictures they owned. The electric light in the centre of the room was partly obscured by a sizeable bunch of mistletoe. Annie had deliberated long and hard whether the inclusion of mistletoe was appropriate since it had strong connotations with kissing and romance. For some reason kissing under the mistletoe had become a source of much fun in recent years.

In the end, following persistent prompting from Eve, she had included the mistletoe.

A cheerful fire crackled away in the fireplace spitting out sparks that were stopped from landing on the one and only piece of carpet in the house by an ancient metal fender. There was ample coal ready in the coal scuttle. The Chadwicks owned but two easy chairs which were now strategically positioned facing the fireplace together with three straight-back chairs. It had been decided the two easy chairs would be occupied by George, as head of the family and their important visitor. The dining room table had been moved up against a wall and contained all the items that Annie believed were required for Christmas drinks. On the table were a bottle of unopened cheap French red wine, four wine glasses that George had successfully borrowed from his boss, four bottles of stout and two beer tankards. Two bottles of lemonade for George Junior completed the range of drinks. They had even remembered to borrow a bottle opener although neither George nor Annie knew how to de-cork a wine bottle.

Annie's three best plates were sitting proudly on the table. One plate contained a special treat of freshly roasted chestnuts, a second plate held small cubes of cheddar cheese surrounded by savoury biscuits and the third consisted of what George referred to as 'manicured' sandwiches. By this he meant that all the crusts had been removed and the fluffy white bread had been cut up into small mouthful-sized triangles. They were jam and honey sandwiches. Annie would have preferred to have had a fruit platter but fruit was virtually impossible

Chapter Nine   The 'Drinks' Party

to procure at this time of year. She had borrowed a set of five matching side plates from a friend up the road and had washed and ironed five napkins. No cutlery was necessary as she was serving finger food only.

The family was dressed to the nines for the occasion: this meant wearing their Sunday best clothes as if they were going to church. Everyone's shoes had been polished and father and son both sported ties and jackets. The ladies had dispensed with their Sunday hats of course but had taken great care over their appearance including applying perfume and a touch of lipstick. Eve's dress might be regarded by some as a trifle too tight fitting for it revealed a generous and shapely figure. Young George was well enough turned out but had regarded this whole rigmarole as a bit 'over the top' and had cooperated somewhat grudgingly.

If the Chadwicks were worried about the evening, Thomas was equally concerned about doing the right thing. He appreciated that he and the Chadwick family originated from totally different strata of British society. However, he had already become fond of Eve in the short time he had known her and was anxious to continue and hopefully deepen this relationship. The last thing he wanted to do was to embarrass Eve, or her parents, in anyway. He was wearing smart mufti which included his regimental tie and a Harris Tweed jacket. As was customary at such functions, he had brought a bottle of good quality Italian wine to give to his hosts.

The door was opened to him by a pleasant looking lady in her late thirties and still attractive. She introduced herself as Mrs Annie Chadwick. Shaking her hand warmly, Thomas realised with a bit of a shock that Eve's mother was closer to his own age than the young woman he was courting. She led him straight through to a small room at the front of the house which was warm and snug. Three people were standing there to welcome him.

'This is my husband, George.'

'How do you do?'

'Glad to meet you, Captain.' They shook hands firmly and Thomas noted the strong calloused hands of a labourer.

'Please, just call me Thomas.'

'And this is me youngest and 'e's called George and all.'

They shook hands. Young George was impressed to find such a strong handsome man looking down and smiling openly at him. He was several inches taller than his father.

'Good to meet you, George.'

'And of course, you know our Eve.'

'Hello, Eve.'

There was an awkward moment of silence before everyone started talking at once and then they all stopped again. Nervous laughter followed.

'I've brought you a bottle of wine.' Thomas moved over to hand the bottle to George Senior.

'Aw, thank you for that. It'll go down a treat. Take a seat Captain... I mean Thomas.' George gestured towards the nearest easy chair and plonked himself down on the other one.

Thomas was sure there was a spring out of place, or perhaps altogether missing, in the seat of his armchair, but he

Chapter Nine   The 'Drinks' Party

ignored the minor discomfort, and opened up a subject that was guaranteed to break the ice: football. Almost everyone in Preston followed football and had a favourite team to support. The two Georges and Thomas were quickly into making comparisons between players and teams and nominating likely players to represent England in the international against France in two weeks' time. Thomas, it transpired, was a Liverpool supporter but the Chadwicks all barracked for Manchester United. Thomas made a mental note to get tickets for the next Liverpool/Manchester United clash and to invite Eve to accompany him.

George Senior was soon called upon by Annie to come and open the bottle of French wine. Seeing he was struggling, Thomas quietly rose to give him a hand, skilfully keeping the football conversation going as he did so. Glasses were filled and handed out whilst the plates of snacks started circulating.

It was George Junior who eventually managed to change the subject to something rather more interesting for the ladies.

'What's it like in the army?'

This set off a whole series of questions and answers that lasted for at least another half an hour. Thomas was in his element. Clearly, he loved life as an army officer and by the time he'd finished George Junior was starting to wonder whether a future as an army officer might be preferable to his long-intended career as an aircraft engineer. Thomas, like most returned soldiers, skirted around his time fighting the Germans, his serious leg wound and lengthy and painful period of convalescence. But he had them all intrigued with some of his stories and Eve felt proud to be associated with this brave man.

Around half past eight, Thomas checked his watch and informed his hosts he needed to leave in order to get to bed early. He had to be out on parade duty at 0600 hours. The evening had been a great success: nothing had gone seriously amiss, and thankfully they had found common ground. They made their farewells and the family discreetly hung back to allow Eve to see Thomas to the door. It was there they exchanged Christmas gifts, each promising not to open theirs until December 25th. Eve had spent almost all the money she had on a pair of gold-plated cufflinks. Thomas's present was a delicate necklace containing a beautiful arrangement of small rhodonite and amethyst semi-precious stones.

CHAPTER TEN
The Relationship Develops

Fulwood Barracks was one of a handful of establishments across the country charged with receiving, equipping and training new army recruits. It provided basic square bashing designed to mould young male recruits into obedient soldiers. At the same time the officers and NCOs weeded out those that would not make the grade or accept army discipline. Batches of around one hundred men came through every two months or so. At the end of six weeks those that made the grade were assigned to their regiments and then might be stationed anywhere in the United Kingdom or overseas.

Captain Dillon was responsible for the training of every second batch of new recruits arriving at Fulwood Barracks. During each six weeks of training the pressure was on and he worked long hours. He made it his duty to get to know the new recruits personally as soon as possible and to follow them through until they completed their basic training. As the officer-in-charge he witnessed an amazing transition from boy to man in most cases. The lads grew up in a hurry or were dismissed. Most nights he held sessions with individual youths who had issues or were struggling with the physical or mental demands. Sometimes he had to break the news to a youngster that he was simply not cut out for army life. Thomas was a strict disciplinarian, dedicated, but caring. His superiors recognised he was excellent at his job.

Whenever one of Thomas's six-week training sessions was in progress there was no time to socialise. If he did have an occasional night off, he was too exhausted to go out. In the short time before Christmas when Thomas had been dating Eve, it had been his six weeks with lighter duties during which he planned for his next intake. Just after Christmas Thomas's next group of recruits would be arriving and he had forewarned Eve that she probably wouldn't see him again until mid-February when this round of intensive training had concluded.

It was a bitterly cold winter. Most of January the polar northerlies blew and the ground was covered in snow and ice. Icicles hung from broken pipes like stalactites and hoar frosts brought down electricity lines. The River Ribble froze over and became the mecca for ice skaters. Walking to work became treacherous for Eve as she negotiated icy paths and pavements. Her father lent her a pair of his thick wool socks which she pulled over her shoes to give her better grip. The long cold snap continued on into February before it finally broke during the second week.

The new recruits at Fulwood Barracks suffered horribly. Gloves were not part of army issue so the young men endured painful chilblains. The heating in their dormitories was almost useless so they shivered through six weeks of intense cold day and night. Thomas ordered extra hot food be provided and lunchtime sandwiches were replaced with a range of hot soups. On a few occasions the blizzard-like conditions forced the abandonment of drill. Colds and influenza broke out keeping the medical orderlies busy. A record number of recruits pulled out or were forced to leave as a result of illness. In deference to his recruits, Thomas never asked them to do anything he wasn't prepared to do. He declined to wear gloves, ate with his charges and never shirked to complete the long-distance runs clad only in a flimsy pair of shorts and a t-shirt. In the evenings he would visit the men in the sick bay.

Eve and Thomas exchanged several letters during January and early February. Thomas's letters were well written and courteous and he described in detail some of the activities he was putting his recruits through. The tenor of his letters was friendly but certainly not romantic, or even hinting at romance. Each letter began simply with 'Dear Eve' and ended with 'Kind regards.' He signed off 'Charles.' There were no kisses or hugs or anything for that matter in his letters to suggest their relationship was to be more than a platonic one. How different were Thomas's letters from some she had received earlier from passionate young lads who wrote sloppy stuff with heaps of endearments and kisses and wrote endlessly of their undying love. Eve replied to each of Thomas's letters in a similar vein.

Their enforced separation provided ample time for Eve and her family to reflect on their drinks party and what might eventuate. Eve's parents were quite taken with Thomas. Her father described him as 'a decent sort of a cove, even though he backs the wrong football team.' Annie felt he was 'a proper gentleman and could be trusted.' Young George envisioned staying friendly with the captain in the hope that one day Thomas could show him the inside workings of armoured vehicles or even a tank. Eve, meanwhile, had placed her beautiful necklace in a special spot in her wardrobe and wondered when she might have a chance to wear it.

Apart from holding hands with Thomas briefly during a frightening scene in Macbeth, there was little to indicate that the captain found her to be more than just an interesting friend. There was no intimacy. She certainly liked and admired him as a person but she was unsure whether their relationship would ever blossom further. Her friends down at June Doyer's, however, were convinced that this was a match made in heaven and when they weren't teasing her about it, they wanted to hear graphic details about their dates. Mrs Moriarty was full of curiosity too. She had even been in contact with some of her old cronies to try and discover more about Captain Thomas Dillon's pedigree.

Chapter Ten The Relationship Develops

By mid-February the weather had returned to being typically damp and bleak with thick fog rolling in from the sea and intermittent rain and drizzle. The snow had melted and the ice on the river was breaking up. Everybody who could afford wood or coal to burn in their fireplaces and cooking stoves were beginning to ration its use, concerned they would run out before spring. The smoke from a thousand fires melded with the fog, when conditions were right, to produce something the scientists were now calling 'smog'. Too much smog, the scientists were saying, could give people respiratory diseases.

It was on one of these miserable gloomy days that another letter arrived from Thomas; he sounded rather more upbeat. The successful recruits had been posted to their regiments and he now had some time on his hands. The Preston Annual Catholic Ball was coming up in a little over a week's time; would Eve like to be his partner? Remembering how well they had combined together on the dance floor at the Army Ball, she had no hesitation in replying positively.

So it was that Eve and Thomas began to go out together regularly. Thomas always made the bookings, provided the transport and paid the expenses. Eve did her best with her meagre salary to make herself presentable and always behaved with the utmost decorum. As the weeks went by her confidence grew and she felt more comfortable being Thomas's 'lady friend'.

Eve had to admit that Thomas arranged some wonderful outings and was spoiling her to bits. Having a car was wonderful and allowed them so much more freedom. They danced the evenings away at both the Catholic and Anglican

Balls, enjoyed three more theatre productions, attended two chamber orchestra concerts, dined at expensive restaurants and picnicked on the moors. The 1926 Australian cricket team was touring and came to play Lancashire at Old Trafford in Manchester. Thomas booked tickets and Eve was surprised at how much she enjoyed her day at the cricket. They took a picnic with them and gorged themselves on strawberries and cream together with glasses of champagne. Eve didn't fully understand what was going on in the cricket, but it was lovely in the warm sunshine and Thomas was very attentive.

As the months rolled by Eve began to wonder where their relationship was going. They enjoyed each other's company, were polite and respectful, avoided any disagreements and had grown fond of each other but that's where it ended. Thomas never attempted to hold hands or showed any inclination to kiss her. She suspected it was his strict Catholic upbringing that prevented him letting go and showing more emotion. For a time, she even wondered if he was a homosexual. She had heard of men who preferred to have sexual relations with other men rather than with women. Perhaps he was just horribly shy and embarrassed about showing affection towards women? She asked him once whether he had any close girlfriends before he started taking her out, but he simply brushed her question aside.

Eve's parents were also confused about what was happening. From time to time, they would question their daughter about where things were heading, but since Eve didn't know herself, she could never give them a satisfactory answer.

Their dating was seriously disrupted during the month of

May by an unexpected event. The 1.2 million coal miners across the United Kingdom went on strike on May 1st. Coal production per miner had been steadily falling over the last few years with the unsavoury result that the miners' pay had been reduced accordingly. Average weekly wages had fallen from six pounds per week to less than four pounds. The sorry plight of the miners angered the heavily unionised workforce around the rest of the country and a General Strike was called for May 3rd by the Trade Union Congress. Newspapers ceased production, but the British Broadcasting Commission ran five news bulletins daily to keep the populace informed. On May 9th the Prime Minister, Mr Stanley Baldwin, declared a state of Martial Law, enforced a nation-wide curfew and called out the military forces to carry out civil functions. Captain Dillon, along with the other troops based at Fulwood Barracks, suddenly found himself serving on the civil frontline. The strike ended on May 12th but Martial Law dragged on until December 2nd. Night duties for Thomas continued throughout May until things quietened down.

Thomas's thirty-fourth birthday was coming up on July 25th and Eve had been wracking her brains trying to think what to buy for him. She knew he was an avid reader so finally she decided a new book from the Preston Book Shop might be something he would really appreciate. Eve had never purchased a book before because spending money on books was a luxury the Chadwicks could never afford. Sometimes she would stop and look enviously at the new books displayed in the window but she had never actually ventured inside.

One day, when she had the afternoon off, she resolved to

walk into town, be brave and visit the town's book shop. A bell tinkled softly as she entered and she found she was in a new and different kind of world. There were shelves and shelves groaning with books all sorted into various categories and a quiet learned atmosphere prevailed. A few people were scattered about thumbing through editions or speaking together in hushed tones. As Eve was taking this in, a bespectacled young man with a mop of unruly hair approached her with a welcoming smile.

'Good afternoon madam. May I be of any assistance?'

'Oh yes, thank you. I'm thinking of purchasing a book.'

'Of course,' he said, 'May I ask what sort of a book you have in mind?'

Eve had absolutely nothing in mind and looked blankly back at her interrogator.

'Is the book for yourself madam, or somebody else?'

'No, it's... it's for a man.'

Relieved to discover this attractive young lady had someone definite in mind, the salesman probed a bit further. 'A young man perhaps?'

Was a man coming up to thirty-four still a young man? Eve asked herself.

'Yes, I guess so,' she replied rather uncertainly.

'And does this young man have any favourite authors?'

Eve panicked under this barrage of questions. The only author she could think of on the spot was Agatha Christie which she relayed to the still smiling salesman.

'Ah, then you are in luck,' he responded enthusiastically. 'We

Chapter Ten   The Relationship Develops

have this week taken delivery of Agatha Christie's latest novel published only last month. It's the third in the Hercule Poirot series called, '*The Murder of Roger Ackroyd*.' A look of triumph came across his face. 'It's already looking like being a bestseller.'

Eve followed the salesman to a side table where about a dozen copies of '*The Murder of Roger Ackroyd*' were arranged in a row between bookends.

'These are selling very fast madam. I can't guarantee there will be any copies left after tomorrow. Hercule Poirot, the Belgian detective, is rapidly becoming a favourite with our customers.'

'Good, I'll take a copy please.'

Eve was rather surprised at how expensive the book was and it must have shown on her face as she dug deeper and deeper into her purse to pay for it.

'Books written by popular authors always sell fast, madam. Everyone wants to acquire a copy and so the price goes up. It's a first edition you see. I'm sure your young man will be delighted to receive this book; an English author too.'

Eve thanked the salesman. Next, she bought a birthday card with a red racing car on the front from the card shop next door before hurrying home to wrap the gift. She was pleased with herself; Thomas was sure to like Hercule Poirot.

* * *

Eve's mother watched as her daughter carefully wrapped up the Christie novel in clean brown paper and used up one of her last pieces of string. As Eve wrote in the card, Annie couldn't contain herself any longer.

'Eve dear, what's happening with Thomas? You've been stepping out with him for over eight months now and he's going to be thirty-four in a few days' time. If he's serious about you then he had better hurry up and do something about it because he'll be an old man soon.'

'Mother, that's an awful thing to say.'

'Well, it's true pet. You're seventeen and he's almost thirty-four. That's double your age! He's almost old enough to be your father!'

'Stop being so horrible. Thomas is a lovely man and has been marvellously kind and generous to me.'

'That may be the case dear, but you both need to think seriously about where this is going. I'm sure there are heaps of young men around your age who would love to take you out and might even be potential husbands. What about Jack up the road? He's been hanging around here for months hoping you'll end it with Thomas.'

'Well, Jack will just have to wait. It's Thomas's birthday on July 25th and then it's mine on August 6th. We have plans for both dates. By the way, I think Thomas would like to come here for my birthday. Would that be okay?'

'Yes, of course dear.'

There were a few moments of silence while Eve put away plates and dishes before Annie spoke again.

'Eve, there is one more thing I have to ask you. Please don't be angry with me, but it has been worrying your father too.'

'What's that mother?'

'I don't quite know how to put this dear. There are some men who take advantage of young girls like you. They want to have sexual relations without getting married.'

'Thomas is a complete gentleman, mother; he would never do anything like that. You have no right to even suggest it. I'm a virgin and I intend to remain so until my wedding night!'

'I'm sorry dear, I didn't mean to offend you, but there really are men like that, and I just wanted to check that Thomas wasn't one of them.'

'He's not, mother. In fact, he hasn't even kissed me!'

With that, Eve grabbed her present and stormed out of the kitchen.

CHAPTER ELEVEN

Birthdays

Fortuitously, July 25th was a Saturday, so Eve finished work at lunchtime and waited for Thomas to pick her up from Miss June Doyer's establishment. The usual ribbing went on as one by one the other girls left the premises. Eve was no longer the junior and now occasionally modelled for Miss Doyer when the seasonal apparel arrived from London and Paris. Her neat, trim figure and willingness to learn ensured she was one of Miss Doyer's favourites. Eve was never late for work and was willing to stay back late some evenings when customers were still present. She always found Miss Doyer firm but fair, and from time to time her boss would allow her to have half an hour off to do some shopping. Best of all, Eve was more than aware of the latest fashions and this helped dictate her taste in clothes.

Never late, the bright red Sunbeam Sports Tourer pulled in at the side of the shop just before 1.00pm. It was a gorgeous sunny day and Thomas had the car's hood folded back. He sat there grinning at her as she approached.

'Happy birthday Thomas.' She leaned over and kissed him on the cheek. It seemed such a natural thing to do that she wondered why she had never done it before. 'Where are we going?'

'Down to the river. My batman has made up a picnic and I have a bottle of wine and glasses as well.'

'Oh wow, sounds like we are letting our hair down, Thomas.' She glanced at him but he had his eyes firmly fixed on the road.

They wound their way down the short track that led to the river bank and parked under a willow tree with its long branches gently waving in the light breeze. Within a few minutes they had the picnic rug down and were sitting on the two cushions Thomas always carried with him in the car. The picnic hamper was opened to reveal the efforts of Thomas's batman. He had excelled, providing them with a selection of sandwiches, fruit cake and a bright red apple each.

Eve had Thomas's present ready and as soon as they had filled their wine glasses, she passed it to him.

'Happy birthday, Thomas. I hope you like it.'

Carefully and deliberately, he removed the string and

Chapter Eleven   Birthdays

unwrapped his present. He was thrilled with her choice and told her he had already read the first two Hercule Poirot books and that Agatha Christie was rapidly becoming one of his favourite authors. But there was no attempt to give her a kiss as part of his thanks.

They enjoyed their picnic, apart from some pesky ducks that insisted on also being fed, and finished off the bottle of wine. Thomas lay back on the rug, closed his eyes and basked in the warm sun. Daringly, Eve lay down next to him but propped herself up on an elbow so she could speak to him and watch his reactions.

'Thomas, can I ask you something very personal please?'

'Depends what it is?'

'This is difficult for me Thomas, so please be patient.'

Thomas raised himself onto his elbow and looked inquiringly at Eve. 'This all sounds horribly serious Eve.' He smiled disarmingly.

'Yes, it is,' she blurted out. 'Thomas, I need to know what your intentions are? Forgive me for saying this, but you are turning thirty-four today and we've been stepping out together for over eight months now. My parents are worrying too...'

A steely look came into Thomas's eyes, the friendly twinkle disappeared and for a moment Eve thought she might have pushed too hard and Thomas was angry. Never, in all the time they had been together, had he ever shown any aggression or lost his cool with her.

'Okay,' he said simply, 'I understand your concern.' He rolled onto his back, closed his eyes and looked as though he was going to sleep.

'No Thomas, it's not okay. It might surprise you to know that there are other young men anxious to take me out. So far I have ignored their invitations because I have been stepping out with you...'

'Eve dear,' he interrupted. 'I said I understand what you are saying and I'll make my intentions clear on your birthday.'

And that was the end of the discussion.

After a time, they packed up the picnic, left the hamper in the car and went for a walk along the path by the river. Eve hung her hand down by her side suggestively and even brushed it up against Thomas's a couple of times in the hope that he might feel moved to hold it. He didn't notice, or deliberately ignored her. Soon they approached the Preston Municipal Park drawn there by the sound of lively music. The Preston Town Band was ensconced in the bandstand playing to a couple of hundred spectators sitting around lazily in deck chairs and relishing the pleasant sunny conditions. They found two empty seats and stayed for half an hour to hear a couple of Gershwin numbers and a Glen Miller medley. A Lyons ice-cream van was doing a roaring trade nearby and Thomas wandered over to buy two vanilla ice-cream cornets.

He dropped Eve back home about six o'clock.

Eve thought long and hard about her situation that night. She sensed that, one way or another, Thomas was finally going to declare his intentions when he came to their house for her birthday on August 6th. She reasoned three things might happen: Thomas would propose marriage, or break the relationship off completely or just continue with his indecisiveness. If he persisted in procrastinating, then she would tell him she was breaking it off. She had been patient long enough and a decision was needed.

If Thomas did propose marriage then Eve was faced with the dilemma of either accepting or rejecting his offer. The man had many positive attributes: he was kind, honourable, respectful, totally honest, generous, intelligent and attentive. She felt safe with him. She didn't think she loved him, but she conceded that might still happen. In addition, he was wealthy and marriage to Thomas would allow her to immediately move into the upper echelons of society, something she had craved for as long as she could remember. Being an army officer would entail postings abroad so she would also get to travel and see the world. Thomas had recently hinted at the prospect of a promotion to major soon, so his career looked safe. Life with Thomas would be secure and comfortable.

There were some negatives though. Whereas she was extremely fond of Thomas, she wondered if that was enough to sustain a marriage. Could a marriage survive on respect alone? And where was the passion and romance in their relationship? Eve had read enough books to know that young couples could be passionately in love and that physical intimacy was part of the magic formula. Would Thomas ever be passionate? Eve wanted to be loved fiercely but doubted Thomas was capable of this. Perhaps he was already too old to be a fervent lover? Would she ever feel emotionally satisfied in a relationship that lacked ardent love-making?

There was also the problem that Thomas was a deeply religious man and would surely insist that she convert to

Roman Catholicism. Presently, she was a hot and cold Anglican but could probably cope with becoming a Catholic so long as Thomas didn't want her to go to mass every week. And then, of course, any children would have to be raised as Catholics too!

Weighing it all up, Eve decided that if Thomas proposed on her birthday, she would accept. After all, she could always change her mind later, provided she did so well before the marriage date. Hopefully their relationship would deepen meaningfully once they were engaged and had committed their lives to each other.

* * *

August 6th, the day of Eve's eighteenth birthday, fell on a Thursday. When the last customer left, shortly before five o'clock, her work colleagues produced a small birthday cake, showered her with little gifts and made quite a fuss of her. It was lovely, but consequently she was late getting home. Her mother was not impressed, as she had been relying on Eve to help prepare the table. Thomas was coming for dinner at seven o'clock. Eve set to and soon had everything organised, then raced upstairs to change into her new dress. She felt strangely calm considering her whole future might be determined tonight!

Eve was back downstairs just in time to welcome Thomas at the front door. He arrived carrying a bottle of wine as a gift for her parents but apparently there was nothing for her. He wished her a happy birthday pleasantly enough but again declined to give her a kiss even though she stood in front of him expectantly. One of the girls at work had given Eve a small bottle of perfume which she was wearing for the first time tonight. It seemed to have no effect on Thomas although before they entered the dining room, he did compliment her on her new dress.

Annie had excelled in the kitchen and produced a roast of beef complete with potatoes, carrots and cabbage some of which had come from her garden. There was even gravy served in a gravy boat that Eve had never seen before; borrowed from a neighbour no doubt. The Chadwicks couldn't rise to a proper carving tray, or the tools to slice the meat, but Annie had done her best out in the kitchen and put the rather too chunky meat slices on their plates beforehand. They asked Thomas to say grace for them.

Conversation didn't flow easily and Eve found herself raising topics and asking questions to try and avoid awkward embarrassing silences. In doing so, she realised how much she had learnt already about playing the part of the hostess, a skill she would inevitably have to perfect if she ever married Thomas. The men talked about football, the recent national strike and Thomas praised the Poirot novel Eve had given him for his birthday. George Junior asked Thomas about cars and life in the army.

The roast was appropriately praised and Annie then produced spotted dick with treacle for dessert. Finally, when the plates were cleared away, a small birthday cake was placed in the centre of the table. Annie had baked it but was disappointed because it had sagged in the middle; she had tried valiantly to cover up the problem with extra icing. They all sang *'Happy Birthday'* to a blushing Eve and then Thomas toasted her health.

Thomas and George Senior then sat down in the two armchairs to chat over a beer while the other three did the dishes. There was still no sign of a birthday gift from Thomas or any indication of his future intentions. Eve, despite this being her birthday party, was feeling despondent. She had put it to Thomas as they lay on the picnic rug that she wanted to know once and for all what his plans were. He had assured her he would let her know tonight but nothing had happened yet.

About half past nine, after tea and biscuits, Thomas thanked his hosts most sincerely for the evening and asked Eve to please accompany him out to his car. For Eve this was the moment of truth. If Thomas proposed marriage she would accept. If nothing eventuated, she would tell him firmly that it was all over and she did not wish to see him again. It was a do or die situation.

It was still reasonably light as they went out to the car and Thomas held open the passenger door for Eve.

'Hop in, we'll go and watch the sunset over the harbour, it should be really pretty tonight.'

This, Eve had not anticipated. She did as she was bid, however, telling herself that this was the last time she would ever sit in Thomas's bright red 1922 Sunbeam 16/40 Sports Tourer that he was so proud about. The hood was down now as the warmth of the day was slowly fading. They sat in silence as he traversed the town of Preston and drove out along a ridge that overlooked the port of Preston with its many fishing boats, coal barges and merchant vessels bobbing up and down gently on the water. There was hardly a soul about, just a couple of old timers fixing their nets in the dimming light. The sun was sitting just above the horizon and the sunset was at its artistic best. Thomas had parked next to a wooden bench located perfectly for watching sunsets.

'Let's sit over on that bench Eve.' It sounded more like an order than a request. Nevertheless, Eve clambered out and followed Thomas over to the bench and sat down next to him. They sat in silence watching the sun slowly dip below the horizon. Eve had never watched a sunset from this vantage spot before and had to admit that it was strikingly beautiful.

The wonder of the sunset must have totally absorbed her until she felt a warm hand take hers. Surprised by this sudden move, she turned to look at Thomas.

'Eve, will you marry me?'

In his other hand Thomas held open a small jewel box in which lay an exquisite engagement ring. The offer of a life with Captain Thomas Anton Dillon was his birthday gift.

CHAPTER TWELVE

The Wedding

Next morning Eve woke early and lay in bed until it was time to get up and go to work. She looked at her hand to check the engagement ring was still there and that she hadn't dreamt everything. It was there alright, bright and shiny; she recalled someone telling her once that diamonds are a girl's best friend.

Last night had been magical. It had been surprisingly romantic sitting in the fading light of the sunset, holding hands. Thomas had planned everything precisely so that they were there on the bench at exactly the right time. Amazingly, he had even lent over and kissed her gently on the lips, just the once. She wanted to throw her arms around him and kiss him hard and long but she held back because he probably wouldn't have approved of such spontaneous, passionate behaviour in public.

When Thomas had dropped her off at her home, she was met at the door by her parents in a high state of excitement. Apparently, when the two men had been having a beer together, Thomas had done the right thing and asked George if he could have his daughter's hand in marriage. Approval granted, and with the precision of an army officer, Thomas had then proposed that the wedding take place on Saturday, November 24th at the Catholic Church of Gregory the Great in Deepdale, a suburb of Preston. He urged the acceptance of that date because his commanding officer had already agreed to allow him a month's leave from that date and changing his leave would be a horribly complicated business. George senior was quite overwhelmed by this sudden turn of events. At Thomas's request, he said nothing to Annie or his son until after Thomas and Eve had left in the car.

They were so thrilled about the proposal they cracked open the second bottle of wine and allowed George junior a glass too, even though he was still only sixteen. It was midnight before they all retired to bed, slightly the worse for wear, after disposing of the second bottle. They had spent an hour or so throwing ideas about for the wedding but had resolved nothing; they were on such a high they were simply not thinking rationally.

For Eve the world now seemed strangely unreal, she floated

Chapter Twelve The Wedding

around doing her morning chores, then left for work. She geared herself up for the lively reception she knew she would receive at work as soon as someone noticed her engagement ring. She didn't have to wait long: as she signed the timesheet there was an excited yelp from one of the girls and next moment, they were all about her with their good wishes and congratulations. The staff had known for months that Eve was dating an army officer but nobody knew him or had even spoken to him. Two or three times, Thomas's red sports car had been seen pulling up outside June Doyer's dress shop when picking Eve up but sightings of the man himself had been virtually impossible. They all insisted that she bring him to the shop one day so they could meet him. Eve, however, was not sure Thomas would be happy about this idea.

At closing time Miss Doyer surprised the staff by producing a magnum of champagne so Eve's engagement could be properly celebrated. There was much speculation about what kind of wedding dress Eve would wear, how many children she wanted, where the honeymoon would be and where they would reside. Eve had no answers to their questions but their speculations brought it home to her that she and Thomas had not yet discussed such details about their marriage ceremony, the honeymoon, or their life afterwards. They were dining out on Saturday evening so she decided to raise some of these matters then.

* * *

Eve and Thomas's very first outing together had been at *The*

Three Nuns and this is where they went for their first date as an engaged couple. Eve recalled how terrified she had been on that earlier occasion and smiled to herself as she realised how much more sophisticated she was today. Dining out now was an enjoyable experience no longer tempered by concerns about whether she was doing the right thing or committing some awful faux pas. It was thoughtful of Thomas, and almost romantic, to take her back to *The Three Nuns*.

The restaurant had not changed since their initial visit almost nine months ago. The same young man relieved them of their coats in the foyer and the menu looked similar, except this time Eve recognised what many of the dishes were and was knowledgeable enough to have an opinion about which bottle of wine to order. She had Thomas to thank entirely for her greater knowledge and maturity. They ordered and Eve placed her hand gently on Thomas's before her opening gambit.

'Thomas, that was such a beautiful way to propose to me on Thursday night. It was magic.' She squeezed his hand. 'We have so much to discuss tonight because the big day is only three months away.'

He was looking at her affectionately and made no attempt to remove his hand.

'Father has told me you have a whole month of leave and don't have to go back to work until December 27th. It will be winter then. Have you thought about our honeymoon?'

'I have indeed. I am about to make some bookings. How would you like to go to London, Paris and Nice?'

'Oh, how thrilling! Thomas, you do know that apart from my

Chapter Twelve The Wedding

outings with you, I've never been out of Preston, except when I was a child and lived in Bilsborough just a few miles away.'

He laughed. 'Then you're going to be absolutely amazed at the places I'm going to take you to.'

'I know London and Paris will be cold in November and December but what about Nice? Is it in France too?'

Thomas laughed again. 'I'll have to give you a crash geography course. Nice is way down in the South of France where, in December, the weather is still beautifully warm and the Mediterranean Sea lovely to swim in. It's near Monte Carlo and Cannes. You'll love it there.'

'I'm excited already, Thomas, but I can't swim.'

'Then I'll teach you.'

'Could you? So, I'll need to pack warm clothes for winter and clothes for a hot place?'

'Correct. My plan is that we take the train to London the day after our wedding, spend a couple of nights at the Dorchester, that's in London, then get the ferry across the channel and have a couple of days in Paris. Next, we board another train from Paris to Nice where we'll spend about two weeks basking in the sun and seeing the sights. Same sort of thing on the way back.'

'Wow, I can't wait to tell my family.'

The entrée arrived and they concentrated on their meal for a few minutes. Thomas topped up their wine glasses.

'I'm going to have to buy heaps of new clothes, Thomas, and I haven't a clue what to wear in Nice.'

'Well, by then you will be Mrs Dillon, so it would only be right for me to purchase these items of clothing for you.'

'Oh, Thomas, would you? That would be such a weight off my mind. Perhaps you could come down one day to Miss June Doyer's to help me choose? The staff are desperate to meet you.'

The thought of waiting about in a lady's dress shop, whilst Eve tried on endless garments, had absolutely no appeal for Thomas and he reacted instantly.

'Buying clothes for ladies is not my thing, Eve. You buy what you want and then give me the bill. I'll trust your good taste.'

'Oh, that's dangerous,' giggled Eve. 'I might spend much more money than you want. Do you know how expensive lady's clothes are, Thomas?'

'No, I'm blissfully ignorant but I prefer to stay that way.'

For a moment or two Eve recalled some of the lovely garments she had happily sold to wealthy customers at Miss Doyer's over the last couple of years. It was almost unbelievable that now *she* would be the customer and no doubt the envy of all the other girls. She would have to handle things tactfully as there might be some resentment.

The main course appeared and they gave it the attention it deserved. Eve was mentally travelling around Miss Doyer's dress shop and trying certain garments on. Indubitably, this marriage business was the best thing that had ever happened to her!

'Thomas?'

'Yes, dear?'

'Where are we going to live when we get back from our honeymoon?'

'For a short time, we will move into one of the officer's

married quarters at the barracks, but it won't be for long because I have a promotion.'

'A promotion, Thomas? How exciting. What does that mean?'

'It means a great deal. As from January 1st I will officially be Major Dillon and can expect to be posted to another barracks in the United Kingdom or even overseas somewhere. So, you see, we will not be living long at Fulwood Barracks.'

'Are you pleased to be moving, Thomas?'

'Yes, I've been here long enough. I need a more challenging position. Promotion also means an increase in salary which will help pay for all your expenses.'

Eve blushed, despite recognising he had said this without malice. For the first time in her life, she was going to climb out of 'struggle street' and start to live the good life she had always dreamt about. It was all so thrilling; she could hardly comprehend how her life was about to change. She sought Thomas's hand again and squeezed it hard.

The waitress reappeared, removed their dinner plates and returned a few minutes later with desserts. Brandy snaps with ice-cream and a strawberry coulis kept them quiet for a little longer, but Eve still had so much to inquire about. Her next question was the most important one and she felt rather awkward asking it.

'Thomas, can I ask you a very personal question please?'

A slightly defensive look flitted across the face of her husband-to-be, 'Go on, Eve, what is it?' he said with a note of caution.

'Have you thought about children?'

'Not really, I guess they'll come along in due course. Remember, I'm a Catholic, and I expect you will convert too before we marry. As practising Catholics, we should avoid using any kind of contraceptive devices. How many children we end up having is entirely in the hands of the good Lord.'

Thomas had answered her question forthrightly enough, but she was taken aback by the realisation that he saw no reason to limit the number of offspring they may produce. Suddenly she had visions of piles of unruly children tramping about their house while she and a nanny tried desperately to maintain some kind of control. Eve had previously come to terms with the fact that she would be expected to convert to Catholicism but she had not fully appreciated that by marrying a devout Catholic she was potentially to become some kind of a 'baby-making machine'. Eve liked children but had no intention of having more than two or perhaps three. Coming from a working-class background she had seen far too many families with eight, nine or ten children and that was definitely not the kind of life she envisaged.

Thomas was watching her carefully and waiting to see her reaction.

Eve skilfully avoided the real issue. 'So, Thomas, dear, when do I start my conversion classes?'

* * *

The ensuing three months or so was a blur for Eve. She continued working at Miss June Doyer's dress shop until the

Chapter Twelve The Wedding

very end. The staff were invited to the church to witness her wedding however, June Doyer was the only one invited to the wedding breakfast afterwards. Outside of work hours, Eve had a seemingly endless number of engagements. Fittings for her wedding dress and organising the costumes for her bridesmaids occupied many hours. Then she had the highly pleasurable experience of purchasing her cold and warm weather outfits for their honeymoon. She was surprised when Thomas insisted on her taking a full medical examination before they wed. He said he would do the same. Pre-matrimony medicals were, he assured her, quite the normal practice for well-to-do couples. He wanted to be sure there was no impediment to their having children and it was also necessary for life insurance purposes, he stressed.

Two evenings a week, for ten weeks, Eve fronted up for her Catholic conversion course with two other people, at the conclusion of which, she was accepted as a full member of the Roman Catholic Church. Eve and her mother handled the invitations and the arrangements for the reception after the wedding but left all the planning for the ceremony itself to Thomas. Thomas also organised the travel and accommodation for the honeymoon and informed Eve he had ordered a guard of honour for the special photograph to be taken as they left the church. Most importantly, Thomas agreed to cover all the wedding expenses, a massive relief for Eve's parents!

In addition to the above activities, Eve was invited to a series of farewells and send-offs. Several of her school friends put on small parties, the Anglican Church she was leaving had a special morning tea, there were a couple of outings at work and even Mrs Moriarty's nursing home organised an afternoon tea. By the time the wedding came round she was exhausted!

* * *

Dawn on Saturday, November 24th, 1926, the day of the wedding, started just like most late November days in Northern England. A weak glimmer of sun tried valiantly to penetrate the fog that had rolled in overnight from the Irish Sea. The view from Eve's bedroom window was of rows of tenements disappearing into the fog as a hundred red brick chimneys belched out a grey sooty waste product to mix with the fog to form the foul-tasting suffocating smog. *At least it's not raining or snowing*, thought Eve, as she pulled on her slippers and headed for her bath.

The house was abuzz as each member of the Chadwick family went about their allotted duties prior to the wedding; the cars were due to arrive at a quarter to eleven. Eve spent the morning in a sort of a cloud, not unlike the outside weather. It seemed unreal that she was finally giving her life to a military man and stepping out into a frightening unknown world. She timidly surrendered to the long line of people arriving to dress her, pamper her, help with makeup, arrange her hair or offer last minute advice. This was supposed to be the best day of her life but she felt overwhelmed. Her mood fluctuated from elation one minute to nervousness the next. Somehow, she had to survive a formal marriage ceremony, a posh reception afterwards and then the first night sharing a bed with Thomas. She didn't know which of these three things terrified her the most.

The evening edition of the Lancashire Daily Post for Saturday, November 24th reported on the wedding as follows.

Military Wedding
Picturesque Ceremony
at St Gregory's Church, Deepdale

A military wedding took place at St Gregory's Church, Deepdale, this morning when Captain T.A. Dillon, formerly of Bolton, and now stationed at Fulwood Barracks, Preston, was married to Miss Mary Evelyn Chadwick of Tulketh Brow, Preston. Father J.L. Prescott officiated at the ceremony and was assisted by Father Leighton of Bolton.

The bride, who was given away by her father, wore a dress of white georgette trimmed with pearls. The bridesmaids, Miss B. Chadwick (sister of the bride) and Miss L. Bateson, wore pink crepe de china with georgette sleeves and trimmed with sequins and brilliants. Colonel W.J. Cranston D.S.O. was the best man.

As the couple left the church, a guard of honour was formed by NCOs of the East Lancashire Regiment and officers of the Loyal Regiment. A reception was held at the Bull and Royal Hotel, Preston.

The honeymoon will be spent in London, Nice and Paris.

Next there appeared this photograph:

The marriage of Captain Thomas Dillon to Mary Evelyn Chadwick, November 24th, 1926. (Photo taken by the Lancashire Daily Post)

In later years, Eve would sometimes look back at this photograph to remind herself of the occasion. Thomas, in his full-dress uniform looked handsome and in control of the situation, as indeed he was, whereas she looked timid and fearful. The Colonel, Thomas's best man, stood behind her husband and her two faithful bridesmaids stood immediately behind her with her older sister, Bell, on the left. Peeping out between the two bridesmaids was her devoted father. Everyone looked rather serious.

The smog had blown out to sea as they set off for the reception at the Bull and Royal Hotel nearby. Once again Eve found it all too much to take in and she did little more than go through the motions as if in a dream. Sixty people were present with around forty being family members from the Dillons and Chadwicks. Several officers and their wives attended. Mrs Moriarty was there comfortable in her wheelchair. Finally, there was Miss Doyer and some good friends from Eve's school days. There were several speeches and as the alcohol began to take effect the reception became louder and louder. Finally, the cake was cut and distributed and Eve and Thomas were invited to move onto the dance floor. As an accomplished dancing couple, they really impressed their guests!

Everyone partied on until the evening, although Thomas and Eve kept to their strict limits of alcohol consumption and remained sober. Around eight o'clock, Eve remembered her bridesmaids helping her to change into her 'going away' clothes even though they were just staying the night upstairs in the hotel's bridal suite. Her luggage had been safely stowed in their suite in readiness for next morning when they would depart on the London Express. She re-joined her husband at the reception and arm in arm they said their farewells to their guests now formed up in a ragged and very vociferous circle around the outside of the room. With much applause, and a few ribald comments from some of the more inebriated, the pair left the reception and made their way hastily up the thickly carpeted staircase.

At the entrance to the bridal suite, they were surprised to be met by a member of staff who inquired, 'Will that be all sir?' and then went on to ask what arrangements they would like for breakfast. Apparently, occupants of the bridal suite were entitled to breakfast in their bedroom, a luxury not extended to other guests. Thomas declined the offer, explaining that they needed to get away early to catch their train to London. He asked to be woken at six.

What occurred in that bridal suite over the next hour or so was not a particularly pleasant ordeal for Eve and she was relieved when it was over. Only dear old Mrs Moriarty had attempted to explain what she might expect to happen on her first married night.

They took it in turns to use the bathroom where they bathed and put on their dressing gowns. Eve went first and then had to wait quite some time for Thomas to complete his ablutions. Thomas insisted on the lights being turned off before they removed their dressing gowns and he eventually climbed into bed next to Eve. Here they fumbled around for a few minutes, both complete amateurs, not knowing whether to kiss, cuddle or fondle. After a few more minutes Thomas succeeded in penetrating, a painful experience for Eve, and then, after a few energetic thrusts, it was all over. As Eve pulled on her nightdress, she wondered why some people raved about the act of intercourse. Perhaps it would improve with time?

CHAPTER THIRTEEN
Married Life 1926-1936

The honeymoon was fantastic with almost everything being a 'first' for Eve.

In London they stayed at the lavish Dorchester where they were waited upon ad nauseam. In 1926, London was still the world's largest city and the political and economic centre of the British Empire. Together they toured London Bridge, the Houses of Parliament, watched the changing of the guard at St James' Palace, visited Peter Pan's statue in Hyde Park and Marble Arch and then, intrigued, watched the world's first traffic light recently installed in Piccadilly Circus, controlling the traffic. They travelled on the underground 'Tube' and sat upstairs on several bright red London buses that charged about all over the city. Eve's only disappointment was discovering that Madame Tussaud's was closed as it had suffered a devastating fire last year.

The *Roaring Twenties* were in full swing and the so-called 'Bright Young Things' had established a dubious reputation around the capital for non-stop partying. These were the wealthy upper-class young adults celebrating peace time after the ravages of war. The more conservative members of society dismissed these young gentry as being hedonistic, decadent and frivolous. Nevertheless, London in 1926 was vibrantly alive with scores of night clubs, jazz clubs and cocktail bars partying on into the early hours. Eve would have loved to have visited one of these places, but her more conservative husband settled for a quiet dinner at the Dorchester where, she had to admit, he did permit her to sample her first cocktail but in rather more sedate surroundings.

Visiting London was the first time Eve fully appreciated a significant difference between herself and her husband. He liked ordered, respectful, decent, genteel behaviour with polite conversation whereas Eve recognised for the first time that she also possessed a wild adventurous streak. At times she yearned to throw away convention and join those Bright Young Things so as to let her hair down. Little Preston offered nothing in comparison to what she knew was here in abundance in London! Already, at times, she felt like a dog on a leash, constrained and controlled. There was a wild side of London and being a teenager, she so wanted to experience it.

After a couple of days, they crossed the English Channel and arrived at The Ritz in Paris, another fabulous hotel. The French capital, although far smaller than London, was just as exciting a place to visit. 1920s Paris had once again become a great centre of art, music, literature and the rapidly developing new world of silent black and white cinema. This was the place to be, where in the streets you could bump into the likes of Picasso, Salvador Dali, Ernest Hemingway and James Joyce. Coco Chanel was already famous for her 'little black dresses' and Chanel No 5. The Parisians referred to the 1920s as 'les années follies' (the crazy years).

Together they viewed the Eiffel Tower, the Arc de Triomphe, toured the Cathedral of Notre Dame and spent a wonderful evening at the Theatre des Champs-Elysees where Eve swooned at the sound of a seductive young man called Maurice Chevalier. They strolled the famous 'Left Bank' where they nearly froze before sampling the best of French cuisine at the fashionable 'Les Deux Magots'. They passed the Moulin Rouge, but Eve rightly predicted that that was as close as they would ever get to seeing the erotic non-stop shows within.

Next it was off by train to the comparative warmth of Nice on the French Riviera. Eve couldn't believe the brightness of the sun in Nice and the fact that the sun shone relentlessly 300 days every year. In Preston it was fog and gloom for 300 days a year! Thomas had booked a room in the huge Hotel Regina which was one of the famous hotels along La Promenade des Anglais. The Promenade had been so named because the English aristocracy were the first to frequent the beach here back in the eighteenth century. The Promenade des Anglais with its palm trees was the place to be seen as it curved elegantly around the Baie des Anges.

Their stay in Nice was far slower paced and therefore more relaxing. They visited the Monastery of Benedictine Monks up in the hills, the striking Russian Orthodox Cathedral completed by Tsar Nicholas III in 1912, several museums, Le Place Massena, Le Casino Municipal and the statue of Apollo with its beautiful fountains. They also travelled the railway line that followed the coast to Monte Carlo. Eve loved the warm elegance of la Cote D'Azur.

Even life in the bedroom improved somewhat. Thomas wanted her every second or third night and was rather more efficient now. She simply submitted to his desires and never refused him. He was unimaginative in his love-making, always using the missionary position and still insisting that the lights be off. She could cope with this rather mundane sex but was convinced there must be more to it; if only she knew what. Thomas never aroused her sexually and she felt no passion for him. It was always, 'lie back and think of England'.

Shortly after Christmas, Thomas (now Major Dillon) and his beautiful young wife returned to bleak, miserable Preston and took up residence in their married quarters at Fulwood Barracks. Their stay would be short-lived, however, for Thomas received notification almost immediately that he and Eve would be sailing for a posting in India on February 1st. Thomas was able to take a couple of days leave to visit his family in Bolton while Eve made the most of the limited time available to spend it with her family and friends.

Eve's parents never seemed to change and remained humble and industrious souls. Her father continued his work as a stonemason and her mother's dressmaking business kept her busy and brought in a valuable second income. They seemed happy enough and were so proud of her. They loved hearing about the honeymoon and the exciting places the couple had visited. Eve had brought back presents for all her family. There was exciting news about her siblings too: Bell was engaged and planned to marry sometime later in the year, young George had won a scholarship to Liverpool University and would commence an engineering degree shortly. Dear old Mrs Moriarty was still doing well at the nursing home.

Eve and her husband departed from Southampton Docks, as planned, on February 1st, 1927. Senior officers and their wives sailed 'POSH' (port out and starboard home) thereby always being accommodated on the better side of the boat with regard to the sun.

Major Thomas Dillon, on his arrival in India, was immediately assigned a specialist role: officer-in-charge of 'Indianisation'. Discontent and strong nationalist stirrings for Indian independence were rife and one strategy adopted by the British Indian Army to try to appease the anger was to allow promising young Indian men to become fully commissioned officers in the army. This new initiative had been approved in Parliament in February 1923 and by 1927 was in full swing.

Thomas had to select Indians who were suitable officer material and arrange for these young men to either become King's commissioned Indian officers trained in India or be sent to the Royal Military College, Sandhurst in Buckinghamshire, England.

There was widespread resistance to Indianisation from many of the British people living in India at the time so a senior British officer with highly developed skills of diplomacy was required to manage the implementation of this controversial strategy. Thomas was an excellent choice and did his work sensitively and conscientiously. He was assigned to the 19th Hyderabad infantry regiment and he and Eve were accommodated in a large rambling bungalow safely located well within the army compound. Eve was surprised to discover she was responsible for organising several servants: they had a full-time cook, gardener and housekeeper. Thomas also had a batman, but what this Indian soldier's duties were, was entirely her husband's business.

Gradually, over the next few months, their life in India fell into some kind of a routine. Thomas's work required him to travel extensively because he was drawing his officer recruits from no less than eight different regiments scattered about the huge colony which meant he was sometimes away for weeks at a time. Eve developed a good working relationship with her three servants but found life could be lonely. Even when he was home, Thomas worked long hours. There was nothing for her to do on the domestic front so she did what all young wives at the base did: she joined in with the activities of the 'expats'. The expats were a lively bunch of women who occupied their time playing bridge, having endless tea parties, playing

Chapter Thirteen Married Life 1926-1936

tennis or simply sitting about gossiping. As the wives of British army officers, they had much in common, although there was a clear pecking order amongst the ladies depending on the rank of their respective husbands. Although, at nineteen, Eve was clearly the youngest in the entire group, she was also one of the most senior since there were only a couple of officers at the base who outranked Major Dillon.

The wives found this anomaly somewhat unnerving. Normally, the wives of the senior military officers were in their forties or older, but here was this slip of a thing, called Eve, who was a mere teenager! The gossip-merchants soon worked out that there was an amazing age gap of sixteen years between Eve and her husband and they didn't think this augured well. Major Dillon was referred to by some of the ladies as a 'cradle-snatcher'. The advice circulating quietly around some of the gossip-mongers was to keep a close eye on your husband lest he develops a desire to get into the pants of this strikingly attractive young newcomer.

Eve, unaware of this scuttlebutt, found several of the younger officers enthusiastically wishing to enjoy her company whenever there was a dance or a cocktail party organised in the mess or elsewhere. The married officers were largely kept in check by their wives, but there was less reason for caution amongst the dashing and more adventurous single men. There were very few suitable young females around for these testosterone-charged officers, so, starved of female company, perhaps understandably, they gravitated towards Eve, who was arguably the best-looking woman on the base.

Eve greatly enjoyed the attention she received from the young studs. These officers were a lot of fun and most were satisfied just to be in her company, sharing a drink, showing her how to play tennis, dancing or horse riding. It was not long though before a couple of the single officers decided to 'try it on'. Married for less than three months, Eve was certainly not expecting such behaviour and strongly rejected their advances. No longer living in the sheltered environment of Preston, she soon realised she was more vulnerable to sexual predators living inside a military compound, despite the fact she was married.

In July she missed a period and the doctor at the base soon confirmed she was pregnant and likely to give birth around February 1928. Thomas was thrilled and couldn't do enough to fuss over her. Eve chatted to some of the ladies on the base who had had babies while posted in India and all agreed that the British-run maternity ward at the Hyderabad Hospital was excellent. The nurses and doctors were from the United Kingdom and could be trusted to care for pregnant mothers just as well as back home.

* * *

On February 15th, 1928, Eve gave birth to a healthy bouncy boy who they named Anthony Michael Peter Dillon (known as Michael). Care at the hospital had been faultless and after a week, Eve returned to their bungalow and the baby became an immediate fascination for their three servants. Soon Eve was receiving visits from other clucking mothers around the base, who, almost without exception, had plenty of advice on what to do for the baby. Thomas was a proud dad and Eve felt that she had become more acceptable to the expat ladies now that she had successfully achieved motherhood.

As was the custom in the 1920s, families that could afford it employed a nanny. Before returning to their bungalow, Thomas and Eve had engaged Nanda, a delightful young Indian lass. Nanda lived in and soon bonded well with little Michael. The new addition to the family never wanted for love and attention. Eve and Nanda quickly settled into daily routines that suited everyone. Michael thrived and Eve was again able to resume an active social life with the other mothers. Thomas continued his extensive travelling, always returning home whenever possible.

* * *

After three fulfilling years in India, Thomas received orders to return to the United Kingdom where he was to take up the post of second-in-command back at Fulwood Barracks in Preston. The couple had mixed feelings about this next posting, however. Eve was thrilled to be returning to her family, who naturally were longing to see Michael, now a boisterous two-year-old. Michael would be able to start at kindergarten in England. It was a good career move for Thomas too, since the second-in-command at such a large barracks had traditionally been held by an officer with the rank of a Lieutenant-Colonel. Another promotion could be anticipated within a year or two of taking up this appointment.

On the negative side was leaving exotic India where they had become acclimatised to the heat and had made many good friends. Saying a final farewell to Nanda and their other loyal servants was distressing too, especially for Michael, who had come to regard Nanda as his second mother. Returning to cold, damp, foggy Preston at the start of what was later to be referred to as 'The Great Depression' was a soul-destroying experience with its high unemployment, widespread poverty and social discontent. Furthermore, Eve now had to resume domestic duties, although Thomas assured her they would still be able to afford to employ a full-time nanny.

The great depression started after the crash of the stock market in New York during October 1929 and its impact spread rapidly around the world. In the United Kingdom, little had been done to modernise the coal mining, ship building and steel industries since the end of the World War, whereas other nations had done so and were already outperforming the British. As conditions deteriorated in the United Kingdom, the government took drastic and highly unpopular steps in an attempt to reduce the national debt: it reduced wages and increased income tax. By the summer of 1931 more than three and a half million were unemployed and barely surviving on the meagre dole. The situation was particularly dire in the north of England in areas such as Preston.

In the same year Thomas was called to attend a special conference in London to discuss the future status of India.

Chapter Thirteen Married Life 1926-1936

As a recently returned senior military man, involved in the 'Indianisation' initiative, his views were considered useful. The conference was high powered and Mahatma Gandhi was the main spokesman for India. Although the conference itself was a failure, it did afford Gandhi an opportunity to meet senior politicians and public servants. He even met Charlie Chaplin! After the conference, Gandhi, who in his traditional robes, had sparked the public's imagination, had a few free days to travel around the United Kingdom and was mobbed when he visited the East End of London. At Gandhi's request, he travelled by train to Lancashire to witness for himself some of the hardship endured by the people of the industrial north. At the last minute, Thomas was called in to organise Gandhi's itinerary in the north and so spent time with the great man. Once again Gandhi was mobbed in the streets as many struggling with poverty were able to identify with the deprivations felt by Gandhi and the Indian people.

One of the ironies of the great depression was that those who remained fully employed became more affluent. This came about because prices of food items and commodities fell substantially so that purchasing power was stronger. Thomas, Eve and little Michael were in this fortunate situation. Horrified at the extent of the misery all about her, Eve volunteered to assist in the soup kitchens where thousands of people queued each day for free hot soup and a chunk of bread. It was there that Eve witnessed malnourished children in many cases suffering from scurvy, rickets or tuberculosis.

Eve's family fared reasonably well during the depression.

Her father had to accept a 15% reduction in his stonemason's wages and her mother found it increasingly difficult to find work as a dressmaker. Fewer and fewer people could afford new clothes: they were forced to tighten their belts. Bell, Eve's older sister, married and continued working as a nurse. Her younger brother, George, graduated as a civil engineer and began work with the aircraft manufacturing company based in Preston. The truly sad news was the passing of Mrs Moriarty at the grand old age of eighty-eight. Young Michael was thriving and becoming a typical mischievous youngster. Apparently, he was considered quite a handful at his kindergarten.

From the time Eve and her husband returned to Preston their relationship steadily deteriorated. They were still civil and polite to each other, but what little chemistry there had been when they first married four years ago, had virtually disappeared. As the depression wore on, they saw less and less of each other and gradually came to live separate lives although living within the one house. This divide was not apparent to other people, although Annie sensed that things were tense in the Dillon household and shared this observation with her husband. Thomas still requested his conjugal rights once a week or so and Eve never refused him, but for Eve it was a duty and certainly not a pleasure. She had mixed feelings about falling pregnant again, although as a devout Catholic, Thomas was expecting to become a father again before long. Eve found Michael already took up much of her time despite having the money to afford a full-time nanny.

As they drew further apart, Eve attended mass less and

less frequently, which was an embarrassment to Thomas. Eve had willingly committed to his faith prior to their marriage but now was seldom honouring it. Thomas decided, however, that as soon as Michael turned five, he would come to mass with him whether or not Eve came as well. Michael continued to attend kindergarten at an establishment called Captain Olsen's where he was regarded as one of the more disruptive boys although he did well at the things he liked: drawing, games and physical training. At the age of six, Michael was enrolled as a day boy at St Christopher's Preparatory School for boys, a new private school located on the outskirts of Preston with extensive grounds and wonderful old trees for climbing.

And so, Eve settled down in Preston as a lady of leisure. Financially they were comfortable and she did not have to work. She divided her time between her blossoming hobby of gardening, frequently visiting her parents, working two days a week at the soup kitchen, caring for Michael, entertaining as required, and attending the social and political activities of the Young Conservatives. She was entitled to remain a member of this last group until she turned thirty. Her parents, die-hard Labour supporters, strongly disapproved of Eve's move to throw her lot in with the 'capitalists' and told her so, but Eve found the group interesting and lively, and besides, there were a couple of young men there she found particularly attractive.

CHAPTER FOURTEEN

'Jacko'

The difficulties in Thomas and Eve's marriage finally came to a head during January 1937. It was mainly brought about by Eve's rapidly developing affair with a young man she had met at the Young Conservatives' gatherings. John Smith, known by his close friends and family as Jack Smith, was a live wire, terrific fun, but in many ways irresponsible. He was, for example, quite proud of the fact that he had smashed up three motor vehicles over the last two or three years and yet been fortunate enough to walk away each time virtually unscathed. He smoked, partied hard and tended to drink too much. Eve, yearning for a more exciting and stimulating social life found Jack, or 'Jacko' as she began to call him, the perfect antidote. Jacko brought out Eve's more adventurous side and within a few weeks of meeting him she realised that for the first time in her life she was falling in love.

Jacko was a couple of years younger than Eve, strongly built and handsome in a rough sort of way. He came from a well-to-do Lancashire family that had made its money from coal and textiles. Jacko's father, Thomas Smith, was the managing director of the Astley and Tyldesley Colliery and had appointed his son Jacko as a colliery salesman with the intention that once he was more mature in his outlook, he would take on a senior management position in the company. Jacko's brother-in-law was, prior to his death, none other than Sir George Holden, Managing Director of Combined Egyptian Mills which controlled thirty-five cotton mills throughout Lancashire. The Smiths were widely recognised as one of the most prestigious and wealthy families in the north of England.

Eve had first met Jacko late in 1936 at one of the regular Young Conservatives evenings. She was immediately attracted to his bright personality and terrific sense of humour. Within a few minutes he would have her in stitches relating some event that he would describe so colourfully and expressively. Eve needed to laugh heartily after years of living with her rather humourless and boring husband.

One night, after a Young Conservative fundraising dinner at which the wine had been flowing freely, Jacko invited Eve to go for a short ride in his new car. She hesitated, aware of his poor record with cars, but then felt there was no harm in a short trip and agreed to go with him. Jacko spent a few minutes showing off what the car could do and then drove straight up to the Preston lookout where he parked in a spot where they could look out across the Preston Port and see the many lights twinkling below. It looked like a night fairyland. Without warning Jacko came on strongly.

'Eve, you are the most beautiful woman I've ever met.'

Eve was quite taken aback and didn't know how to respond.

'I have felt this ever since I first laid eyes on you about eight weeks ago.'

'That may be so Jacko, but just remember I'm a married woman with a young child.'

'So what? I suspect your marriage is not a particularly happy one? Am I right?'

'Jacko, the state of my married life is none of your business.'

'Oh yes, it is. If I find you irresistible it's very much my business. Am I right about your marriage? Come on, tell me. I've heard you're married to a stodgy old major and your life is deadly boring?'

Again, Eve was lost for words. Nobody had ever dared to confront her like this before about her marriage. She knew Jacko was absolutely right, her marriage was a marriage in name only. She and Thomas just existed together; there was no genuine love or passion in their relationship. It was young Michael that was keeping them together. He was as unruly as ever, but they both loved him to bits. Unsure how to respond, Eve remained silent.

'Eve, I've had a few girlfriends over the years, but I've never met the right one. I think you are the beautiful woman of my dreams.' He took hold of her hand, moved closer and looked deeply into her eyes.

Eve felt strangely aroused by this full-on expression of affection. Thomas had never told her she was beautiful, but suddenly, here was this man she had known for only a few weeks and to whom she was already strongly attracted, ready to seduce her. Eve had enjoyed a few glasses of wine and her adventurous streak was fighting to get out. She would love to be kissed by this man and nobody else would ever know. She held his gaze.

Slowly Jacko moved closer until she could feel the warmth of his face next to hers and then his lips were searching for hers. She resisted, pulling away, everything in her being telling her she should not be doing this; she was a respectable married woman with Michael to care for. As his lips found hers, it was so heavenly that she couldn't resist any more and letting go she responded, enthusiastically. She knew she wanted more; just kissing was not enough. Her heart was beating strongly and her breathing was wildly out of control. Why not surrender to him totally here, now, in the car and release the many years of passion she had bottled up for so long? Nobody would ever know. They were alone together, nobody else was about. Why not, she *so* wanted to?

'Eve, I've told you how I feel about you. I think I'm falling in love but I don't want to make love to you in my car. We should go somewhere special together for a weekend and really get to know each other properly. Would you like to?'

'Oh, Jacko, this all very sudden. You're a single man but it's much more complicated for me. I have a child to care for. I can't just go away for a weekend.'

'So, you are not saying you *don't* want to go away with me, you're saying you *can't*.'

'I guess so.'

'Come on, use your initiative, Eve. Think about how you can get away for a weekend. I know, next month is the Young Conservatives District Conference. Let's put our names down for the conference, but instead go off together somewhere else? That way it will seem perfectly legitimate. I'm sure your husband would be happy to look after young Michael for a couple of nights. What do you think?'

Eve was not sure how much the wine was doing the talking for her when she replied. 'That's a clever idea, Jacko, I think we could do that. But... I do need to organise what I'm going to do with Michael.'

'You are wonderful, Eve. You make your booking for the conference and I will too. I'll organise where we spend the weekend. Sound okay?'

Before she could answer, he leant over and kissed her sensuously again. This time she knew for sure that she desperately wanted to have a weekend away with Jacko.

* * *

That night when she arrived home Thomas wanted sex, but the thought of surrendering to his tedious sexual needs yet again disgusted her, and for the first time in over ten years of married life, Eve bluntly refused him. Angry, shocked and feeling rejected, Thomas reacted.

'You've been drinking again, Eve. I can smell it. I've asked you before to limit your drinking.'

'What I drink, Thomas, is my business, and you have no right to dictate to me how much I can, or cannot, drink!'

'As your husband, I have *every* right to ask you not to come home half drunk!'

'Go to hell!' and Eve stormed out, went to the wine cupboard and helped herself to another drink.

Thomas didn't follow her out and retired to his bedroom furious and frustrated. Half an hour later, Eve retired to her bedroom and fell into a restless disturbed sleep. Now there was one thing she was sure about: she would definitely be putting her name down for next month's Young Conservatives conference.

* * *

The strained relationship between Eve and Thomas lasted for only a few more days until the major made the astonishing announcement at breakfast one morning that he had purchased a small house at 3 Clifton Grove, in the suburb of Holme Slack in Preston and he wanted Eve and Michael to move there forthwith. Thomas argued that there was nothing to be gained by the two of them remaining under the same roof anymore and in order to retain a semblance of civility between them they should permanently part company. As a devout Roman Catholic, he refused to entertain any talk of a divorce; they would be 'separated' only. Thomas also insisted that he be permitted to visit Michael at any time and that Michael be encouraged to visit his father at the barracks whenever possible. Eve accepted these conditions and moved with Michael to 3 Clifton Grove two days later.

The separation came as a huge shock to Eve's parents still living at 195 Tulketh Brow. George, no longer a fit man, took the news particularly hard. At the age of fifty-four the many years working out of doors as a farm labourer, a gardener and finally as a stonemason had taken its toll. He was riddled with arthritic pain and recently had developed respiratory problems caused, no doubt, by clouds of dust created when grinding and working in stone. A determined man, he assured everyone that he was well enough to keep working until sixty when he could retire. Annie was well, but increasingly concerned about her husband. News of Eve's marriage breakdown was hard to take. They were particularly concerned to shelter Michael from any unpleasantness.

The third weekend in February was the time of the Young Conservatives conference to be held in Manchester. A bus had been hired to transport the Preston contingent to the event but, to the surprise of many, Eve was not on it. Shortly after lunch on Friday, Jacko parked his car outside 3 Clifton Grove and entered Eve's new place of residence for the first time. She showed him around briefly before they departed taking nine-year-old Michael with them. Eve had arranged for Michael to stay with his best friend from St Christopher's for the weekend.

After dropping Michael off, they continued driving north to a secret location booked by Jacko at the foot of Beacon Fell, the highest point around. He had selected a romantic little sixteenth century hotel near the start of the path that wound its way up, snakelike to the summit of Beacon Fell. They booked in as Mr and Mrs Smith and were shown to their snug bedroom upstairs. The room was quite adorable with white-washed walls, natural wooden beams and full of nooks and crannies. Old horse brasses stood on the mantlepiece above the fireplace where a welcoming coal fire crackled. A small lattice window looked out over the wintery garden scene below where they could see bare trees waving their branches in the fading light and a fishpond, still frozen over. Thrushes, sparrows and blackbirds flitted about in the undergrowth and a robin with a bright red breast sat momentarily on a gate post. Heavy clouds obscured the summit of Beacon Fell: the BBC weather forecaster had warned of possible snow storms during the weekend.

Dinner was not served until six-thirty. They didn't bother to unpack for they both knew what they desperately wanted.

Afterwards, as they lay together naked and fulfilled, Eve told Jacko that this was the first time she had ever enjoyed the act of love-making. Jacko knew how to arouse her to heights of exhilaration she never dreamed possible. He said nothing but his hands glided all over her body again until she cried out for more. They were ten minutes late for dinner.

* * *

Chapter Fourteen 'Jacko'

The BBC forecaster was right: snow began falling silently that night and when they looked out in the morning they were greeted by a wintry wonderland. All was quiet and still with a few large flakes still falling lazily. The only sound was the scraping noise of the hotel proprietor clearing a path to the front door. There remained a glow of hot embers in the fireplace and Jacko soon had the fire roaring again. They enjoyed a relaxed full English breakfast in the dining room but were obliged to cancel their plans to walk to the top of Beacon Fell as it had started snowing again. There was a comfortable lounge for hotel guests and they were invited to make use of the extensive range of board games and books available there. Eve and Jacko looked at each other but both knew there were other more exciting games to play in their bedroom.

Their affair continued unabated throughout 1937, and before long Eve realised she was hopelessly in love with this larrikin man. They did their best to keep their relationship quiet and secret, but in a small place like Preston, where Eve was so well known, they inevitably became the talk of the town. Gradually, however, people lost interest in them as other interesting and more current scandals arose, or important national or international events occupied their minds and conversations.

The first major distraction of the year was the coronation of King George VI and Queen Elizabeth on May 18th. The King had reluctantly stepped up to the throne following the abdication of his older brother, King Edward VIII in 1936. The massive coronation celebrations held throughout the British Empire were soon followed by the controversial marriage of the Duke of Windsor (previously King Edward VIII) to the divorced American, Wallis Simpson, at the Chateau de Cande on June 3rd. Then there was an unsuccessful IRA assassination attempt on the newly crowned King as he toured Belfast.

Shortly afterwards came the horrendous explosion of the Flying Ship Hindenburg which effectively ended all efforts to promote and sail these gargantuan transports. Later in the year the papers reported Japan had invaded China and captured Peking and Shanghai, in the process massacring over 200,000 innocent citizens. Finally, on November 5th Chancellor Adolf Hitler ominously disclosed his plans to 'acquire more living space' for the German people. The steady rise of Hitler and the Third Reich, less than eighteen years since the end of the World War, was already haunting the British people.

Jacko continued to work as a colliery salesman throughout the year. Whenever he had a spare weekend, he would travel down to visit Eve at 3 Clifton Grove. He was as infatuated with her as she was with him. They now hoped that Major Dillon could eventually be persuaded to agree to a divorce. Jacko got along famously with young Michael and would always make time to take him to the park for a kick with a soccer ball or a hit at cricket. Michael was showing encouraging signs of being athletically gifted.

Jacko still displayed his larrikin streak and at times behaved quite irresponsibly. He found open roads irresistible for speeding and was in trouble with the police on more than one occasion. Whenever Eve was driving with him, she managed to modify his behaviour somewhat and was a steadying influence.

Jacko also introduced Eve to all sorts of sexual positions and activities she had never even dreamed of, most of which she found arousing and deeply satisfying. Jacko, she realised, had 'slept around' extensively before meeting her and he would become very guarded if Eve ever tried to ascertain further details. Eve was convinced, however, that their relationship would be lasting and Jacko's womanising would then become a thing of the past.

CHAPTER FIFTEEN

Christmas 1937

John Smith (Jacko) was not without substantial means and in October 1936, before he had met Eve, he had teamed up with a friend, John Harrap, to become joint tenants of a boathouse at Pull Woods, Brathay, on the shores of Lake Windermere in the county of Lancashire. Jacko and John had been friends for about five years. John Harrap was a director of the firm, John Harrap, based in Manchester. The boathouse was small but reasonably well furnished and could comfortably accommodate two visitors. There was a bedroom with a double bed and another small trundle bed for a third person if required. The boathouse was located on the estate of Pull Woods and was approximately half a mile downhill from Pull Woods Mansion where the caretaker, Robert Fox, lived with his wife. It was a remote beautiful place ideal for anyone who wished to take the boat out for some fishing on the lake or, as Jacko had discovered, ideal for bringing willing young ladies for a weekend.

In the time Jacko had been courting Eve, he had never had an opportunity to bring her to the romantic boathouse: either something else would be happening, or John Harrap booked the boathouse first. Finally, as Christmas 1937 approached, Jacko persuaded Eve to come away with him over the Christmas period and stay at the boathouse. Eve had been reluctant at first, because she had expected she and Michael would join her parents for the festive season and her young brother, George, would be there too. Jacko, however, was most insistent and persuasive. In the end she relented and apologetically arranged for Michael on his own to stay with her parents over Christmas. Eve organised her Christmas presents and cards in good time and was packed and ready when Jacko arrived to pick her up on Christmas Eve.

They dined at a small pub en route and arrived at Pull Woods Mansion around seven-thirty. Earlier in the day Jacko had sent a telegram to Mr and Mrs Fox, the caretakers, confirming their arrival later that evening. John Harrap had vacated the boathouse only that morning so Robert Fox and his wife had been busy throughout the afternoon changing the sheets, making up the beds and cleaning.

Chapter Fifteen   Christmas 1937

It was pitch dark and flurries of snow were falling lightly when Jacko parked the car under the welcoming electric light outside the main entrance of the mansion. He introduced Eve as 'Mrs Smith' and, armed with torches that Robert Fox handed them, they set off walking down the rough track that led to the boathouse. Mr Fox carried Jacko's heavier suitcase and Jacko took Eve's. Eve was wearing a good pair of shoes and found it difficult scrambling down the rocky path. In places slippery roots were exposed and loose stones made the track treacherous. They heard mysterious little animals scurrying about in the undergrowth. Nevertheless, they arrived safely and Robert Fox unlocked the door and ushered them in.

It was bitterly cold and the snow was coming down more heavily now. Robert set to and had a roaring fire going in the grate within minutes whilst Jacko found some glasses and poured the three of them a full glass of red wine. With the suitcases safely stowed in the bedroom and their coats shaken out and hanging up to dry, Jacko invited Robert Fox to stay and have a drink or two with them. It was Christmas Eve after all, and Robert had always looked after Jacko's interests professionally and discreetly. They chatted affably for an hour or so before Robert excused himself saying he must get back to his wife who was up at the mansion and alone. It was still snowing when Robert left and a light dusting had settled on the ground around the boathouse as he trudged back up the track.

The little boathouse was beautifully warm. Jacko switched off the electric lights and led Eve over to the fireplace where he sat her down on the thick wool rug. Joining her there he slowly, deliberately and lovingly began to undress her, pausing from time to time to admire the way the light from the fire played on her hair and skin. They were both beautifully relaxed by the wine and hungry for what was coming. Eve insisted on reciprocating and gradually removed layer after layer of Jacko's clothing. Soon they were sitting in front of each other wearing only their underwear.

'Jacko I can't wait any longer. Take me to bed.'

Instead, he lent forward and gently and skilfully removed her bra and then slipped her panties down her legs. He felt for her special place and they made love passionately and wildly there by the light of the fire.

Sometime later, and still lying naked together, Jacko suddenly sprang into action.

'Come on Eve, get your gear back on. I want to show you something.'

Eve would have far preferred to have retired to bed to sleep but Jacko was full of energy. Perhaps he wanted to give her his Christmas present? She had his present wrapped and ready to give him if he really wanted to exchange gifts straightaway. By her reckoning, it was by now the wee small hours of Christmas day already.

'Have a look at this Eve,' Jacko walked over to the side of the fireplace where he picked up a gun and brought it over to where Eve was standing.

'This is my double-barrelled shot gun. What do you think of it?'

Chapter Fifteen Christmas 1937

'Oh, Jacko, I don't like guns. Thomas has to go off to a firing range to practice shooting sometimes but I prefer to keep right away from them.'

'Well, they're perfectly safe Eve, when you know what you're doing. Look I'll show you.'

She watched warily as Jacko picked up a small cardboard box and took out some cartridges which he then loaded.

'Come on, I'll fire it outside. Come and watch.'

Jacko was so anxious to demonstrate his gun to her that Eve didn't feel she could refuse. She grabbed her coat and shivered as soon as he threw open the door leading out onto the balcony. Outside it was pitch dark, apart from the light coming from the boathouse, and she could barely see as far as the water's edge. It wasn't snowing but it was horribly cold.

'Okay, listen to this Eve.'

Jacko raised the shotgun, paused, then fired out across the lake. The sound was louder than Eve had expected and she recoiled; there was no way she wanted to be around such a ghastly weapon.

'Let's get out of the cold and I'll show you how to fire it. Come on.'

'I don't want to fire that thing Jacko!'

'Yes, you do, it's easy. I'll show you what to do. It doesn't hurt.'

Eve followed Jacko back into the boathouse making sure the door was firmly closed behind her and much relieved to get in from the biting cold. She hastily kicked her shoes off and removed her coat as it was gorgeously warm inside.

'Now, I'll show you. You hold the gun like this. No... like this.'

Yes, that's better. Now point the gun up to the ceiling. See if you can hit that beam. Put your finger on the trigger.'

'I don't want to do this Jacko, I'm scared,'

'Absolutely nothing to be scared about, Eve dear. It'll make a hole in the ceiling but that's not a problem. Are you ready? Are you aiming at the beam? Okay, come on, pull the trigger.'

'I can't.'

'Yes, you can, I promise you it won't hurt. Come on, fire!'

Eve tensed herself, checked the rifle was pointing up towards the beam and pulled the trigger.

The gun went off, a small piece of plaster fell from the ceiling and there was a kind of a burnt odour that Eve had never smelt before.

'Fantastic Eve! Well done! It's so easy, isn't it?'

'I guess so.'

'Now the gun's empty and perfectly safe. If it's got no ammo it can't go off, can it?'

'No, I suppose not.'

'See, hold the gun up again and point it at my chest. Pull the trigger, it's empty. It's quite safe. Go on...'

Eve squeezed the trigger, there was an explosion and Jacko collapsed to the floor.

'Oh, come on Jacko, stop fooling about. Get up!'

Then Eve watched in horror as a small circle of red began to ooze out of her lover's chest.

CHAPTER SIXTEEN

Tragedy

Jacko lay motionless and the ghastly red stain on the left of his chest continued to grow ominously.

Eve now realised this was no joke; the injury was serious, so she threw the hateful gun onto the closest arm chair. She knew she must get a doctor for Jacko urgently. Panicking, she charged out of the boathouse, not bothering to put on her coat or shoes or take a torch, to run the half mile back up to the mansion to get the Foxes to call for medical help on their telephone.

The trip up to the mansion was the most terrifying of

journeys, one she would never have dreamt of attempting, if it wasn't for the thought of the man she wanted to marry lying helpless on the floor of the boathouse. As she began her hazardous way through the woods, tripping and stumbling and desperately scrambling up again, she realised she should have checked first to see if Jacko was still alive. No time to go back, time was of the essence.

Eve lost count of the number of times she fell to the ground. She blundered on through patches of stinging nettles, scratched by blackberry brambles and ran into small whip-like branches. A couple of times she believed she was lost but reasoned that as long as she was climbing upwards, she must be heading roughly in the right direction. Coming up over a small rise she saw the outside light of the mansion glowing in the distance. Thankfully the light had been left on showing her the way.

At times she completely lost her footing and fell on her hands and knees so that she was almost crawling. Eve was vaguely aware of painful scratches and bruising and her ankle was hurting but nothing could stop her desperate plight to get help for Jacko. An owl screeched and flew so close she believed it was going to attack her. Shielding her face, she fell once again but picked herself up painfully and struggled on.

Eve had no idea how long she had taken blundering around in the dark before she finally arrived at the small yard outside the entrance to Pull Woods mansion where the lone light offered a smidgin of hope. Looking down at her clothing, she noticed her garments were badly torn and her hands and legs covered in blood from cuts and scratches. She remembered thinking she must have looked like some crazy mad woman, dishevelled, dirty and bleeding. But her appearance didn't concern her, it was Jacko that mattered.

Hobbling painfully from her injured ankle she approached the main entrance and started screaming. She yelled and yelled with all the energy she could muster and kept on screaming until lights started coming on upstairs. It seemed to take forever for someone to unlock the solid wooden doors and appear in front of her. It was Robert Fox. Eve ran forward and grabbed his arm, quite hysterical by now.

'Jacko, Jacko, blood... fetch a doctor, quick!'

'Okay, calm down, we'll help you.'

Mrs Violet Fox joined her husband on the doorstep wearing a dressing gown and holding a torch. Eve moved towards her and fell on her knees, pleading, 'Jacko, Jacko, I've shot him! I didn't know the gun was loaded. Help me please.'

'Yes, of course we'll help you dear, but please try to calm yourself down.'

'Come with me, Mrs Smith. I'll walk down with you to see how Mr Smith is while my wife rings for the doctor. Violet, can you lend Mrs Smith a coat please, it's very cold.'

'Yes, of course, dear.'

Violet gave the torch to Robert and hurried back indoors to find a spare coat, re-emerging a moment later with an old winter coat she used when out walking in the woods.

'Here dear, put this on. Are you okay to walk down with my husband?'

Eve nodded. *Perhaps,* she thought, *this is all just a terrible dream and when we get back down to the boathouse Jacko will be sitting up and smiling. Possibly he was only stunned and I panicked unnecessarily. Please God let it be so.*

The trip back to the boathouse was far quicker. Robert had a good torch and he knew the way. Eve, in her hysteria, had missed the track completely and instead had headed up a crazy way through bracken, undergrowth and trees. As they hurried down the proper track, she kept up a relentless nervous chatter explaining to Robert Fox what they had been doing with the gun and how she loved Jacko and how they were going to get married.

Robert said little, sensing that Mrs Smith needed to keep talking in an attempt to ease some of her tension. The more she jabbered on, the more it confirmed in Robert's mind what he had strongly suspected from the previous evening that this was not 'Mrs Smith' at all, but somebody masquerading as the wife. Robert had, over the last eighteen months, welcomed two or three other young ladies who were escorting Jack Smith to stay in the boathouse, although this was the first time Jack had brazenly announced that this was 'Mrs Smith.'

Eve's ankle was not troubling her now as she followed Robert down the track but her numerous cuts and scratches were hurting. Soon they saw the light shining from the boathouse window and again Eve prayed that she would find Jacko was only injured and that this whole ghastly nightmare would end.

'Would you prefer to wait outside, Mrs Smith, while I go in?'

Eve was confused. Why was Robert calling her Mrs Smith? She thought to tell him that she was actually Mrs Dillon.

'Mrs Smith? Are you prepared to come in with me or do you wish to stay outside?' Robert repeated gently.

'I'll come in,' she muttered.

Now that he had her answer, Robert moved quickly. The door of the boathouse was wide open; in her haste to call for help Mrs Smith must have left it that way. He entered and was immediately confronted by the sight of the body of a man lying spreadeagled on his back with his head towards the door. There was no sign of life. A circle of blood, about the size of a side plate, covered his chest. The man's face was a sinister ashen white. Robert knelt down next to the body and could tell just by looking that Jack Smith was dead. He heard Mrs Smith collapse into an easy chair behind him and cry out in anguish. She knew the awful truth too.

Robert was a pragmatic man. He looked around the room, noting that Jacko's gun had been left on an easy chair and that a small piece of the ceiling had fallen down on the floor. On closer inspection the ceiling appeared to have been shot at. Realising that the boathouse was now a crime scene, and nothing should be disturbed, Robert walked over to where Eve was seated and, bending down, said kindly, 'Mrs Smith, I'm sorry, there's nothing we can do here. Let me take you back up to the house. We need to call the police.'

'I want to stay here with Jacko. We were only fooling around; it was a terrible accident.'

'I'm sure it was, but we can't stay here. Come with me and we'll see if my wife can clean up some of your cuts and grazes.'

Robert was fully aware that he was now in the company of

a possible murderer, although he could hardly imagine a less likely killer. The young lady, whoever she was, was so distressed he wondered if she was going to pass out. It would be wise to try and walk her back up to the mansion where she could rest more comfortably, have her wounds attended to, and remain until the police arrived.

'Come on Mrs Smith, let's get you back to the mansion. No point in staying down here.'

Still sobbing, and in a kind of a trance, Eve wobbled to her feet, and taking one last long look at the man who had so passionately made love to her only a couple of short hours ago, she turned and shuffled towards the door. Robert took her arm and gently guided and supported Eve back to the mansion. Several times she appeared on the verge of collapsing and it was all he could manage to half-carry, half-support her. She moaned softly and made a few incoherent comments as together they made their slow journey back.

It was around two in the morning on that fateful Christmas day when Eve and Robert finally stumbled in through the heavy wooden doors of Full Woods mansion. Violet met them at the door and helped to convey Eve to a comfortable chair over which she had placed a large sheet to protect the chair from dirt and blood.

'Here dear, sit down and I'll get you a brandy. Oh my, you have some horrible cuts and scratches. I'll put TCP on them for you.'

'I can't think why he did it. It was so silly. We were so happy.'

'Don't talk about it now dear. You will have to tell the police

Chapter Sixteen Tragedy

when they get here. I rang them after I rang for the doctor. Here you are, it's a brandy, just sip it slowly and it will warm you up.'

'We don't need a doctor anymore, Jacko's dead,' she cried.

There was a knock at the door. Robert opened it to find a tall be-whiskered gentleman with a stethoscope hanging around his neck and carrying a leather medical bag.

'Good evening. I'm Dr Quarmby. I had an urgent call from a Mrs Fox to attend to an accident here.'

'Yes, that was my wife. It happened down at the boathouse. There's only a track down, so we will have to walk, I'm afraid.'

'That's okay, I'm wearing sturdy walking boots.'

Dr Quarmby and Robert set off together and Robert filled the doctor in with the background as they walked.

The doctor duly pronounced Jack Smith dead and indicated he had died approximately two hours earlier from a gunshot wound to the chest inflicted at very close quarters. The shot had penetrated the heart causing death, probably instantly. Anxious not to spoil the remainder of his Christmas day, Dr Quarmby left hastily, assuring Robert that he would have a report ready for the police later in the day and that he would arrange for the removal of the body to the morgue in readiness for a post-mortem.

Robert had only just farewelled Dr Quarmby when there was another knock at the door. A portly, red-faced policeman greeted him this time, holding his police helmet tucked safely under his arm.

'Good evening sir. I'm Sergeant Galley and this is PC

Rawcliffe. I understand you've had a spot of bother here tonight, sir?

'Yes, indeed sergeant. Would you like to come in?'

'It's important that I go to the crime scene straightaway sir before anything is disturbed, if you don't mind sir?'

'Yes, of course, sergeant. I'll take you down.'

'Now, I understand that a young lady was involved. Whereabouts is she, sir?'

'She's in my lounge room having some of her nasty wounds attended to by my wife.'

'With your permission sir, PC Rawcliffe will remain with the lady until we return.'

'Yes, that's fine sergeant. She's very shaken up and badly cut about. I'm sure she won't try to escape.'

'I'm sure you are right sir, but we do need to take necessary precautions.'

PC Rawcliffe, who looked like a pimply teenager, removed his helmet, wiped his boots thoroughly on the foot scraper and entered the mansion relieved to escape the cold while his superior walked down to the boathouse in the company of Robert Fox, now making his third trip there since his guests had arrived.

* * *

Violet Fox was a kindly soul and her heart went out to this troubled young woman. She didn't wish to be judgemental. Irrespective of what had transpired down there in the boathouse, right now this young lady needed some motherly help and support. No sooner had Violet managed to get the young lady settled comfortably on an easy chair with her legs up on a foot stool, and a large glass of brandy in her hand, than she heard a nervous cough from the doorway. Looking up, she saw the fidgety young policeman standing there unsure what to do with himself.

'Can I help you, officer?'

'Ur... yes, madam. Sergeant Galley has asked me to keep an eye on this lady while he visits the crime scene.'

'Very well, take a seat officer.'

'I prefer to stand, thank you madam.'

'Very well, suit yourself.'

Violet was annoyed this young policeman wanted to remain standing in the room when she could see that there were nasty scratches and bruises all over the young lady's arms and legs. If she was to put antiseptic on all these wounds, she would have to lift the lady's dress up which would be most immodest and embarrassing.

'Constable, would you mind standing just outside the room please? I need to give this lady some first aid and I can't do it with you watching.'

'Very well, madam,' and the twitchy young policeman removed himself back into the hallway.

For nearly an hour, Violet cleaned the extensive wounds with warm water and cotton wool and then applied diluted TCP to the worst of the cuts. Her patient groaned and gave little yelps of pain as the TCP stung. Violet thought that there were a couple of quite deep cuts that might need stitches and bruises were already starting to appear on the knees, shins and elbows where she had fallen and virtually crawled through the undergrowth. Violet wished now that they had asked Dr Quarmby to take a look at her because the young lady needed more medical care than she was able to provide by just washing the wounds and applying antiseptics.

As soon as Violet finished, the young lady fell into an exhausted sleep, only to be woken five minutes later by the return of the sergeant with Robert and the nervous young constable trailing along behind them.

Sergeant Galley was not in an amiable mood. Being called out to investigate a serious crime on Christmas day was not to his liking: he had family duties to attend to and wanted to be home when the children woke up and explored their exciting Christmas stockings at the end of their beds. Looking at his fob watch, he noted it was already well past three in the morning and now he must interrogate the one and only suspect who was draped out on an easy chair in front of him. Sergeant Galley, quite understandably, was also feeling tired. He was someone who needed his eight hours beauty sleep every night and found it hard to adjust when called into action outside of normal working hours. All this did not portend well for the impending interrogation.

The sergeant grabbed a straight-backed chair and plonked it down just a few feet away from Eve so he could eyeball her closely. From his fob pocket he now extricated a tattered notebook and a short pencil. Thumbing through, he finally located a number of unused pages towards the back.

'PC Rawcliffe, you're to take notes as well. Afterwards we'll compare them. Is that understood?'

'Yes sir,' responded the hapless constable, fumbling about looking for his notebook and pencil.

'Now, madam, you and I need to have a little chat. What is your correct name, in full please?'

'My name is Mary Evelyn Dillon.'

'Are you married?'

'Yes.'

'What is the full name of your husband?'

'Major Thomas Anton Dillon.'

'Are you happily married, madam?'

'Not really, we live apart.'

'Do you have children?'

'Yes, a son, Michael. He's nine.'

'Would you care to tell me why you were staying the night at the boatshed with Mr John Smith?'

'We are in love and plan to get married. Well, until this awful thing happened.'

'Now, Mrs Dillon, I want you to take me through exactly what happened down in the boatshed.'

For the next twenty minutes Eve provided a detailed account of what had happened in the boatshed, punctuated only by the occasional probing question from Sergeant Galley whenever he wanted further clarification. Finally, the sergeant seemed satisfied. He rose to his feet, cleared his throat and looked straight at Eve and announced in a monotonous voice, 'Mrs Dillon, I'm arresting you for the murder of Mr John Smith.'

CHAPTER SEVENTEEN
Preliminaries

PC Rawcliffe moved towards Eve and assisted her into a standing position. The pain of Eve's multiple injuries was now more severe and she found she could barely walk. Violet Fox took pity on her and came to her aid offering an arm to lean on. Eve shuffled slowly and with considerable difficulty towards the front door where Violet placed the same old gardening coat gently around her shoulders. Sergeant Galley, thankfully, had decided that Eve was no risk of trying to escape so did not insist on handcuffs.

The freezing cold night air stung Eve's cuts and scratches

and her sore muscles stiffened so that she tottered out to the police car like a wooden soldier. With some difficulty she was placed in the back seat with PC Rawcliffe for company. The sergeant took the wheel and they moved off with light snow starting to fall again. Eve cried and whimpered much of the way and PC Rawcliffe, who had no idea what to do to try to comfort her, pretended it wasn't happening.

It was well over an hour later that Sergeant Galley pulled up at the entrance gates to Strangeways Gaol for women in Manchester. A sleepy guard opened up and permitted him to drive through before hurrying back to the warmth of his small guard room. It was ten minutes past five.

Eve was, by this stage, in such a poorly state that she couldn't walk through the main entrance to the prison and PC Rawcliffe was obliged to carry her holding her clumsily like an oversized, heavy laundry basket. The duty officer at the gaol was none too pleased to have to admit a prisoner at such an early hour on Christmas day. She fumbled about for the requisite papers and a fountain pen. Eve, who had been left standing there while the duty officer organised herself, suddenly collapsed in a heap on the floor. With an effort, she managed to get herself back up onto one elbow like a boxer almost down and out for the count.

Observing this, the duty officer picked up her phone and rang someone in the prison's hospital ward. She barked a couple of orders, which resulted in the appearance of two male hospital orderlies carrying a stretcher. The exhausted and groaning Eve was unceremoniously dumped on the stretcher and carted off to the prison's hospital ward. It was left to the unfortunate Sergeant Galley to provide the duty officer with the details of the newest prisoner as best he could from the notes he had assiduously taken.

As Eve was being checked into the hospital ward, she was on the verge of becoming delirious. The night nurse, seeing the state she was in, placed her in a room of her own and administered a mild sedative to calm her down and help her sleep. The nurse then superficially examined Eve's injuries and placed Eve's name on the list of patients for the prison doctor to visit later on in the day when he came to do his daily rounds.

Eve fell into a deep but troubled sleep. Hours later, having lost all track of time, she awoke to find a woman bending over her and examining the wounds. For a moment or two Eve remained completely nonplussed. Where was she? Who was this person? Why did she feel so utterly exhausted? And then the awful memories hit her and it all come flooding back. She started to call out and scream and then felt a sharp prick in her arm. The sedative only took a couple of minutes to take effect and she fell back into a kind of a stupor before sleep completely overtook her again.

The next time Eve woke she found her wounds had been treated with ointments, plaster and bandages and a couple of female orderlies were dressing her in a plain brown prison uniform. What remained of her clothes had been removed. There was a cup of strong tea on offer, which she relished for she was thirsty. Once dressed, the orderlies placed her on a chair and left her there. A few minutes elapsed before another nurse turned up and informed Eve she was going to be taken to court to answer a charge of murder. She was told she would be provided with a wheelchair as she was not yet fit to walk into the court unaided. The guards would be picking her up shortly.

As Eve sat there confused and alone, she gradually began to appreciate the dreadful situation she was in. Try as she did, she didn't seem to be able to concentrate on anything for more than a moment or two before feeling sleepy and drifting off again. In her more lucid moments, she knew the police thought she had murdered Jacko and that she was being taken to a court to answer the charge. Alarmingly, there was nobody to help her, nobody to defend her. Possibly nobody even *knew* she was in a prison somewhere. She must try to get a message out to her parents. And poor Michael, what was happening to him? He must be worrying about her by now.

Two grumpy male orderlies turned up a little later pushing a wobbly wheelchair. From them she learnt that she was in Manchester at the Strangeways Prison for Women, that it was four o'clock in the afternoon on December 27th and that she was being taken to appear in a Manchester court to be formally charged for the murder of Mr John Smith.

Eve must still have been under the influence of sedatives when she was wheeled into court to appear before the magistrate because she remembered little about the hearing except that she was surprised and delighted to find her husband was there to meet her. Somebody presumably had contacted him and he had left whatever Christmas festivities he had been attending to immediately drive over to Manchester to be by her side. He told her Michael was happily staying with a school friend for a few more days.

Chapter Seventeen   Preliminaries

The solicitor representing John Smith at the inquest was a Mr W Boydrill. He opened the proceedings by announcing, 'Mrs Dillon, you are formally charged with feloniously killing John Smith, aged about twenty-seven, at Pull Woods boathouse, Brathay, on the shore of Lake Windermere, between the hours of 9.30pm on December 24th and 1.30am on December 25th, by shooting him with a double-barrelled shotgun.'

The only evidence given then was that of the arrest.

Thomas explained to Eve afterwards that it had been necessary for her to appear before a magistrate so that she could be formally charged with murder. Apparently, it was illegal to imprison a person if they had not been formally charged. Eve was next ordered to appear before a magistrate at Hawkshead in three days' time to answer the charge of murder. Thomas told Eve he was already contacting lawyers to defend her and that he was most hopeful the charge could at least be downgraded from murder to manslaughter. If this happened, Eve's lawyer might be able to argue for bail and she could be released into his custody.

Although Eve no longer wished to live with Thomas as his wife, she was deeply grateful that he had come to support her in her time of need.

* * *

Eve remained in the hospital ward for the next three days as her injuries required regular dressing changes. The matron told her the prison authorities were expecting she would be granted bail which would mean she would not have to be moved to the normal cells of the prison. Eve was more than thankful to hear this.

On the morning of December 30th, a nurse attended to Eve's wounds for the last time and provided her with a pair of brown stockings that Eve managed to carefully pull up over her several dressings. She no longer required a wheelchair and could walk slowly unassisted. Eve was clad in the normal unflattering uniform worn by all prisoners at Strangeways. For the first time in years, Eve had no access to makeup, creams, lotions or powders and it showed. Looking at herself in the one small cracked mirror in the ablution block depressed her. For Eve this was a massive fall from grace. A few days ago, she still enjoyed the respect of all around her as a lady from the better classes; now she was reduced to being sneered at and ridiculed as a murderer. Some of the prisoners and staff in the hospital ward appeared to enjoy witnessing her demise and had little or no sympathy for her plight.

Mid-morning, two burly policemen came to her room. They checked she was Mrs Eve Dillon, handcuffed her and marched her out, albeit slowly, to a waiting car. They hardly spoke on the journey and treated her with disdain. She felt like a nobody, as if she was merely an object to be delivered somewhere.

This time she was driven to the small township of Hawkshead where she was to appear before a different magistrate in the town hall used for such events. They arrived early, which was fortunate, as she was taken indoors to be met by Thomas and a barrister from Bolton by the name of Mr Cyril Morris. A small, cold, sparsely furnished room had been allocated for their use. There was an old table and a few metal chairs, no carpet and no heating. Eve was asked to sit on one side of the table, with Thomas next to her, and Mr Morris sat on the opposite side behind a small pile of papers he had brought with him. The two policemen stood guard like sentries at the door.

'Eve, this is Cyril Morris, a barrister from Morris, Speidel and Walton, a firm based in Bolton. Cyril and I went to school together many years ago. I can assure you Eve, you will be well represented. Cyril is highly regarded in the legal profession.'

Mr Morris smiled warmly at Eve. 'What a pity, Mrs Dillon, that we have to meet under such unfortunate circumstances.'

Eve immediately warmed to this man, who conveyed an aura of quiet confidence and was the sort of man you knew was worth listening to as soon as you met him. He was not exactly stout, but clearly enjoyed a comfortable lifestyle. Smartly dressed, with grey, thinning hair, he exuded a sense of authority. His soft, well-manicured hands contrasted markedly with Thomas's hands roughed up from army service.

Mr Morris turned to the two policemen and spoke softly, 'Now, gentlemen, before we start, Mrs Dillon is not going to start running away, so we can remove these handcuffs please?'

To Eve's surprise, one of the policemen obediently stepped forward, silently removed the offending item and resumed his place by the door, sticking the handcuffs in a pocket as he did so.

'Now, we've twenty minutes before this case is due to be heard. I want to listen to your story please Mrs Dillon, every single detail right from the very beginning.'

For the next twenty minutes Eve described everything that had happened on that fateful night and answered several of the barrister's probing questions. In deference to Thomas's sensitivities, she omitted to disclose the beautiful love-making in front of the fire. Thomas sat and listened, totally absorbed, because, of course, it was the first time he had heard the full story too. Finally, Mr Morris cleared his throat and announced confidently, 'I believe we can reduce this murder charge to one of manslaughter and we can get you out today on bail, Mrs Dillon,' and he gave Eve another of his warm comforting smiles. Next, the barrister briefed Eve and Thomas on the likely order of proceedings during the hearing before the magistrate.

The hearing lasted only half an hour. The intricacies of the legal arguments were largely lost on Eve and Thomas. The good news was the magistrate accepted the charge against Eve should be altered from murder to that of manslaughter. In his brief summing up the magistrate ordered Eve to reappear at Hawkshead on January 6th, 1938. Furthermore, the magistrate agreed to release Eve on bail on the surety of her husband for two hundred pounds.

Eve was still legally married to Thomas and, although they did not live together, he believed it remained his duty, as her husband, to protect her and care for her in her hour of need. Consequently, he had no hesitation in providing surety and was happy to promise the magistrate that he would have Eve back to face her full trial at the appointed time on January 6th.

Although he did not mention it to Eve, Thomas earnestly hoped they might try again to live together as husband and wife along with their son, particularly, because he had recently been interviewed about a possible appointment in Africa. A fresh start, in a wildly different part of the world, might be the exotic stimulus and re-charge their marriage required. But first, Eve needed to be cleared of the charge of manslaughter and a verdict of misadventure brought down instead. Barrister Cyril Morris assured them he was quietly confident that a verdict of misadventure was a strong possibility.

As Eve gratefully climbed into Thomas's car immediately following the hearing, she was a bundle of mixed and confused emotions. She was grieving deeply for Jacko, the man she had agreed to marry if she could persuade Thomas to grant her a divorce, or find some other legal way around the problem if Thomas continued to refuse. And now, like a knight in shining armour, Thomas had come to her rescue. He had procured a top-notch barrister, provided surety and was now taking her somewhere safe for the few days before she had to reappear in court. Eve always knew Thomas was a man of the highest principles but she also knew she did not deserve such devotion and attention. In fact, she felt a deep sense of shame as she sat silently in the car with her husband.

News of the tragic events that had transpired in the boathouse on Christmas day had been splashed across the front pages of every local newspaper and had even made it into the national papers. It was a major scandal: the wife of a senior army officer accused of murdering a man in a desolate boathouse on the shores of Lake Windermere! Tongues wagged strenuously. Had Mrs Dillon been abducted? Had she shot John

Smith in self-defence? Was Mrs Dillon in the boathouse of her own freewill? Was this a clandestine affair? Had there been an argument? Few people entertained the idea that it was merely an accident. Only some of the better-informed denizens of Preston town knew that Jacko and Eve had been having an affair for some months.

Whereas the death of John Smith was an intriguing topic of conversation nationally, it was massive news in Preston, Eve's hometown. The Lancashire Daily Post, always desperately short of any significant news over the Christmas New Year period, was having a field day. In almost every edition, the creative journalists at The Lancashire Daily Post managed to come up with a new twist on the story, or a snippet of additional information was disclosed. Many of the letters to the editor discussed at length what the writer believed had happened in that lonely boathouse. Some contributors had already found Mrs Dillon guilty of pre-meditated murder, others were less sure. There was an even more farfetched claim that it was Eve's husband, who, long aware of the illicit relationship, could stand it no longer and had sneaked down to the boathouse in the dead of night and committed the crime.

While Eve was being treated in Strangeways, Thomas arranged that if Eve was released on bail, she could come home to Preston and stay with her parents. It was important, they all felt, that she had supportive family around her and her parents could also provide any continuing medical treatment should that be required. Eve was pleased with this idea and looked forward to a few days of rest and recuperation, although she was worried about the reactions of the close neighbours. Thomas had also arranged that young Michael would stay with him at the barracks until things calmed down. Their son had, naturally, taken a huge interest in what was going on and was constantly asking questions, some of which were difficult to answer honestly. He was now quite capable of reading The Lancashire Daily Post.

Thomas and Eve pulled up outside number 195 Tulketh Brow at about three o'clock in the afternoon. There was a damp mist hanging over the town, and try as it may, the sun was incapable of breaking through to give more than a glimmer of light and warmth. Eve was still wearing the unflattering brown prison garb she had been issued in prison because Thomas had not thought to bring her a change of clothing. Inevitably, as she waited at the door to be admitted, she was spotted by one or two of the neighbours and the word was out that Eve was back. Small groups of nosey neighbours spent the afternoon wandering along to number 195 where they would hobnob with other neighbours on a similar mission. A couple of the more forthright women yelled out 'Murderer' loudly and one drunk man on his way home from the pub kept up a barrage of rude and suggestive comments about what Eve was doing in the boathouse.

After an hour or so, Thomas, satisfied that Eve was as comfortable as possible, arranged a time to pick her up on January 6th and letting himself out, walked to his car. In doing so, he had to endure a number of rude and unpleasant questions from the vocal group still hanging about outside;

'what's it like to have a murderer for a wife, mister?' and, 'can't you bloody satisfy her, mate?' from the drunk. Thomas ignored the jibes and drove back to his barracks and Michael, who had been out riding his bike all day and was due back before dark.

Thomas's main concern was that his army career was now quite possibly in jeopardy. Top brass did not look kindly on officers experiencing marital problems, and an officer with a wife suspected of murder had to be considered a troublesome black mark against his name. He knew he was under consideration for a senior posting to Africa but the tragic events of the last few days might mean he would be passed over for another officer who did not have such a besmirched background.

Having Eve recuperating at number 195 was not easy for George and Annie either. For the first couple of days each time they left their premises they were subjected to abuse. Eve never ventured out, fearing her appearance would only exacerbate matters. Gradually, interest waned until by the end of the third day few, if any neighbours could be bothered to hang about outside to harass them. From time to time there would be a knock on the door from a journalist wanting to have access to Eve to get her story. Wisely, they didn't open the door to any visitors except a couple of times when Thomas brought Michael down to see his mother.

Eve now had plenty of time to think about things. She started to doubt whether she had really been in love with Jacko. Indubitably she had been infatuated with him and the sensuous and beautiful sex they had savoured so many times was something she had never experienced with Thomas. It had been so fulfilling and exciting that she had found herself desperately longing for more. Perhaps that was all their relationship had ever been; two people with an intense physical attraction, but nothing else?

Eve also needed to focus on her future. If she was found guilty of manslaughter what could she expect? Interestingly, nobody had discussed this possibility with her and the mood had remained upbeat and optimistic as though being found guilty was out of the question. Would she get ten, fifteen, twenty years behind bars? It didn't bear thinking about. She shuddered to think how such a decision would impact Michael. He was already showing signs of stress.

On the other hand, if she *was* cleared of the crime, what would she do with herself? Her reputation would be sullied for many years to come and job prospects in and around Preston would be impossible. June Doyer wouldn't want her as a customer, let alone an employee. Her number one priority would have to be to leave the district and settle somewhere else as far away as possible where she would be persona non grata.

There was, however, one other possibility. She and Thomas were still legally married. Could she cope with being his wife again? When Thomas had driven her back to Preston after the preliminary hearing, he had mentioned that he was being considered for a senior posting somewhere in Africa. In Africa she could start afresh: nobody would know about her past. She could be legitimately seen as the wife of a senior army officer and accorded the respect such a position demanded. Michael, she knew, would be thrilled if they came back together as a family. The more she thought about it, the more this seemed the best option. However, she was getting ahead of herself. Going to Africa, as Thomas's wife, was concomitant on escaping a guilty verdict, Thomas being prepared to take her back and his move to Africa being approved. Was this really a likely trifecta?

CHAPTER EIGHTEEN

The Trial

The proceedings of Eve's trial were well covered by *The Lancashire Daily Post* for Thursday, January 6th, 1938. Some extracts from the newspaper are reproduced in this chapter.

From before dawn, dozens of villagers started to assemble at the entrance to the Hawkshead Courthouse, such was the intense interest in this case. Sadly, only about thirty locals were admitted into the public gallery because the courthouse was so small, and a large army of newspaper men, witnesses and others associated with the case had priority. It was a chaotic scene as officials tried to sort out who should be permitted to enter and who must be turned away. Those who were fortunate enough to squeeze in were obliged to stand.

BOATHOUSE SHOOTING DESCRIBED
MRS DILLON ACCUSED OF MANSLAUGHTER
'EVIDENCE CONFIRMS HER STORY'

Mrs Mary Evelyn Dillon, the 29-year-old Preston wife of Major T.A. Dillon, a British Army officer, and second-in-command at Fulwood Barracks, Preston, made her third appearance before the Hawkshead magistrates today on a charge of shooting a man at a bungalow on the Lancashire shore of Lake Windermere early on Christmas morning.

After the hearing on December 30th, Mrs Dillon, who was released on bail, went away with her husband, who stood surety for her, to some unknown destination.

The charge against Mrs Dillon, who is defended by Mr C. Morris, barrister of Bolton, is the manslaughter of John Smith. of Long Meadow, Culcheth, near Warrington, at Full Woods, Brathay.

Eve arrived in a closed car, accompanied by Thomas and her barrister, Cyril Morris, and a legal secretary, about half an hour before the case was due to commence. The small party entered the Hawkshead Courthouse unnoticed through a rear door.

Michael had just returned to St Christopher's Preparatory School but this time as a boarder. His parents felt he would be less troubled by the ongoing legal proceedings if he was a full-time boarder. They would, of course, take him out at weekends whenever possible. Eve's parents had chosen to remain in Preston as George did not wish to take any unnecessary days off. His increasing emphysema meant he was already forced to take days off for sick leave when his breathing became too laboured.

Apart from her wedding, this was the most important day in Eve's twenty-nine-year life. Her wounds were virtually healed, although she still had a slight limp eleven days after her terrifying scramble through that snowy wood to beg for help. She had had more than enough time to consider her future and was now committed to returning to Thomas if she was cleared of the charge of manslaughter. Thomas, meanwhile, had been tipped off that he remained the first choice for a promotion to a senior position in Africa in the new year and hoped to have final confirmation any day now. They had discussed the possibility of getting back together as husband and wife on the drive up from Preston and Thomas appeared to like the idea. It would be a loveless reunion, a marriage of convenience for them both. Escape to Africa would mean the three of them could escape the unpleasantness of remaining in Preston and Thomas would be able to rely on his wife to organise and host any social events he was called upon to provide.

When Eve was led into the courthouse she was struck by how densely packed the room was. Every chair was occupied and the public gallery looked more like the floor of a Promenade Concert at the Royal Albert Hall, though on a far smaller scale. Her entrance was greeted with a buzz of excitement and a few in the public gallery yelled out comments that she didn't catch. Eve was wearing a blue hat and a camel hair overcoat. She was accompanied by a police matron and sat on a chair in front of the dock, immediately behind her counsel. As she arrived at her seat, the clerk of the court ordered all to stand, the side door opened and two elderly male magistrates and a younger female magistrate entered bedecked in their appropriate wigs and gowns. The presiding magistrate, Major H. W. Boddington, invited those that had seats to sit and immediately chastised the few loudmouths in the public gallery who had deigned to call out when Eve entered. Eve was surprised the presiding magistrate was a retired British officer and wondered idly whether Thomas had somehow influenced his selection.

When everyone was settled, and silence prevailed, Major Boddington called upon Mr Parham to open the case for the prosecution on behalf of the Director of Public Prosecutions. Mr Parham rose to his feet, but was a man of unusually short stature, so that many had to crane their necks to find him. Even though Mr Parham was to put the case against her, Eve immediately liked the look of this genial little man. Tubby, with a mop of greying hair, and wearing a slightly scruffy suit, he smiled generously at all around him as if he was at a cocktail party rather than in a court of law. He spoke with a strong, clear Yorkshire accent.

'Thank you, your Honour. You will hear that about 12.45am on Christmas Day three shots were heard down by the lake, and the evidence indicates that Smith met his death by gunshots from a double-barrelled shotgun, at a time that he and the accused woman were the only persons in the boathouse. It is clear from the evidence that the gun must have been fired at a very short range.

On the evening of Christmas Eve, Mr Smith and Mrs Dillon arrived at the boathouse. They were expected to stay over Christmas. There is a Mr Fox, who will be called before you as a witness. He is the caretaker at the lodge at Pull Woods, and he had had a telegram and was prepared for the arrival of these two persons, who duly arrived about 7.30pm on Christmas Eve.'

Mr Parham clearly enjoyed being the centre of attention. He went on to detail how Mr Fox had welcomed the couple and even shared a drink at the boathouse with them before retiring around 9.30pm and returning to the lodge. The prosecutor was a gifted speaker and held his audience's attention well. After recounting the traumatic scene when Mrs Dillon had turned up in a hysterical state outside the lodge yelling for help and the subsequent arrival of the doctor and then the police, Mr Parham began to draw some tentative conclusions.

'It should be made clear that not only are the prosecution unable to disprove the story the woman has told, but the circumstantial evidence available completely confirms it.'

This important statement was met by a flurry of spontaneous conversations breaking out throughout the courtroom. Clearly the prosecution saw no reason to dispute Mrs Dillon's account of what had happened. There was so much noise at hearing this opening statement from the prosecutor, that Major Boddington had to call for 'Order!' in a loud and commanding voice. 'Please continue Mr Parham.'

For the next five minutes the prosecutor ran through the statements that Eve had made after the incident. He followed this up with more or less verbatim quotes from Mr and Mrs Fox, Dr Quarmby and the police who had attended the scene and later taken detailed notes at the time of Eve's arrest. The statements were remarkably consistent.

'Your honour, ordinarily the handling of a firearm, without taking the precautions a reasonable person would take, would constitute manslaughter. But on the evidence of the case that Mrs Dillon was relying on the word of Smith that it would be safe, it would be a matter for the bench to consider whether there is any evidence of reckless, wicked or culpable negligence which must be used to carry the case across the line and make it manslaughter. Unless that were so, it would be their duty to find for the accused.'

Again, there was a rumble of comment and chatter that rolled through the courtroom and the presiding officer was once more obliged to call for 'Order!'

The first evidence called was that of the two county police photographers who testified to the authenticity of the photographs taken at Pull Woods boathouse and later at the post-mortem examination on Smith.

The next witness was John Harrap, a director of the firm John Harrap Ltd., living at Fallowfield, Manchester. He said he had known John Smith for about five years, and since October 1936, he and Smith had been joint tenants of the boathouse at Pull Woods.

A gun in a cardboard box was then produced and the

witness identified it as Smith's property which was usually kept at the boathouse. Harrap reported that he spent the night of December 23rd at the boathouse and left about 10.30am on the 24th. The gun was then leaning up against the wall by the fireplace and he left four packets of unused cartridges and some loose ammunition in a drawer at the sideboard.

Mr Parham asked the witness, 'Were he and she [sic] always very happy and friendly together?'

'Yes.'

'I think you have heard her say she was fond of him and would look after him?'

'Yes.'

'I think she had rather a good effect on him, had she not?'

'She had.'

'Had you ever seen her handle a gun?'

'Never.'

'Thank you, Mr Harrap. You may stand down.'

Mr Harrap's valuable evidence was followed by the lengthy prosecution's examination and questioning of Mr Robert Fox and then Mrs Violet Fox. Mr Parham dwelt at some length on some of Mrs Fox's testimony much to the chagrin of Eve.

'Mrs Fox, would you please take a look at these garments? Hold them up so they may be seen, and then tell the court if you have seen them before?'

Mrs Fox was handed a bag containing a bundle of clothes. Much to Eve's embarrassment she proceeded to hold up one item after another. There was a skirt, a blouse and a cardigan.

'Have you seen these garments before Mrs Fox?'

'Yes, I have.'

'To whom do they belong?'

'They are the clothes Mrs Dillon was wearing on the night of the accident.'

'How do you know that Mrs Fox?'

'Because they are badly torn and I helped remove them from Mrs Dillon and give her something else to wear. Her stockings were so damaged that I burnt them.'

'Thank you, Mrs Fox. Did Mrs Dillon tell you she was not married to Mr Smith?'

'She did.'

'What else did she say about her relationship with Mr Smith?'

'She said, *'but we were so happy, and I loved him so'*.'

Once more the courtroom erupted into noise until called to order.

'Anything about getting married or a divorce?'

'She said, *'when my divorce is absolute, we were to be married'*.'

Again, the noise in the courthouse had to be quelled by the presiding officer.

Dr Quarmby testified next that he had found the deceased with a hole in the chest wall over the heart and about an inch in diameter. He believed it was consistent with a gunshot wound fired at close range.

The final witnesses were several other police who had been involved in the case.

Major Boddington then adjourned the court for lunch and immediately a queue began forming outside the public entrance of people wanting to hear the afternoon's proceedings.

Chapter Eighteen   The Trial

Eve was ushered out by the police matron to join her barrister and have some lunch. She was far too fraught to want to eat but welcomed a hot cup of tea. Cyril Morris was highly optimistic that the magistrates would rule in favour of Eve and did his best to cheer her up.

He was right. No sooner had everyone reassembled and the court called to order than Major Boddington rose to his feet and briefly addressed the gathering.

'Learned Counsel, Ladies and Gentlemen. During the luncheon adjournment we three magistrates have discussed this case at length. We have carefully considered all the evidence before us and we see no reason to prolong this unfortunate case any further. We wish to extend our heartfelt condolences to Mr Smith's mother and his family who are here today. If there is a lesson to be learnt from the tragic events that occurred at the boathouse on Christmas Day, it is the need for the utmost care whenever handling firearms.

We find that this was a case of misadventure and that the charge of manslaughter laid against Mrs Dillon cannot be upheld. Mrs Dillon you are free to leave.'

CHAPTER NINETEEN
Another Chance

Two weeks after Eve's court case had concluded so satisfactorily, several things happened. First and foremost, Thomas and Eve agreed to share their lives together again. Although Thomas had never expressed his feelings about Eve leaving in the first place, he felt the manslaughter charge had actually helped to bring her to her senses. Their marriage might not be a perfect one but he felt there were distinct advantages from cohabiting again. Thomas was prepared to forgive Eve for her many liaisons with Jacko and the affair soon became virtually a taboo topic. Number 3 Cropley Drive was put up for sale and Eve moved back into the married quarters at Fulwood Barracks. They even resumed their mundane sexual relationship.

Young Michael was delighted his parents were back together again but had now discovered he thoroughly enjoyed being a boarder at St Christopher's so his parents agreed he could continue. They promised to take him out at weekends and he remained a lovable scallywag, reasonably intelligent but often up to mischief.

Michael Dillon, aged 11.
(Photo donated by Michael Dillon)

In mid-January, on a rainy morning, Thomas received a telegram summoning him to the War Office in London. It read: '*Report War Office London 1500 hours Wednesday STOP Discuss posting with KAR commencing February STOP RSVP urgently STOP.*' It was signed by Lieutenant-General Ames. Not surprisingly, Thomas telegrammed back in the affirmative within the hour.

Eve was delighted they might soon be moving to Africa.

Chapter Nineteen Another Chance

Since the manslaughter charge, some of her friends had dropped her completely and others were lukewarm. She could count on one hand the genuine, faithful friends that were prepared to overlook her affair and still offer her sincere friendship and support. Whenever she went to town to shop, she sensed people around her whispering and giggling as she went about her business. A few even confronted her with nasty comments which she did her best to ignore. After two weeks she had expected people would get over it and forget her misdemeanours, but there was no sign yet of the sniggering gossip declining. For Eve, therefore, a move to Africa was a wonderful chance to live a more normal life again.

Thomas was thrilled about the prospect of joining the Kings African Rifles (KAR) and spent valuable time with a junior officer who had served with the KAR and had only recently returned to the UK. Thomas reasoned it would be sensible to know something about the KAR and its history before meeting Lieutenant-General Ames in two days' time. Thomas learned the KAR was formed as a regiment on January 1st, 1902. Its origins were interesting. During the nineteenth century, five European powers were scrambling to colonise the 'dark continent' of Africa: Britain, Germany, Italy, Belgium and France. The avowed aim of each country was to end slavery and bring Christianity, civilisation and commerce to the hundred million native people. As the land grab proceeded, each of the five colonising nations established formidable trading companies. In 1888 the Imperial British East Africa Company was granted a Royal Charter and given the responsibility of administering a vast expanse of the African continent along the lines of a Crown Colony.

It was not long before it became apparent that some form of military or police force was needed to assist the British company's endeavours with the administration of its territories, to prevent inter-tribal conflicts, protect trading operations and suppress the Arabs' slave trade. Small bands of tribesmen were recruited, armed and led by agents of the British East Africa Company. Over the years these groups of tribesmen steadily increased in size until they were equivalent to small regiments. At the turn of the century, it was recognised by the British Government that these disparate groups of fighters would become more effective if they were incorporated in some way into the British Army under British trained officers. So, in 1902 the groups were combined into one large regiment to be called the Kings' African Rifles led by seconded British Army officers. This new regiment comprised six battalions and officers were expected to serve a five-year secondment away from their normal British regiments. The KAR served with distinction in the first world war where they defeated the German forces based in German Africa.

Armed with this background, Major Thomas Dillon travelled by train to London to meet with Lieutenant-General Ames. This was the first time Thomas had had business at the War Office and he was pleased he arrived half an hour early because the place was like a massive rabbit warren with seemingly endless corridors and offices. Finally, he arrived at Room B421 which displayed a sign announcing, 'Lieutenant-General Ames,

Chapter Nineteen   Another Chance

OBE, Commander-in-chief KAR'. Thomas knocked and was surprised to hear a young female voice inviting him to enter. The General's secretary was seated behind a desk with her hands poised on a typewriter. She looked up and smiled.

'Major Dillon?'

'Yes, that's me.'

'Please take a seat, Major. I'll let General Ames know you're here.' She tapped an intercom and in a quiet, subdued voice relayed the information of his arrival.

'He'll be ready in a few minutes, Major. May I get you a cup of tea?'

Thomas declined the offer and tried not to stare at this highly attractive blonde who served as the general's secretary. He didn't have to wait long; the door to the office swung open and the general came out to welcome him.

'Major Dillon, great to meet you. Good trip?'

'Yes, thank you sir.'

'Come on in. Jane, no interruptions for half an hour please.'

The general was of medium stature, deeply suntanned with steely blue eyes that seemed to bore into you when he looked at you. Some might find this penetrating stare off-putting, but it didn't worry Thomas. They shook hands, both delivering the other an iron grip. Thomas reckoned the general was in his early fifties, very fit and with not a spare pound of flesh anywhere. His smart uniform sat comfortably so that he cut a handsome figure. There were impressive crows' feet around his eyes, a fastidiously neat moustache and hair that was just starting the thinning greying process.

'Take a seat, Major.'

'Thank you, sir.'

'Major Dillon, your name has been given to me to consider for a possible senior posting to the KAR. How do you feel about this idea?'

'I'd be delighted to serve with the KAR, sir.'

'Why?'

'Variety is the spice of life, sir. I've been stationed at Fulwood Barracks for a few years now and it's time for something more adventurous. Besides, working in Africa sounds an interesting challenge that I'd relish. My wife would welcome a change too and my young son is old enough now to cope with an overseas posting.'

'Forgive me for being personal for a moment Major, but I understand you and your wife have had a spot of trouble?'

'Yes, that's correct sir, but everything is A1 again now.'

'I hope you're right. Living in Africa can be harsh and difficult for wives you know. I have to ask you... will she manage?'

'I believe so, sir. She is very keen to give it a go and she handled everything well when we served in India a few years ago. She knows what it's like being away from England for an extended time.'

'Indeed. Now, what do you know about the KAR?'

Thomas recounted everything he had learnt from his fellow officer at Fulwood Barracks.

'Good. Glad to hear you have done your homework. If I appoint you Major, I shall expect you to serve the full five years. This will not be a push-over job you know. Adolf Hitler

Chapter Nineteen Another Chance

is looking increasingly as though he wants a scrap. Africa could well get involved again as it did in the Great War. The KAR fought the Germans with great distinction from 1915 to 1917 and have a fine record to maintain. The Italians are a troublesome lot too. Mussolini's intent on empire building and has amassed a large force of troops in Eritrea, Italian Somaliland and Abyssinia under the command of the Duke of Aosta. The Italian navy is threatening to take control of the Red Sea and parts of the Mediterranean and The Duke of Aosta can call upon strong support from the Italian air force. If hostilities break out, we can expect one hell of a shindig and you, Major, will be in the thick of it!'

The general was searching Thomas's face to try to gauge whether he was up to the task. Things could get very nasty for the KAR and he wanted to be sure he had the right man for the job. He knew from the military records that Major Dillon had fought in the Great War with courage and had led his men intelligently and with distinction. You don't get mentioned in despatches unless you have performed exceptionally well. But that was twenty years ago. Now that Major Dillon was married and had a son, would he still have what it takes to lead a much larger fighting force? In short, did he have the mongrel still?

'Major, you are forty-six years old and you have a family. Some officers in your situation would not be keen to see active service again and, perhaps understandably, would be seeking a desk job or something else that avoided direct warfare. Putting it bluntly, you have experienced war and been wounded at the Somme. Are you really prepared to front up again?'

'Certainly sir. It would be a great honour to serve my country overseas again, whether or not war eventuates.'

'Very well, Major. There will be a three-day briefing, orientation and exercises for you and a couple of other senior ranks next week starting Tuesday. Ask my secretary, Jane, for the details and travel passes. Following the successful completion of the three-day course you will be promoted to the rank of Lieutenant-Colonel. Welcome aboard! I look forward to working with you next week. Expect to fly to Nairobi sometime next month.'

'Thank you, sir. I look forward to joining the KAR.'

* * *

The three-day orientation course at the London War Office was an eye-opener for Thomas and the two other senior officers who attended. General Ames chaired the sessions but called upon the expertise of several other KAR officers to handle some of the specifics.

Thomas learned he had been appointed commanding officer of the KAR regiment responsible for Kenya's Northern Frontier District (NFD). The NFD extended from Lake Rudolf to the Somali border and consisted of about one hundred thousand square miles of acacia scrub, lava desert and broad areas of sand desert almost twice the size of England. Termites' towers, like crude sculptures, grew tall in their thousands from the baked earth and the only trees were the shadeless thorn trees. In the heart of this flat and inhospitable landmass was the amazing volcanic outcrop called Marsabit. Marsabit consisted of mountains, forests, plantations and maize fields. The elevated altitude of Marsabit offered a somewhat cooler climate and it was here that the headquarters of the NFD was located. The commanding officer's house was next door to the District Commissioner's home and consisted of a spacious bungalow with five bedrooms, staffed by three full-time servants. Thomas was relieved to hear about the bungalow on Marsabit as it should afford some home comforts for Eve and Michael.

Thomas would be commanding British officers and non-commissioned officers (NCOs) and around a thousand African tribesmen known as 'askaris'. The askaris had been recruited mostly from Kenya but some came from farther afield. The language spoken by the tribesman was predominantly Swahili and British soldiers serving with the KAR were expected to learn at least rudimentary Swahili within six months of joining the KAR so they could communicate effectively with their troops. Thomas was no exception: he was expected to pass his Swahili examination in six months' time like all other British personnel.

The askaris had been recruited to serve 'Kingi Georgie' (King George VI) with promises of adventure, good pay, a uniform and good food. Many askaris came from impoverished villages where more often than not only small quantities of milk, blood and beans were available. Army life provided three regular meals a day with plentiful meat, maize, meal, rice, beans, lentils, fruit and green vegetables, tea and sugar, a miraculous transition from a state of want to a state of plenty. High above all the material advantages of army life was the intangible, but immense and lifelong prestige of being selected to serve in the King's African Rifles.

A balanced diet, combined with army discipline and intensive physical training, made the askaris fit and strong and capable of astonishing endurance. They enlisted as the rawest of recruits but quickly and enthusiastically learnt the infantryman's trade. By the time they had completed their basic training they were proficient in the use of the rifle, the bayonet, grenade, Bren gun and mortar. The askaris had already proved their fighting qualities in the World War and in defeating the Italians in 1935 when the Italians had invaded Abyssinia. In short, the askaris made superb soldiers and were proud to be a part of the British Army.

The majority of the three-day orientation program was devoted to discussions on military tactics to be employed in the desert conditions of the KAR, logistics, transport issues and the future intentions of the Italians under Mussolini and Hitler's Nazi Party.

At the conclusion of the three-day program, Thomas was given the date on which he and his family would fly out to Nairobi, Kenya's sprawling capital. They would spend a few days there staying at the Officers' Club in the centre of the city for final briefings. Nairobi was the HQ for all the KAR regiments. Finally, they would depart by road for Thomas's regimental command centre located high on the central plateau of Marsabit.

* * *

Chapter Nineteen Another Chance

On his return to Preston, Thomas relayed much of what he had absorbed whilst in London to a family gathering that included Eve, Michael and Eve's parents, George and Annie. His news was received with a mixture of excitement and anxiety. Young Michael could only see the thrill of adventure in living in Africa and bombarded his father with questions whenever he had the chance, quizzing him about lions, hyaenas, puff adders, spitting cobras, spiders and vipers. Eve, however, was more concerned with domestic matters. She probed her husband for more details about their house in Marsabit, the climate there, and how big the expat population would be. Was their house already furnished? Thomas wished he could answer her questions more adequately, although he did know that the bungalow was fully furnished. Eve's parents were more concerned about the diseases in Africa: they had heard of nasty maladies such as malaria, dengue fever and cholera.

The Dillons had a little over three weeks to pack and prepare for their five years' sojourn in Kenya.

CHAPTER TWENTY

Kenya

The Dillons departed for Kenya on March 20th 1938, a glorious early spring day in Preston. Those with gardens were proudly displaying snowdrops, primroses, daffodils and crocuses and there were signs that the early blossom trees were waiting to burst out into colour. Blackbirds and thrushes sang heartily and a weak sun glimmered above the township. Eve loved the English countryside at this time of year. Looking out of the window it suddenly struck her that she would not be able to enjoy these rustic English scenes for five long years; the scenery in Marsabit she knew would be totally different.

Thinking about this new chapter in her life, Eve was comforted by the knowledge she had survived a few years in India well enough after they had first been married back in 1926. Then she had been a naïve nineteen-year-old; now she was a far more worldly and mature thirty-year old. If she had coped reasonably well twelve years ago, this posting to Kenya should not be too demanding. Thomas had explained to her that the size of the territory he was to be responsible for was massive (twice the size of England) and he would be away visiting his troops much of the time. She could cope with his absences provided there were some other European women in Marsabit for company. She realised she would have to play the role of the wife of the commanding officer and attend to his social agenda and any other duties that the position entailed. This should not be too irksome though and she rather enjoyed planning and socialising. Three fulltime servants to help was a godsend!

Despite the dreadful stresses and strains of the last three months, Eve still presented as a beautiful woman. Wherever she went men's eyes followed her, or she elicited wolf whistles from the tradesmen who were far less inhibited. Privately, she had to admit she rather enjoyed being ogled and whistled at; it made her feel good about herself. Having borne only one child had helped her to retain the wine-glass figure she knew was so appealing to men. Sadly, Thomas rarely appeared to fully appreciate her beauty for he seemed reluctant to compliment her on her looks even though she did her best to look attractive. They had resumed infrequent intercourse but poor Thomas really had no idea how to satisfy her. He might be a fine soldier but he had no idea what to do in the bedroom. If only Jacko was still about...

Eve still had nightmares about that awful time at the boathouse when they had so foolishly played around with the rifle. In many ways she and Jacko had been well suited, but marriage might never have worked because Jacko was such a restless soul and he would probably have become bored with her after a time. She missed him awfully, but getting away to Kenya and starting afresh would, she hoped, help to lessen the pain.

Michael was full of enthusiasm for the big adventure ahead and jabbered away excitedly about how he planned to go out hunting wild animals on safari. He was going to milk snakes and learn Swahili so he could play with the Kenyan boys. His father tried to explain that they would be living most of the time in semi-desert conditions and that they may see little of the wildlife he desperately craved. In fact, Michael would be enrolled at a boarding school, Kenton College, far away in the capital, Nairobi, a school that catered for the sons of British officers, wealthy white landowners, colonial officers and other British families working in Kenya.

1938 was an ominous year with tensions steadily increasing across Europe as Hitler continued to flex his muscles. The main items of news always seemed to revolve around disturbing events that heightened everyone's concerns. In January, the famous psychoanalyst, Sigmund Freud, fled Vienna and arrived safely in London. He was to be followed by many others. On February 14th the impressive brand new British naval base in Singapore commenced operations. On March 12th, shortly before the Dillons left for Kenya, Hitler declared 'Anschluss' the total annexation of Austria to form a 'Greater Germany'. The Fuhrer argued this unification would create a nation state of like-minded citizens who shared a common language and ethnicity.

On June 1st, the British army announced the Bren light machine gun was now fully in service wherever its personnel were based. Then, as a sure sign of the expected troubles ahead, every British civilian was issued with a gas mask during July, although many found it was more useful as a picnic box. The Munich Agreement was signed in September by Neville Chamberlain, the British Prime Minister and Adolf Hitler. It was an agreement that was supposed to guarantee that any disputes between the two parties would be resolved peacefully. In December, HMS Ark Royal, a magnificent aircraft carrier, was commissioned into the Royal Navy. Perhaps the only good news for the English people in 1938 was Len Hutton's world record score of 364 not out in a test match against the old foe, Australia.

* * *

When moving to a new country to live, it is wise not to have lofty expectations. It is better to be pleasantly surprised overall when you arrive at your destination than to discover the place is a hell hole compared with what you had envisaged. Being comprehensively and honestly prepared beforehand for any major move is best practice, but only Colonel Dillon had received such an induction. The army had fully, and accurately, appraised Thomas of the kind of environment he would be entering into, but neither Eve nor Michael had been included in any such briefings. Thomas was, on the whole, a poor communicator and had done little to realistically prepare Eve or Michael for what their new lives in Kenya might be like.

Everything started off well enough. They flew via Cairo to Nairobi where they were met by a staff car and driven to a well-appointed, quality hotel run by a British hotelier. Four nights were spent there whilst Thomas received his final briefings. There was a generous and well-maintained swimming pool and Michael was quick to join the other expat children there to escape the heat. Eve found a few mothers with little to do except lounge around the pool drinking gins and martinis and enjoyed a few lazy days living the life of the wealthy elite being waited on by African staff and ogled by the men. Eve and Michael ventured into Nairobi one morning to visit the preparatory school, Kenton College, where Michael was enrolled and would continue his schooling in two weeks' time, but were really shocked by the noise, the pollution and the squalor they encountered about them on the streets of Nairobi. The school itself was like an oasis surrounded by trees and a six-foot-high fence. Eve was greatly relieved that Michael immediately took a shine to his new boarding school.

At the crack of dawn on only their fifth day in Kenya, the Dillons were picked up by a convoy of two army trucks and a staff vehicle to commence the long journey to Marsabit along dirt roads that were in a deplorable state. An escort of two trucks was considered essential in case of breakdowns, but more importantly as protection against the Shifta. Marauding Somali Shifta bands roamed the desert around Marsabit armed with captured and discarded Italian type 91 model rifles, pillar box-red grenades and submachine guns with their heads festooned with bandoliers. These were ruthless outlaws who killed for the sake of killing, holding human life cheap if it stood in the way of rape and pillage. A lone vehicle would stand no chance against them. Each truck carried a driver, six askaris (African soldiers) and a British officer. These were well trained men, practised in the procedures necessary to defend a small convoy against attack. The convoy moved off slowly with the staff car sandwiched between the two trucks.

It was Shifta custom to hand their prisoners over to their women to deal with. By all accounts, capture meant certain death. The women were known to tie their victims to a tree, then rip open their stomachs with a razor-sharp dagger so that the intestines fell in a heap at their feet. Progressive unspeakable mutilation then followed until death came at last, hours later. Understandably, none of these gory, horrific details were passed on to Eve or Michael.

As the convoy trundled relentlessly north, the country gradually became drier and drier until they were into semi-desert. Few people lived in this arid environment apart from nomadic herders, occasional camel traders and the people who lived in the small market townships of Isiolo and Archers Post. The convoy pulled up in both towns for a toilet stop, to consume their army rations, give the drivers a break from the arduous task of trying to keep the trucks on the road and to undertake routine maintenance checks. Fortunately, no Shifta were encountered along the way and they completed the 550 gruelling kilometres in just under twelve hours for what was considered by the officer-in-charge to have been an 'excellent' journey. It was dark when they finally arrived and were made welcome by Major Williamson, the second in command. They enjoyed an evening meal prepared by the native chef before collapsing, exhausted, into bed.

* * *

When Eve woke next morning, she was more than anxious to discover what sort of a place she had landed up in. Last night, after dark, she had been so tired she was aware only that they had spent at least half an hour climbing steeply up out of the desert and into a cooler mountainous region. Michael was equally keen to start the next part of his African adventure. Major Williamson called at their home at eight o'clock and whisked his new commanding officer off to the nearby HQ. Before he left, the major asked Eve and Michael to be ready by nine o'clock so they could spend the morning with Sergeant Stephenson who would show them around Marsabit and the surrounding countryside.

Sergeant Stephenson arrived on time in an open jeep and turned out to be a jovial young man from near Bath, in Somerset, or *'Zomerset'* as he pronounced it. He insisted on being addressed as 'Johnno' and proved to be good company and a mine of information. He had already spent a year with the King's African Rifles and was in charge of the army vehicles based at Marsabit. There were not many vehicles, he told them, but it was an uphill job trying to keep them all roadworthy considering the shocking state of what passed for roads and the difficulties in procuring any spare parts. He said that he was forced to improvise much of the time.

Eve was surprised at how insignificant the fledgling township of Marsabit was; back in England it would barely merit even hamlet status. Its continued existence appeared to revolve around the small British army base which consisted of a huddle of poorly constructed huts set around a small parade ground where the Union Jack fluttered in the cool breeze. Johnny explained that all up there were three or four offices, a communications room, several storage sheds and a dormitory-like building that could accommodate up to twenty men if necessary. There was a kitchen and a small dining room that served meals suited to the tastes of the askaris. Within the compound were four bungalows, the largest of which, with five bedrooms, was for the commanding officer, the next, with four bedrooms, was occupied by the second in command, Major Williamson, and the third and fourth bungalows with three bedrooms each were for any other white personnel needing a bed at the base. Johnno, a bachelor, lived permanently in one of the two small houses. Major Williamson, Johnno informed them, was a married man with three young children under the age of eight. His wife, Janet, home schooled the children and was apparently rather disappointed to learn that the Dillons did not have young children of a similar age.

Leaving the army compound, it took but a few minutes to run around the rest of Marsabit. The only substantial house in town was that occupied by the district commissioner and his family. His two teenagers attended private schools in Nairobi. According to Johnno, the district commissioner's wife was an alcoholic, and no use to anyone. There was a small ramshackle Catholic church with a presbytery next door occupied by an elderly priest who was thought to be in his eighties. Mass was held there every Sunday for the handful of native adherents. Scattered about were a number of wood or tin shacks in front of which a few children played in the dirt; Marsabit was yet to boast a school. In the centre of town was a dusty clearing where half a dozen tethered goats nibbled whatever they could find. On one corner was a roadside stall that sold a few basic items to the locals, the first signs of commerce in town. Camel traders also appeared from time to time in town to sell their wares.

Eve had to admit that she was bitterly disappointed at what constituted Marsabit. She was one of only three white women in town, one of whom was reputably an alcoholic, and the other, Janet, would probably have her hands full most of the time looking after her three youngsters. When Thomas was away on his rounds and Michael at Kenton College, she feared she would become desperately bored and lonely alone in their large house. She was still haunted by the tragic Christmas of

1937 and Jacko's awful death. Nightmares were not uncommon, and she often battled deep feelings of guilt about their affair and how she had betrayed her husband. There was nobody she could share her darkest thoughts with.

Johnno was prattling on still about Marsabit, delighted no doubt, to have the pleasant company of a beautiful woman and her son. He relished the opportunity to be their guide and mentor and seemed well informed. According to the local Borona Oroma people, who spoke a Cushitic language, Marsabit derived its name from a farmer called Marsa who was persuaded by the British back in the 1920s to commence farming maize and millet up on this plateau. He had been successful and others soon followed. Marsabit simply meant 'home of Marsa'. Johnno scoffed at an alternative theory that a British explorer called Donaldson Smith when passing by back in the 1890s thought the area looked like 'Mars a bit'.

Johnno, it emerged, was an enthusiastic naturalist and loved the plateau on which Marsabit was struggling to be recognised as an emerging township. He explained to Michael, who was lapping it all up, that the plateau was an extinct shield volcano and that it was covered in basalt from lava flows from millions of years ago. Its altitude of around 4,500 feet created a year-round cool climate, and this, together with the rich basaltic soils made it ideal for farming. Johnno had explored much of the plateau, mostly on foot, with a couple of native guides, and said it was covered in cinder cones, forested craters and crater lakes (maars). He was worried that in time this beautiful country would be deforested to make way for more farms.

Johnno told a wide-eyed Michael that on his explorations of the plateau he had encountered many wild animals and went on to list elephant, zebra, buffalo, blue monkeys, leopards, baboons, gazelle and striped hyenas. The birdlife, Johnno claimed, was also abundant, with vultures, falcons, buzzards, kites and African Fish Eagles all common. Johnno was not such an expert on the flora but still described miles of yellow acacias and huge strangler figs.

This extraordinary insular ecosystem rising up in the very heart of the Chalbi Desert had first been documented by two American filmmakers, Martin and Osa Johnson in the 1920s who described the plateau as having the 'best preserved wildlife in Africa'. Johnno said he was determined to do his bit to try to persuade the authorities to declare the whole plateau a national park. Michael was so excited by all that Johnno was recounting that he urged him to take them out of town straightaway to see some of the wild animals. Johnno, however, had the two trucks and a staff car that the Dillons had travelled in yesterday from Nairobi to attend to. After journeying over such rough country, he insisted, they were bound to be in need of comprehensive servicing. So, by ten o'clock, Michael and Eve were back at their new home ready to start unpacking.

First though, Eve wanted to become better acquainted with the three servants who they had inherited from the previous commanding officer and who all came highly recommended. In charge was Tomasi, known as the 'butler', a fine-looking man in his fifties with short greying curly hair and the biggest smile imaginable displaying a perfect set of gleaming white teeth. Tomasi had been trained as a butler by a senior British administrator living in Nairobi some twenty years ago and had, over the years, perfected his skills. During his long service his reputation as an honest, loyal, thoughtful and hard-working man had grown and grown and Eve felt more than privileged to have him. Tomasi's English was excellent too, and he gave every impression of liking the ways of the English gentry with whom he had spent so much time.

The cook/cleaner was Tomasi's wife, rather large in the beam, but a delightfully happy character. Nothing was ever too much trouble for Mary and she was a natural in the kitchen. She was never happier than when concocting interesting dishes in her warm part of the house. For a time, Mary had struggled reading and understanding English recipes and, of course, she seldom had all the ingredients she required. However, being a great improvisor, and not adverse to throwing in a bit of her own African culinary skills, she never failed to produce tasty well-presented meals.

The third member of staff was the gardener/handy man, who, intriguingly, was called Innocent. Much younger than Tomasi and Mary, he had only been in the employ of the previous commanding officer for three years and was still learning his trade. With the excellent climate for growing vegetables and the help of the previous colonel's wife, he had established an extensive vegetable garden at the back of the house with a wide and commendable selection of crops. Eve was thrilled to see this garden paradise for she herself had been involved in gardening before coming to Preston and later on with Mrs Moriarty's large property. The young lad was keen to learn more and Eve immediately took a shine to him.

Disappointed as Eve was with most of what Marsabit could offer, she was thrilled with the quality of her staff.

CHAPTER TWENTY-ONE

Life in Marsabit

Eve spent her first two days, with the help of Tomasi and, to a lesser extent, Michael, unpacking and getting the house sorted the way she wanted it. Mary and Eve discussed at length the following week's menu, something that Mary stressed was necessary because purchasing meat from local nomadic farmers was a precarious matter. Innocent had chickens freely running around in the back garden so eggs and chicken meat were always available, but procuring buffalo or goat meat depended on whether a nomadic farmer was in town and had an animal ready for slaughter. Non-perishable food and other basic supplies came up from Nairobi aboard the fortnightly supply convoy.

Eve was concerned about how to keep Michael usefully occupied over the next eight days until he would be escorted back down to Nairobi to attend his new boarding school. Fortunately, Michael enjoyed reading and they had thought to bring a substantial collection of books for him. However, Michael happily took himself off to join Johnno in the garage where he and a couple of the askaris were working on servicing the vehicles that had brought them to Marsabit. The three men seemed quite pleased to have Michael hanging about and he began to develop an interest in the vehicles and their maintenance. Johnno also promised that, if his parents agreed, he would take Michael with him to see some of the wildlife over the weekend. Michael could hardly wait and seemed happy enough.

On the third afternoon, Tomasi came into the lounge where Eve was composing a list of items she needed when the convoy next travelled down to Nairobi.

'Excuse me madam, Mrs Williamson and her three children are here to see you. Would you like them to come in?'

'Oh yes, of course, Tomasi. Please show them in.'

Tomasi opened the main door and with a smile and a little bow, invited the Williamsons to please enter.

'Do come in, you are most welcome. My name is Eve.' Eve extended her hand but then realised that Janet, with a baby in her arms would find a handshake difficult.

'How do you do Eve, lovely to meet you. I'm Janet and here is my little tribe. I do hope you don't mind me intruding on you like this when you're probably still busy unpacking?'

'Not at all Janet, it's lovely to meet you. I was wanting to come and visit you but I didn't know when would be a convenient time what with three little ones to look after.'

'Yes, it's busy, but I do have a nanny who comes and helps every day and she's even teaching the children to speak the local Cushitic language. She has very little English herself so the children are teaching her our language. It's working well.'

'That's splendid. Now would you like a cuppa? Would the children like a drink of lemonade?'

'The children have just had an afternoon snack, but I'd love a cuppa please. This is my eldest, Charles, who is seven, this is Maud, who has just turned five and baby James is almost one. He was born out here, which we didn't plan. Quite a palaver, I can assure you!'

'I can't imagine how you coped. Did you go to Nairobi to have James?'

Tomasi politely asked Eve if she would also like some tea and then disappeared silently into the kitchen to organise the refreshments. Charles was keen to go and see the chickens and see if he could find some eggs and Innocent promised to look after him. Snakes and poisonous centipedes lived on the plateau, although they were rarely seen around buildings. Maud was soon busy drawing and baby James, having just been breastfed, was content to stay asleep. Eve and Janet had time for a good chat.

The Williamsons were almost half way through their

five-year posting and already starting to look forward to the time when they could return to the UK. Janet was brutally honest about life in Marsabit: it was not much fun for the wives! Although Janet got along well enough with the locals, she yearned for the company of other white women. The only social life she enjoyed was when visitors (always army officers) came to stay, or they shared a meal with the family of the commanding officer. Once or twice a year, when her husband got his annual leave, they escaped to Nairobi, Johannesburg or Cape Town for a more sophisticated lifestyle where they could luxuriate in a classy hotel. These holiday breaks were the special treats that kept her going, Janet said.

'What about the district commissioner and his family, do you see much of them?'

'No Eve, that's a sad story. The DC is a nice enough fellow but he's seldom here. Can't say I blame him as his wife's a no-hoper. She's only happy when half-sozzled and that's quite often. The locals all know her because she leaves her house and goes wandering off all over the place. Mark, the DC, now pays a couple of local men to be guards when he's away. She could easily get into the bush and be attacked by wild animals if they didn't keep an eye on her.'

'That's so sad. Does she ever come over to your place?'

'We invited them both over for dinner shortly after we arrived here more than two years ago now. It was an awful evening. She arrived drunk and spent the whole time being abusive to us and the staff. I don't think she ate anything at all. I felt so sorry for Mark. After a couple of hours, he had to ask my husband to give him a hand to walk her back home. John, that's my husband, said it was worse than capturing a prisoner of war.'

They both laughed.

'So, there's no real social life here then?'

''Fraid not. You're younger Eve, so it's going to be tough for you. I guess the extreme loneliness is what sent Fiona, the DC's wife, round the bend. You have to find a hobby or something to keep you busy. Thomas will be off visiting his outposts, or going to Nairobi most of the time. What interests do you have, Eve?'

'Well, I'm a bit of a social animal, Janet. I love parties and dances, having dinners and going for outings but those things are simply not going to happen here, are they?'

Janet shook her head and shifted James into a more comfortable position.

'I enjoy reading and gardening. We have an excellent garden behind our house so I plan to work with our young gardener to develop it more. Perhaps I can come over to your place occasionally Janet, to help with the children?'

'That sounds an excellent idea, Eve. I would welcome that. I have quite a few books too so we can have a book exchange. As you can imagine, there are virtually no books in Marsabit!'

'What about the DC and the ancient Catholic priest? Do they have books to share about?'

Janet smiled, 'To be perfectly honest, I stay away from the DC's place for fear of encountering his dreadful wife. As for the elderly priest, most of his books are probably religious texts. Perhaps I should have tried him though?' Janet added.

'I'll make a point of going to see the priest, although we are Catholics and no doubt he will expect us to join his flock. Thomas is a strict Catholic and will want mass every Sunday.'

'Well, the priest's name is Father Peter. He's been in Africa for decades and will die here I expect. He seems pleasant enough. We are Anglicans. Lord knows where *our* nearest church is; Nairobi most likely.'

Eve was enormously relieved there was a woman in Marsabit she could relate to and with whom she could develop a friendship. Janet was a motherly soul, now in her early forties perhaps, with a pleasant round face and quite buxom figure. She had made an effort to look nice before coming to visit and had applied bright red lipstick and a little eyeshadow.

Janet felt the same sense of comfort in having somebody else around to share things with. Looking after John, when he was home, and caring for and educating their three young children kept her more than usefully occupied.

* * *

Next day, Thomas and John knocked off early. The vehicles were fully serviced and roadworthy again, according to Johnno, in readiness for a trip starting early the following morning. They were headed 170 miles to Moyale on the Kenyan-Ethiopian border. In addition, there were three minor outposts en route, each expecting a visit from their newly appointed commanding officer. John estimated the round trip would take five or six days if all went well, however, if they were attacked or had breakdowns it would be longer. The wives and children were warned that the men would be away for an uncertain time and urged not to get stressed. By the time they returned, young Michael would have been escorted on the long journey back to Nairobi to start at Kenton College, his new school. Johnno, who was in charge of this particular operation, would take two army lorries with eight armed askaris on board each vehicle.

That evening, with a couple of hours to spare, Thomas invited Eve and Michael to stroll with him down the road to visit Father Peter. Thomas was keen to meet the elderly priest and find out what the arrangements were for mass on Sundays even though he would still be away on manoeuvres for his first Sunday in Marsabit.

Even in this remote part of the world, Lieutenant-Colonel Thomas Dillon insisted he be dressed smartly in uniform and he cut an impressive figure as he left the bungalow. The few locals sitting about watched the trio with a keen interest. It was difficult to gauge what they thought of the small British base that had quite suddenly sprung up almost twenty years ago and had ever since provided the nucleus for this fledgling settlement. The locals smiled or waved shyly as the Dillons wandered by.

The small church was in better condition than they expected. Constructed from local timbers with open glassless windows, Eve observed that if there was rain it would be important to sit in the centre of the wee church. The tiny building boasted only seven rough-hewn pews since few of the locals had been persuaded so far to give up their beliefs in animism and other primitive deities. A wooden cross stood in the centre of the largest opening at the end of the church behind a white-sheeted table that served as the altar. It was all beautifully simple.

They walked on past the church and knocked on the door of the presbytery. It was opened by an elderly native woman with a warm welcoming smile.

'How you do?' she inquired, revealing a mouth barely half full of teeth.

'How do you do?' replied Thomas leaning over to speak to the shortish woman, 'May we see Father Peter please?'

'Father Peter?'

'Yes, Father Peter.'

'Father Peter sleep,' and the good lady gave a commendable imitation of a person sleeping.

'Oh. I'm sorry, we will try again another time,' Thomas responded.

The lady seemed unable to understand this last sentence and stared back blankly. They turned to leave when a male voice called out from farther back in the presbytery. Now it was the Dillons turn to be nonplussed for the speaker appeared to be speaking Cushite, the local language. Whatever was said, it worked, and the elderly lady flashed them a generous smile and ushered then in.

She led them to a dark room where they found Father Peter standing but leaning heavily on a walking stick. He greeted them warmly and apologised for his meagre surroundings. After introductions all around he offered them his three upright chairs and in Cushite spoke briefly to his elderly housekeeper.

Appreciating there were not enough chairs to go round, Michael saw his opportunity to escape what was sure to become yet another lengthy, boring grown-up conversation. Politely, he asked to be excused, and permission granted, hurried back to the bungalow.

'Thank you for calling,' began Father Peter, 'I fully intended to come and visit you, however, my leg is particularly painful at the moment and I'm not sure I would have managed it.'

'We quite understand Father and are sorry to hear your leg is giving you trouble.'

The three adults sat down and Eve took the opportunity to look around the small room. It was clearly a building erected in a hurry and she didn't like its chances in a bad storm. There was one decent-sized window but it was covered by what appeared to be an old blanket making the space dark and gloomy. Against one wall was a wooden desk with a table next to it. Across both pieces of furniture, papers, books and manuscripts were strewn about as if abandoned. A large painting of the Last Supper hung on one wall and a photograph of the current pope on another, but there was little else in what was a spartan room.

'Please excuse the mess, I'm putting together next Sunday's homily and it has to be in Cushite as none of my parishioners speak English,' Father Peter apologised.

'Well, Father, we are going to be part of your flock for the next five years,' Thomas replied.

'And that, my dear Thomas, presents me with a conundrum. I have six regular native adherents with a few others who come along occasionally out of curiosity, or because they have sinned, so mass is no longer in Latin but is delivered in the local language. When you attend mass, you will perhaps expect me to speak in Latin?'

Hearing this was enough to convince Eve that she would not attend mass in Father Peter's church. Several years ago, she had gradually slipped into becoming a 'lapsed Catholic' despite Thomas's angry protestations. These days Eve considered herself an agnostic. Poor Michael was left in a quandary for his parents were not in agreement over religion. He loved them both and wanted to please them both, but didn't know which way to go. Usually, he went with his father to mass and Eve just accepted this, but he always felt uncomfortable about the situation. He was only ten, too young to try to grapple with different belief systems.

Thomas cleared his throat and replied, 'I will be away often Father, most Sundays in fact, so it would be unfair for me to expect you to conduct any services in Latin just for me. I know the mass well enough anyway.'

'That is most considerate of you,' replied Father Peter, 'and what about you Mrs Dillon?'

Eve coloured with embarrassment although the darkness of the room offered her some protection. She felt an answer was called for and sheepishly muttered, 'I may not be coming to mass, Father.'

Father Peter looked disappointed, 'And what about young Michael?'

'He'll be coming with me when I'm home,' Thomas declared, before Eve could think of an alternative response.

'Well, at least we all know where we stand then,' commented the elderly priest.

'Changing the subject Father, we have brought a pile of books with us, which we would be more than happy to lend to you if you wish.'

'That's very kind of you, my dear,' replied the priest, noticeably lightning his mood. 'I have a large number of Agatha Christie's books if you are interested? Rather dog eared, I must confess, but still quite readable.'

'That sounds excellent,' smiled Eve. 'I'll drop a couple of books into you tomorrow.'

They left the old priest shortly afterwards and returned home. Thomas was anxious to get his gear packed for his first tour of duty starting early next morning.

CHAPTER TWENTY-TWO

Ennui

Lieutenant Colonel Thomas Dillon and his second-in-command, Major John Williamson, together with two of their escort vehicles, departed for Moyale at 0800 hours. Their families were there to see them off. Previous experiences away on army manoeuvres had convinced the two senior officers that it was unwise to commit to a firm date on which they would return. 'Around three weeks, maybe more, maybe less...' was as specific as they were prepared to be.

Normally, the two most senior officers would never travel together in the same vehicle. This was a safety precaution.

Should the vehicle be attacked by Shifta, or some other bloodthirsty tribesmen, or be involved in a serious crash, it was preferable to lose only one of the two most senior men in such an incident. However, the two men still had much to discuss and plan so they decided this time to break from convention and ride together. Uppermost in their minds was the need to put their troops on a war footing. Whilst Hitler was posturing in Europe, his colleague, Mussolini, was building up his Italian forces in the Horn of Africa. Clashes along the Ethiopian-Kenyan border, where Moyale was located, looked increasingly likely in the months ahead.

Eve was unmoved by her husband's departure. They had been reunited for some four months already but any love they had once felt for each other had not been rekindled. It was a largely empty, hollow relationship. They rarely argued, but did little more than tolerate each other at the dining room table. Always polite, they kept up the pretence of being a devoted couple. Last night Thomas had requested his conjugal rights and Eve had grudgingly obliged. They didn't make love, they had sex. Eve still longed for the magic touch and the chemistry she and Jacko had found so pleasurable and satisfying. Her husband had rescued her in her hour of need, and she would be forever grateful for his generosity of spirit, but he was no help to her when she felt depressed about the events at the boathouse or wanted to talk about that terrible night.

Michael felt the departure of his father more deeply, however. Although only ten, he was starting to take an interest in all things military. Working with Johnno during the last few days on the army vehicles and being around a few of the athletic askaris had influenced his thinking. His departure for boarding school in a couple of days meant he would not see his father again until the end of term, three months hence. Michael was becoming interested in the wide range of badges, medals, ranks and other uniform attachments worn by those serving in the army. He was proud of his father: lieutenant-colonel and commanding officer of the 1st Battalion was a grand sounding title. Nobody else around was entitled to wear a crown and a pip on both their shoulders.

Eve put her arm around her son as they wandered back indoors. Together, they now had the task of packing his school clothes, purchased in Nairobi a week or two back, into his trunk and filling up his 'Tuck' box with tasty non-perishable snacks that hopefully would last him for weeks. Mary had been busy for days sewing name tags onto every item of Michael's school clothing. There could be other Dillons at the school so the name tags had to read 'A.M.P. Dillon' for Anthony Michael Peter Dillon. Kenton College was for British children only and was run strictly along the lines of the best known preparatory and public schools in the United Kingdom.

Corporal Spratt, Johnno's assistant, arrived on time on Sunday morning driving one of the two lorries that would be travelling down to Nairobi to see Michael safely delivered to his preparatory school. Eight well-armed askaris sat quietly in the back of each vehicle ready for action should it be required. The askaris were always more than happy to escort a vehicle to Nairobi because they then had a couple of days leave in town before making the hazardous return journey. Eve would have liked to have gone with them too, so she could do some shopping in Kenya's capital city, but Thomas had refused permission. With the Shifta still active he would only condone what he termed 'essential' travel and shopping was not included in this category.

Michael put on a brave face. Travelling 550 miles alone over an atrocious road, and constantly in danger of being attacked by the Shifta, was a big ask for a ten-year-old without his parents for company. On arrival he then had the challenge of adjusting to life in a totally foreign school environment. Michael didn't know any of the teachers or his peers and somehow would have to fit in. The term lasted for almost fourteen weeks so he would not be coming 'home' to Marsabit until the end of July. His parents had assured him they would do their best to come to Nairobi for half term, but this would depend on the military situation at the time which was entirely unpredictable.

Eve and the servants missed Michael and the house fell eerily quiet. As so often happens when a close member of the family leaves, it is only then that those that remain really appreciate their normal presence. Naturally, Eve missed her son dreadfully, but the three servants did too. Fortunately, Eve had already formed an excellent working relationship with her three servants and treated them well. So, domestically, it was a happy household.

It was not long, however, before loneliness and boredom began to get to Eve. A vivacious young woman stranded high up on a volcanic plateau in the heart of Kenya with virtually nobody to mix with and few interests to pursue did not auger well. Despite the respectful attentions of her three servants, Eve was becoming depressed. She felt cheated that she could not enjoy the pleasures of life that other young women of similar age and status experienced back home in England. Here there was no dancing, no theatre, no cinema, no shops, no parks, no restaurants. There was nothing! She was trapped for five long years in a God-forsaken social wilderness! When Eve felt depressed her thoughts returned to Jacko and the guilt she still experienced: deserting her husband, mishandling that shotgun and the ghastly Christmas at the boathouse.

At first, she made some attempts to occupy herself usefully. She took a special interest in Innocent and his garden, even giving him some suggestions on improvements and ways of extending the area under cultivation. At least once a week she visited Janet and her three little ones and sometimes babysat the children so Janet could have a sleep for an hour or two or have valuable time to herself. Eve spent many hours reading, or writing letters to her family and friends back home, but it took three or four weeks for letters to arrive in England and about the same time for a letter to come back. There was no reliable radio reception in Marsabit which further added to Eve's sense of isolation.

Thomas returned from his first tour of duty after three weeks, stayed a week and then was off again to visit another string of outposts to the east across the Chalbi Desert. These inspections continued for a couple more months until every military site had been visited. On the occasional Sunday he was home, Thomas attended mass with Father Peter, but Eve politely declined to accompany him. They did manage to take a few days off to visit Michael during half term and Eve's mood lifted once they arrived in Nairobi. Michael appeared happy at school which was a great relief.

Once the initial inspections had all been completed, Thomas remained for a time in Marsabit. It was then that he told Eve they must prepare to entertain visitors from time to time. And so, after Michael had returned to school after his two-week holiday in July, a succession of British army officers began to appear at their bungalow to stay for a night or two. This was one means whereby Thomas could stay in touch with his senior staff in the field and at the same time offer them a brief break from their duties. Most of the visiting officers were company commanders with the rank of captain, and without exception, they welcomed this short interlude away from the frontline.

Mary excelled in the kitchen and Tomasi relished the opportunity to play the part of the English butler. Innocent did his best to maintain a nutritious supply of vegetables from his garden and Eve especially welcomed the visitors for she enjoyed hearing their fascinating stories from the front. Most of the young men that came to their house were single and no doubt envied their commanding officer for his stunningly attractive wife and domestic comforts. A couple of the officers even risked their careers by making a pass at Eve, but she ignored them. By the end of 1938, almost all the company commanders had made an appearance at the Dillon's home in Marsabit and only a handful remained to still make their visits. These last few officers were scheduled to arrive one by one after Christmas during the months of January and early February 1939.

Eve found the arrival of another young officer every two or three weeks was enough to keep her depression under control: it was something to look forward to. Sometimes Major Williamson, or his wife, Janet, were invited for the evening meal and they all ended up having quite a jolly time. Thomas always insisted that a couple of good bottles of wine were on offer, together with a decent whisky and gin and tonic for those that craved it. Neither Eve nor Thomas ever drank to excess although occasionally one of the visiting captains went overboard and had to be assisted back to the spare bedroom. Officers were expected to be able to hold their drink and know their limits, and drunkenness in the home of the Colonel inevitably resulted in a black mark being recorded in that officer's file.

Christmas in Marsabit in 1938 was a bizarre occasion. The concept of Christmas meant nothing to most of the local population, unless they were among the very few who had accepted Christianity and become part of Father Peter's small flock. The tiny community of British nationals did its best to celebrate in the traditional ways and observe the customs of the festive season. Father Paul was persuaded to open up his small church for a carol service on Christmas Eve and it was well supported by the DC and his two boys, the Dillons and Williamsons. Johnno came along too, with Corporal Spratt, and surprised everyone with a very passable baritone voice. Even Tomasi, the butler, attended, intrigued to discover more about the strange customs of his white masters. The DC's wife was a notable absentee. All in all, it was probably the largest congregation Father Peter had ever experienced in his small Marsabit kirk.

A few days before Christmas, the locals were puzzled when Johnno and Michael dug a large hole in the middle of the clearing in the centre of their small community and placed a tree in it. They watched on in amazement as the two whites then proceeded to cover the tree with small shiny objects and long paper chains in different colours. Next, a star-shaped object was fixed to the top of the tree. Even more surprising was the arrival of several buckets of water that were emptied into the hole around the tree. A few of the old-timers were highly suspicious of this peculiar object that had been erected in the middle of the community and were somewhat relieved when a couple of weeks later it was just as abruptly yanked out of the ground and unceremoniously dumped in the bush. Some of the shiny adornments were cautiously collected by the more daring of the locals and ended up decorating the walls of their humble homes where they became talking points for weeks afterwards.

With the assistance of Innocent, Eve and Michael set up a much smaller tree in a bucket in their dining room. Under the tree they placed a pile of Christmas presents. A few presents had arrived from England but the majority were for the family and their three servants. In addition, there were some presents for the Williamsons who would share Christmas dinner with them. Mary had learnt from the previous Colonel's wife how to prepare a Christmas dinner and was excited to be able to once again show off her skills. Three of their largest chickens were slaughtered, dressed and prepared for the feast along with an assortment of roast vegetables. Mary considered herself an expert on gravy and even knew how to prepare breadcrumbs and stuffing. Eve did, however, help her with the Christmas pudding which had to be appropriately pre-loaded with a few threepenny bits and sixpences. They even had brandy sauce. They did their best to celebrate Christmas in style!

The preparations for Christmas brought Eve out of her depressive state for a short time, but she knew she was in for a really hard time next year. Thomas had told her that he would be travelling most of the year as the tensions were increasing with the Italians who were marshalling more and more troops along the border. Estimates were that the Italian colonial army now numbered around 250,000 troops. The KAR was hugely outnumbered. According to Thomas's latest statistics he had 94 British officers, 60 senior British NCOs and slightly fewer than 3,000 askaris. Askari reinforcements were expected towards the end of February, shortly after the last of the company commanders had made their visits to Marsabit to see their commanding officer.

Michael happily returned to his boarding school a few days after Christmas leaving Eve to once again face a life predominately of boredom whilst struggling to contain her depression.

CHAPTER TWENTY-THREE
1939: War Declared

Any hope that war with Nazi Germany could be averted steadily faded during the first part of 1939. A succession of events in the United Kingdom in the early months of the year confirmed this. Improved communications meant Eve and her few colleagues in Marsabit could now stay abreast of events thanks to the recently instigated BBC Foreign Service. Eve was intrigued to hear what was happening back home.

During February 1939, Anderson Shelters were issued free of charge to families earning less than five pounds a week. The Anderson Shelter was an air-raid precaution and could be installed underground in the garden or in a cellar if it was well sandbagged. Eve's parents qualified for an Anderson Shelter which they installed in their back garden. It was large enough for George and Annie to sleep there if necessary.

On March 31st, Britain pledged to support Poland militarily if it was invaded by Germany.

April 27th saw the passing of the Military Training Act, whereby all men aged 20 or 21 were conscripted to undertake six months of basic military training. On July 1st, the Women's Land Army was re-formed in readiness for taking over much of the agricultural work throughout the country. A mysterious organisation known as the Government Code and Cypher School came into being at Bletchley Park in August, an organisation later to be recognised as being crucial in the breaking of secret German codes. By late August most of the priceless paintings held at London's National Gallery were transported to a safer, secret location in Wales.

On August 24th the nation's army reservists were called up and the Civil Defence put on alert. Operation Pied Piper began on September 1st which involved the evacuation of thousands of children from London and other major cities to live with volunteer families in the safer countryside. On the same day, blackouts were imposed across the nation. Most serious of all, however, September 1st was the day the Germans marched into Poland.

Chamberlain, the British Prime Minister, declared war on Germany on September 3rd and the rest of the British Empire followed immediately. A war cabinet was established in London, with Winston Churchill appointed as first Lord of the Admiralty. National Service was introduced whereby all fit men between the ages of 18 and 41 were called up.

With Britain and the Empire now at war with Germany, tensions were exacerbated with Italy, one of the Axis powers in league with the Nazis. The war cabinet, aware of Italy's expansionist intentions in North Africa, acted quickly to bolster the KAR. By March 1940 there were over 21,000 well trained British and African troops based in North East Africa. Lieutenant-Colonel Dillon, as the officer in command of the 1st battalion, was largely responsible for the training and rapid deployment of these additional troops — a massive and exhausting undertaking.

CHAPTER TWENTY-FOUR

'Freddy'

Whilst a series of dramatic events was happening in the United Kingdom and across Europe during 1939, Eve's life also underwent a startling development with the arrival of a young army officer named Captain Frederic Drummond. It all began innocently enough. Captain Frederic Drummond, who was based in Moyale, located on the Ethiopian/Kenyan border, was almost the last of the company officers scheduled to report for his briefings at Marsabit during the first week of February.

Close to thirty young British army officers had already been through the ordeal of being interrogated by the colonel as he sought to get to know his company commanders better. Most had found the experience beneficial and had received valuable advice from their senior officer. Almost without exception, Thomas had found these young men homesick for their families, girlfriends, their local pub, football and cricket and everything else that was important in their lives back home. In addition, the young officers were struggling to hold leadership roles in hot, harsh conditions with virtually no creature comforts. As local commanders, they were never completely off duty, needing to respond to a variety of incidences at any time of day and night. Obliged to learn Swahili to better communicate with the askaris, they found working with the Africans very different to working with tommies (British soldiers). Sometimes, the challenges of living rough in the bush for months on end almost broke the young officers, and a short escape to Marsabit for a decent bed and grub for a couple of nights gave them the lift they needed to keep going.

And then there was the lovely Eve who floated gracefully about the bungalow and made the visiting officers feel like real young men again. Starved of female company for months on end, the soldiers couldn't keep their eyes off their hostess. Eve, however, had steadfastly resisted any suggestive behaviour and had maintained a level of decorum befitting of the colonel's wife at all times. This, however, was about to change.

According to the timetable of visits that Thomas had prepared many months ago, a Captain Frederic Drummond was expected to arrive from Moyale on the afternoon of

February 3rd. Like his predecessors, he was to stay two nights and then return to Moyale on the morning of February 5th. As usual, Eve made sure the three servants were aware that they would be having a visitor so that an extra place was laid at the table for meals and a bottle of wine was in the cooler, together with a selection of other alcoholic drinks, and the spare bedroom was properly prepared. All was in readiness.

Early in February, Thomas was under enormous pressure. He was receiving telegrams almost on a daily basis as the situation in Britain and Europe steadily deteriorated. The War Office was warning him that plans were being formulated to recruit and train thousands of extra askaris and that hundreds more British army officers and senior non-commissioned officers would be gazetted shortly to be seconded to the KAR. Thomas was faced with a number of challenges. Where were they to be based? What additional living quarters would be needed? How could these men and supplies be safely transported to their various destinations? Preparing for the arrival of so many additional troops in the months ahead was a logistics nightmare and it had all landed in Thomas's lap.

The relationship between Eve and Thomas had cooled even further too. They spent less time together as Thomas's workload increased. Tired and worried much of the time, Thomas had become snappy and less patient with her. He was never overtly rude, just curt and dismissive. In the bedroom all activity had ceased. Eve put Thomas's lack of libido down to the combination of his stress and exhaustion. The last time she could remember they had had intercourse was on Christmas night. Thomas certainly wasn't having an affair; there was nobody to have an affair with!

Eve and Thomas were skilled at giving the impression that they were a devoted couple. Visitors would have had to have been exceptionally observant and to have stayed for more than a couple of nights to detect any disharmony. The only person who had had some suspicions was Janet next door. On one occasion, Janet had plucked up the courage to ask Eve if all was well between her and her husband, but Eve had been quite taken aback that she would even think such a thing and had strongly denied any friction.

After the first few company commanders had come and gone, the whole household had fallen into a well-rehearsed routine. The officers arrived sometime during the afternoon, tired and dirty after their long journeys, and would be met by Tomasi who welcomed them, showed them to the bathroom and their bedroom and invited them to come to the drawing room for pre-dinner drinks at 1800 hours. They were also invited to leave soiled clothes out for Mary to launder. Evening wear was smart mufti. On the bed the officers would always find a timetable for the next two days together with any other information relevant to their stay.

Thomas and Eve made sure they were in the drawing room well before 1800 hours to welcome their latest guest. They were an impressive looking couple in their formal evening attire, Thomas wearing the regimental bow tie, dinner jacket and a bright red cummerbund similar to that worn by the askaris. Eve had a wide range of fashionable full-length evening dresses to call upon, all of which helped to reveal what a beautiful young woman she was. Despite battling depression from time to time, Eve had maintained her hour-glass figure and had the grace and poise to go with it. Tomasi hovered at the door ready to introduce the visitor to Colonel and Mrs Dillon. Thomas felt this rather formal opening evening helped to lift the spirits of the young officers and reminded them that such a life still existed back in the old country.

As soon as the guest appeared, drinks were dispensed and the three of them would sit about in the easy chairs with Tomasi moving about to fill glasses as required. Thomas and Eve did their best to put their guest at ease, which was often easier said than done, since the occasion was quite an ordeal for many. After about half an hour, Tomasi would announce, 'dinner is served, sir' and they would duly adjourn to the dining room, where Mary would be waiting with her trolley, eager to serve the first course, a soup, together with freshly-baked bread rolls and butter. Mary always looked the part with a smart white apron, white gloves and a neat maid's cap. Thomas insisted on saying grace before the meal began, a moment that Eve found fascinating, for she could learn something about their guest according to how he reacted to this show of religious devotion from the colonel.

Without exception, the visiting commanding officers had attended the Royal Military College, Sandhurst, where learning to behave like an officer at all times was drummed into the recruits. Behaviour befitting of a gentleman was demanded at the college, and failure to live up to this expectation would lead to an official warning followed by dismissal from Sandhurst if it occurred a second time. Boozy, boisterous displays at formal functions led to serious trouble and the recruits quickly learnt. Such behaviour, the visiting officers knew, would not be tolerated by their colonel. Tempted as they were by the sudden abundance of plentiful alcohol after weeks, or perhaps months, remaining totally dry, most young men still carefully monitored their intake.

As usual, when they had a visitor, Eve retired to her bedroom to bathe and dress at about five-fifteen so she could be in the drawing room before six o'clock. It was a warm night so she decided to wear her bright red dress, which was a bit daring since it had a plunging neck line that revealed rather more of her cleavage than Thomas thought appropriate. Thomas was running late dealing with some last-minute problem over the phone. When he finally arrived, he was quick to voice his disapproval of Eve's choice of dress, but it was too late for Eve to change now. She looked at herself in the mirror and personally was well satisfied with her appearance. Most husbands would have found her irresistible and she knew it. Sadly, she realised that Thomas would be most unlikely to rise to the occasion and show any interest in the bedroom later that evening. At least she could make herself look desirable, and feel she was an attractive woman even if a barren evening was sure to follow.

Realising that Thomas was not going to be ready by six o'clock, Eve left for the drawing room at ten to six so as to be able to properly welcome their visitor, Captain Frederic

Chapter Twenty-Four 'Freddy'

Drummond. Tomasi was already there and smiled politely as she entered and gave her a slight respectful bow.

'Good evening madam, a very warm night?'

'Yes, it is Tomasi. Do you think this means rain is coming?'

'Most likely madam. The ants are building, usually a sign of wet weather.'

'Everything is looking neat and tidy and that flower arrangement is just lovely.' Eve lent over to smell the scent of a wild red rose revealing a bit more than just her cleavage to the ever-attentive butler, who, of course, pretended not to notice.

'May I pour you a drink, madam?'

'Oh, yes please Tomasi. A sweet sherry would be perfect.'

Tomasi moved over to the drinks stand and started to decant a new bottle of sweet sherry. Eve found her favourite seat, sat down elegantly and watched the butler carefully. They were so lucky to have his services. Eve had never actually had a butler before, except briefly in India. She believed Tomasi was exceptional and could hold his own against any of the snobbier ones back home. She wondered whether there were any competitions for 'best butlers.' She felt sure theirs would be a medal prospect. It wasn't just that Tomasi had learnt his trade so thoroughly, but he was also polite, discrete, observant and pleasant to have around. She wondered, idly, where he had learnt his trade as Tomasi approached with his silver tray, a sweet sherry and an assortment of cheeses and savoury biscuits.

'Tomasi, the colonel will be a few minutes late this evening. Some problem came up that he had to deal with.'

'Thank you, madam. I'll just go and warn the cook that dinner may be a little bit late tonight.'

Eve chuckled to herself as Tomasi disappeared; he always correctly referred to his wife as 'the cook', never 'Mary' or 'my wife'.

Eve was enjoying her first relaxing sips of sherry when there was the sound of a person politely clearing their throat. Jumping to her feet, she turned to find Captain Frederic Drummond standing expectantly at the entrance to the drawing room. Eve was immediately struck by his looks. Slightly above average height for an Englishman, he was extremely solidly built, muscle not fat, and his sun-tanned face bespoke of a man at the peak of physical fitness. He was well groomed with short, neatly brushed dark hair receding ever-so-slightly and the hint of a moustache. It was Frederic's eyes, however, that captivated Eve most. She instantly recognised friendliness, honesty and fun there, as well as the bright twinkle of intelligence. Eyes are a giveaway and Frederic's were immediately engaging.

It's amazing how much the mind can absorb in that split second when first setting eyes on someone. Apart from Frederic's obvious facial good looks, Eve saw a smartly dressed officer in a suit and tie with shiny black shoes. He appeared perfectly at ease and bowed ever so slightly.

'Good evening, Mrs Dillon. I hope I'm not too early?' A slight smile played across the captain's face but he held Eve's gaze with his fascinating eyes.

'Good evening Captain Drummond, and a warm welcome to Marsabit.'

'Thank you, Mrs Dillon. May I say what a pleasure it is to be welcomed by such a beautiful hostess?'

Eve was not accustomed to their visitors being quite so forward in their opening remarks, in fact, Captain Drummond, she thought, was bordering on being flirtatious. Her heart skipped a beat; it was actually rather exciting to receive such a lovely compliment from this fine-looking soldier.

'May I get you a drink, sir?' The spell was broken because Tomasi had returned and was performing his butler's duty.

'You certainly can. A dry sherry, please.'

'Very well, sir,' and Tomasi retreated to his drinks stand.

'Colonel Dillon has been delayed for a few minutes, but will be here directly.' Eve smiled.

For his part, Captain Drummond was totally captivated by the gorgeous woman who stood before him. His fellow officers had warned him Mrs Dillon was a strikingly beautiful woman but in Captain Drummond's mind there were simply insufficient superlatives to describe her fine looks. He fancied himself as a man of the world who had been about a bit, and met many attractive women, some of whom he had bedded, but Mrs Dillon topped them all for looks.

'And how do you enjoy living in Marsabit, Mrs Dillon?'

'Oh, call me Eve, please,' responded Eve, realising as she said it, that this was the first visitor to whom she had granted such familiarity.

'And my name is Frederic, but my friends call me Freddy.'

'Well Freddy, I have to admit that at times I do find it depressing living here.'

Freddy appeared to be genuinely concerned, 'Why's that Eve?' Whilst Eve was considering how best to answer, Tomasi delivered a dry sherry with savouries to the captain.

'It's very lonely here, Freddy.'

'I wish I could keep you company, Eve,' was the quick-fire response.

Eve was taken aback by Freddy's forwardness, but at the same time felt a stirring of excitement at this man's boldness. Two other visiting army officers had tried this flirtatious approach with her during the last year, but she had not been attracted to either of them and had abruptly snubbed them both. But this Freddy Drummond was different; she felt strangely drawn to him, even though they had met but a few minutes ago.

'Good evening, Captain Drummond.' Colonel Dillon bowled into the drawing room looking resplendent in his dinner suit.

Eve and Freddy jumped to their feet and turned to face the colonel.

'I do apologise for arriving late. A bit of a scrap between some askaris over at Buna.'

The two men shook hands warmly, as if they had known each other for years.

'I trust my wife has been looking after you well?' the colonel inquired.

'Indeed, she has been the perfect host,' Freddy replied with enthusiasm, stealing a look at Eve.

'Please be seated. Tomasi, a gin and tonic for me, please.'

'Very well, sir.' And the ever-willing butler scurried off again.

'Now tell me Drummond, did you have a good trip?'

Chapter Twenty-Four 'Freddy'

'Apart from a couple of blowouts, it was plain sailing, sir.'

'Glad to hear it. Any sign of the Shifta?'

'None on our journey, sir, but they have been causing some minor problems around Moyale. We've had a couple of night time raiding parties in the last fortnight. On the second occasion we chased after them and gave them a bloodied nose. It's all in my written report, sir.'

'Jolly good.'

The next fifteen minutes was taken up with further discussion about the various exploits of the Shifta. The colonel revealed that he was considering a daring, ambitious plan to try and incorporate the Shifta into the KAR later in the year, if only he could pin down their leadership to discuss the proposal. Freddy was sceptical about the idea, believing that the Shifta were too wild and untamed to ever accept army discipline.

'Ladies and gentlemen, dinner is served.' They rose and moved to the dining room with Eve taking her husband's arm.

* * *

Mary excelled as usual and provided a most satisfying three course meal, while Tomasi circulated refilling the wine glasses, collecting the plates and generally fussing around. Eve noticed that Freddy was drinking considerably more than she and her husband. Throughout the meal he took every possible opportunity to make eyes at Eve and Eve had to take care not to hold his gaze for fear her husband would notice. Thomas, as always, was sociable and chatty, totally unaware of Freddy's behaviour.

Captain 'Freddy' Drummond circa 1939. (Photo donated by Ted Knights)

From experience, Thomas had found the easiest way to let his visitors relax and enjoy themselves was to have them talk about their families and personal background. It never failed, and he soon had Freddy opening up, aided considerably by his intake of wine. Eve always enjoyed hearing about the officers' families and backgrounds but was particularly interested to hear about Freddy's. Because she felt strangely attracted to this young man, she hung on his every word.

'I was born on December 17th, 2007 in Fulham, London, and was educated at Wellington, one of the smaller public schools. The Drummonds, as you may know, are a famous Scottish family.'

'I do know of the Drummond family,' Thomas responded. 'Are you in anyway related to the banking Drummonds?'

'Aye. I have a pile of relatives from that side of the family.'

'What a coincidence! My family has had business dealings with Drummond's Bank for many long years. I have frequently been to the head office at Charing Cross to do my banking.'

'Naturally sir, all the Drummonds, and there are a great many of us, are loyal to Drummond's Bank, myself included.'

'Yes, of course, of course.'

Eve was pleased to see that Thomas had really warmed to Freddy now that they had discovered they had something in common. She also noted that Freddy was only a year older than her, and that he came from a famous and obviously very well-healed family.

The coincidences didn't stop there, however. As they finished their main course, the conversation turned to rugby. 'The game they play in heaven,' laughed Freddy. Eve knew that her husband was a rugby union enthusiast, but now she discovered that Freddy was an outstanding player with an enviable record.

'So, who have you played for?' asked Thomas, leaning forward with his elbows resting on the dining room table.

'I've played for my regiment, the Leicestershire Regiment, Leicester County, the British Army and so far, have had thirty games for The Leicester Tigers.

'Thirty matches for The Tigers! I knew I'd heard of you somewhere before. Of course, I've probably seen you play then. I've watched The Tigers several times.

'Army life is not particularly kind to sportsmen, sir. I played for The Tigers in the 1929-1930 season and then had to wait until the 1935-1936 season to play with them again.'

'Overseas posting?'

'Yes, sir, India.'

'And now you're stuffed again, Freddy, serving in this goddam part of the world!'

'Correct, sir. I'd like to think Hitler and Mussolini will come to their senses and stop all this aggression. That would let peaceful guys like me get back to rugby.'

'Well, thirty games for the Leicester Tigers, one of the best Club performers in Europe, is no mean feat. Congratulations!'

'Thank you, sir.

'You must have been getting close to selection for England?'

'Indeed, I was, sir. I was invited to trial for England just before being sent out here.'

'Bad luck, my boy.'

Eve had never watched a game of rugby in her life, but she knew it was a highly prestigious game played predominantly in private schools across the United Kingdom as well as many countries overseas. Coming from her working-class background she had had virtually no opportunities to pursue

Chapter Twenty-Four 'Freddy'

sporting interests herself until she reached high school and then it was an expensive 'extra' her parents couldn't afford. She had learnt dancing and had developed into an excellent dancer, which made her wonder how accomplished she might have been had she been given the chance to play sports. She was full of admiration for Freddy though, and now understood why he had such a muscular physique, something she admired in a man.

Clearly, Thomas was impressed with this young man too. Apart from being a member of the renowned Scottish Drummond clan and an exceptional rugby player, there was something very likeable about his boyish looks and pleasant disposition. Eve was conscious she was getting a bit of a crush on Freddy, something that hadn't happened to her for a couple of years since she had fallen head over heels for Jacko. She stole another quick glance at the captain and caught his eye. He winked, and she looked down at her plate, hoping that the warm blush of embarrassment she felt in her cheeks didn't show.

'Tomorrow, I'm going to spend some time with you, Freddy, outlining the very considerable expansion of the KAR that will take place over the next few months as we move to an enhanced war footing against Mussolini's threats from Ethiopia. I shall be looking for some outstanding officers to be based here in Marsabit to take command of a number of battalion-wide logistics. I'll need capable officers to oversee the erection of new barracks, promote askari training and take responsibility for transport, medical facilities, weapons and supplies for a start. Perhaps you would be interested, Freddy?'

Eve's heart leapt. If Freddy was appointed to one of these newly created positions, and was then based here in Marsabit, they couldn't avoid seeing a lot more of each other. The very thought that this might happen lifted her spirits.

'I certainly would be most interested, sir.'

'Excellent, we'll explore the matter further tomorrow, then. You may have noticed a new building going up on the compound when you came in? That will be the accommodation for up to eight senior officers who will be based here at HQ to handle the logistics I just mentioned.'

'Sounds exciting, sir.'

Eve was aware that Freddy was looking directly at her as he said this. She wondered, for a moment, what it was that was *really* exciting Freddy.

CHAPTER TWENTY-FIVE

Yes or No?

Over the last few weeks Eve had adopted a new strategy for bedtimes. She made sure that the exhausted Thomas was safely in bed and asleep before she joined him there. He had shown no interest in her sexually since Christmas and she preferred to keep it that way. Not only was Thomas overburdened with work and stress but he was sixteen years her senior, so perhaps it was understandable that his libido had all but dissipated. For a time, after Michael was born ten years ago, she had thought another baby would be welcome, but then when they drifted apart, she changed her mind. Looking after Michael on her own was quite enough for her to manage. She and Jacko had always taken careful steps to avoid pregnancy and she had continued this safe practice when she had returned to live with Thomas and came out to Africa with him. At forty-seven Thomas possibly felt he was now too old to start fatherhood again anyway.

Eve liked to wear sexy nightwear: it helped her feel good about herself, to feel she was still young and desirable. Thomas had retired to bed half an hour ago after staying up and having a final drink with Freddy. She always left the men to have a drink together and made herself scarce. Tonight, she had been tempted to make a late appearance just so she could see Freddy again but then thought better of it. As she slipped into her nightdress, she heard the steady rhythm of Thomas's breathing and knew he was fast asleep. Carefully she slid beneath the covers making sure she didn't disturb her sleeping husband.

Tonight, sleep evaded her; pleasant thoughts of dining with Freddy kept her wide awake. Nothing had been said about his marital status, although she had not noticed a ring. Many married men didn't wear rings anyway, so this was no proof. Perhaps he was divorced? One thing Eve felt quite sure of was that Freddy was a ladies' man and that he would be very experienced in the bedroom. She resolved to see as much of Freddy as she could over the next day or two before he had to return to Moyale. She knew she was probably playing with fire to get involved with this man, yet she yearned for strong male company and instinctively knew they were well suited. What's more, she was sure Freddy was attracted to her.

Chapter Twenty-Five Yes or No?

Tomasi knocked on their bedroom door promptly at seven hundred hours. Normally Eve would remain tucked up in bed until sometime later and then make her way to the dining room for breakfast after the men had finished theirs and left for work. Today, the chance to spend a little more time in the company of Freddy motivated her to rise early so as to join the men for breakfast. Thomas was wearing uniform and Eve selected a pretty light blue dress with earrings that matched. She deliberately allowed Thomas to leave for breakfast before her so she could take a few extra minutes to carefully apply makeup and then make an appearance in the dining room on her own.

Eve timed it to perfection. She sailed into the dining room to find Freddy sitting at the table with a well-stacked plate in front of him. It looked like a full English breakfast with tomato, sausage, bacon and eggs. Both men stood as she entered and extended greetings of the morning. She smiled generously at them both and moved to the sideboard where Tomasi also welcomed her. Tomasi knew her tastes but always politely checked before serving. Yes, she would have the usual, a scrambled egg with half a tomato and a piece of toast together with a cup of tea with milk. While Tomasi was attending to her breakfast order, she sat down at the table, opposite Freddy. She was pleasantly surprised to see him eating heartily after having enjoyed a few drinks the previous evening. Like all good army officers, he knew how to hold his grog.

'I trust you slept well, Mrs Dillon?'

'Only fair to middling,' she responded with a smile.

'And what are you up to today, my dear?' inquired her husband.

'I think I'll spend some time with Innocent in the garden. He has a decent crop of strawberries and gooseberries ready to pick. Then we can have strawberries and cream for dessert tonight. Do you like strawberries, Captain Drummond?'

'Who doesn't love strawberries?' responded Freddy. 'Last year I scoffed punnets of strawberries at Wimbledon. If your strawberries are half as good as those at Wimbledon, then I can think of no better dessert.'

'Ours will indeed be better than Wimbledon's,' boasted Eve, 'I serve our strawberries with a special liqueur.'

'I'm salivating already,' replied Freddy as he polished off the last of his English breakfast.

'Okay, time to get cracking,' declared Thomas, pushing his chair back. 'Enjoy your breakfast, dear. I'll be thinking of you and your liquored strawberries all day.'

Freddy stood, and politely pushed his chair back against the table, all the while looking at Eve who held his gaze with a hint of seduction. She watched him follow Thomas out of the room, a fine-looking man in his officer's uniform. As he reached the door he glanced back at her and gave another of his mischievous winks.

Eve felt her heart throbbing; she hadn't felt this way since she and Jacko were dating over fifteen months ago. As Tomasi refilled her tea cup, she fell to thinking about the possibility of encouraging an affair with Freddy. She had only met him last evening, and yet here she was falling for the man. Eve had sometimes heard about couples who claimed to have fallen in love at first sight, but frankly, she didn't really believe it was possible. Eve knew very little about Freddy yet felt strongly drawn to him. Was it some sort of instant infatuation that would just as quickly disappear? Clearly, Freddy was discreetly flirting with her, but she was a respectable married woman and couldn't fall for another man a second time. What a scandal it would be if a colonel's wife was discovered to have had an affair with a junior officer!

Eve decided to have a second piece of toast and asked Tomasi to get it ready. As she sat there waiting, feelings of guilt began to trouble her. For years her marriage had been a marriage in name only, and she had used this as the justification for having an affair with dear Jacko. That relationship had ended in a horrific tragedy. Surely, she mused, she should have learnt from that experience that disloyalty was unforgiveable, and yet, Thomas *had* forgiven her and taken her back. He was a saint of a man, to stand steadfastly by her in her time of desperate need and, amazingly, to then welcome her back into his life. Could she really do this to him a second time? She was fond of Thomas and certainly didn't wish to hurt him again.

By the time Eve left the breakfast table she had decided she must definitely end this silly affair forthwith. One affair was bad enough, a second one was inexcusable. She would discourage Freddy's advances and just be the polite hostess befitting the wife of a colonel in the Kings African Rifles.

* * *

Eve spent a pleasant couple of hours with Innocent in the extensive kitchen garden at the back of the bungalow. The rich red volcanic soils and the kindly climate of the Marsabit plateau meant it was ideally suited to the growing of vegetables and certain fruit trees. In the ten months since the Dillons had arrived in Marsabit, Eve had introduced a range of new vegetables and fruit trees for Innocent to care for. Her own gardening background had been most valuable in this regard.

The strawberry patch was producing well. Nobody had picked strawberries for a few days so there were plenty of well-sized ripe ones for tonight's dessert. Thomas had invited John and Janet to join them for dinner, so Eve would need to pick sufficiently to feed five at the dinner table and enough also for Tomasi, Mary and Innocent to enjoy on their own in the kitchen afterwards. Eve had already briefed Mary about how to prepare the desserts and promised to come to the kitchen to oversee the process. After picking a full bucket of carefully selected strawberries, Eve showed Innocent how to pinch out the laterals on the tomato plants and helped him tie them up to the stakes he had hacked and fashioned from the nearby bush.

Thomas and Freddy worked throughout the day in the colonel's office and Tomasi brought them sandwiches, fruit and tea for lunch. Eve had lunch alone. In the afternoon Eve called in on Janet and helped her with the little ones. She found her thoughts slipping back to Freddy from time to time but just as quickly she dismissed them. She had been shamefully unfaithful once and once was more than enough. Tonight, she determined, she would ignore Freddy's subtle advances.

Chapter Twenty-Five Yes or No?

Dinner was an enjoyable affair with lively conversation and much laughter. Eve's desserts were well received. Despite Freddy's best efforts, Eve studiously ignored any attempt he made to flirt and remained a polite, entertaining hostess. Thomas noted, with considerable satisfaction, how well Eve fulfilled her duties these days. She had matured and grown into her role as the wife of a colonel and he was proud of her. She looked stunning tonight.

Towards the end of the evening Thomas proposed two toasts, the first was the loyal toast to king and country which was followed by a toast to Captain Freddy Drummond and his company based at Moyale. Everyone retired early because Freddy would have to be up with the lark to start the slow and torturous journey back to Moyale.

As usual, Eve delayed her bedtime until half an hour after her husband had retired, expecting him to be soundly asleep by the time she came to bed. This night, however, she got it wrong, Thomas was still awake when she quietly entered the bedroom. Annoyed with herself for coming in prematurely, Eve disappeared into the bathroom to get undressed fearing Thomas might have some ideas about intimacy. She needn't have worried, Thomas only wanted to talk.

'Fine young man that Freddy Drummond, don't you think, dear?'

Eve was immediately on the defensive. Had Thomas sensed that Freddy was interested in her? Perhaps he had spotted Freddy winking at her last night? Or possibly he had seen them making eyes at each other the previous evening?

'Do you think so, dear?' Eve replied casually, and in a voice that sounded as disinterested as she could manage.

'Yes, he'll go far. A fine athlete and a natural leader of men.'

'I'm sure you're right, dear,' Eve mumbled in her rather bored tone.

'I'm going to appoint half a dozen of my best officers to run the logistics for the massive number of additional forces coming under my leadership over the next few months.'

'That sounds nice, dear.'

'I reckon young Freddy has to be one of them.'

'I'm sure he would be happy about that,' Eve responded.

'So, he'll be based here for a few months as we deal with the influx of thousands of extra troops.'

'Where? Here in Marsabit?'

'Of course, this is the battalion HQ. It makes perfect sense to have the officers in charge of logistics working cooperatively together here. They can bounce ideas off each other and ensure there is no unnecessary duplication. I can keep an eye on everything as well. I'm going to appoint Freddy as one of these logistics men.'

'That sounds a good idea.' Eve allowed herself to sound mildly interested, but inside her heart was racing. Freddy was going to be living virtually next door for months on end. How thrilling! But then she promptly reminded herself that she had said a definite 'NO' to the prospect of another affair.

CHAPTER TWENTY-SIX

Still Undecided?

The new officers' accommodation in Marsabit was erected in near record time, and by the second week in May, Thomas issued orders for his six specially selected company commanders to take up their new logistical posts as soon as possible and no later than May 20th. Relieving company commanders were despatched to take their places in the field and they only required a day or two for orientation and briefing. True to his word, Thomas had appointed Captain Freddy Drummond to be the inaugural transport officer in charge of the ever-expanding fleet of army vehicles assigned to the KAR 1st Battalion.

Freddy was thrilled to receive notification of his new posting, and needed only a couple of days to introduce his replacement, a young captain on his first overseas appointment, to the company based at Moyale. Freddy felt confident the young man was competent to handle matters capably enough. He set off for Marsabit with an appropriate armed escort early next morning and arrived at his destination late the same day. He was too late to request an evening meal and had to make do with another meal of basic army rations.

Freddy's meeting a couple of weeks back with the lovely Eve Dillon was very much on his mind as his convoy bumped and scrunched its way along the dirt track that boasted grandly that it was the Moyale to Nairobi Highway. Freddy was convinced Eve was a lonely woman, bored out of her brain and longing for some adventure and spice in her life. On the first evening she had certainly encouraged his not-so-subtle attentions, although, for reasons best known to Eve, she had been far less responsive the second evening. Had her husband noticed their flirting and chastised Eve? He didn't think so; Colonel Dillon was so preoccupied with his increasingly demanding workload that half the time he was unaware of what was going on around him. Freddy liked the old colonel, he was a thoroughly decent sort of a bloke, but was guilty of seriously neglecting the needs of his attractive young wife.

Freddy had been promoted to the rank of captain early in 1937 and now, over two years later, he was hopeful of making it soon to major. The fact he was one of just six company commanders selected for Battalion-wide duties was a welcome feather in his cap. If he performed well, and impressed the colonel, he felt sure his name would be put forward for promotion. Marsabit was a far pleasanter location to be based than Moyale stuck out in the furnace-like heat and dust of the desert. But above all else, this posting afforded Freddy the opportunity to get to know Eve better and he was really looking forward to that!

Freddy knew he was attractive to women. His manliness, lively sense of humour and ability to be the life and soul at a party endeared him to the fairer sex. Now, aged thirty-two, family and friends were intensifying their efforts to get him to marry and settle down, but Freddy was still having too good a time with his rugby, tennis and other sporting outlets as well as enjoying life in the British Army. Until coming out to Kenya recently, he had always enjoyed the company of women and had had a long succession of girlfriends. In fact, he had earned himself a reputation as a ladies' man. But here in Kenya, the chances of finding a girlfriend were as arid as the relentless desert around him. He couldn't remember such a long time without the intimate company of a woman and this was frustrating the hell out of him. True, there were tribal women living around Moyale, but touch one of them and you were likely to end up skewered on the end of a spear. Other than the occasional leave once or twice a year, the only time he had laid eyes on a desirable woman was when he had met Eve a little over a fortnight ago. Moving to Marsabit would give Freddy the opportunity to renew his acquaintance with Eve and hopefully develop a deeper, more satisfying, relationship.

Having arrived a couple of days early, Freddy was free to

find his own entertainment until he and his brother officers were to report to the colonel at 0900 hours on May 21st. Two of the other captains had arrived, and at breakfast the three of them teamed up to go looking for wildlife on the plateau. Marsabit already had a reputation as a superb area for viewing, or hunting, elephants, buffalo, camels, leopards and zebras as well as smaller game. The three officers were united in that they wanted to procure a vehicle from transport for the day but whether it was to view or shoot the wildlife was a matter of contention. One of their number, Captain Bruce Ainsley, was a crack shot who had been to Africa on leave a couple of years ago and had spent two weeks on safari shooting wildlife. Ainsley was keen to try his luck again on the plateau to add to his trophies.

Freddy and the third officer, Captain James Hardcastle, were opposed to the shooting of game, arguing that preservation was the way of the future and that some animals were already endangered. Bruce, however, was difficult to convince, protesting that there was abundant game and that his killing of a couple more animals was neither here nor there. Just as it looked as if they would never agree, Bruce came up with a compromise. He consented to fire only if they were in danger of being attacked. This seemed more than reasonable and the three of them commandeered an open jeep shortly after breakfast. Johnno was not comfortable about the three officers new to Marsabit going off on their own without a guide, but could not spare one of his mechanics for the day. With considerable trepidation, Johnno handed the keys to James, who had volunteered to be the driver, and tried to explain where they might go to have the best chance of spotting some wildlife.

As they cruised about, they came across a wide variety of animals and bird life. They were not sufficiently knowledgeable to know the correct names for the particular breeds of animals they saw but they recognised monkeys, gazelles, a pack of hyenas, a group of vultures devouring a carcass, a loan eagle circling above them and a tribe of incredibly noisy baboons carrying on amongst the trees. They were slowly edging towards a herd of grazing zebra when they came across the most exciting find of the day: a leopard in the throes of stalking a young zebra. James stopped the vehicle so they could watch, but regrettably, they had already spoilt the magic moment. The young zebra, seeing the vehicle, frisked off back into the safety of the herd to find its mother and the leopard broke cover, snarling its annoyance that its efforts had come to nothing.

A thunderstorm broke early in the afternoon bringing heavy rain and lightning. The red volcanic soils quickly turned slippery and they still had several miles to travel across open country to make it back to the central track. The rain showed no sign of easing and driving conditions steadily deteriorated. James locked the jeep into a low gear to better handle the quagmire: slow and steady was the only way to keep the vehicle moving through the mud. Despite James's best efforts they became bogged within sight of the central trail. The more he tried to move forward, the deeper the jeep sank into the red basalt soil. The only way they would be likely to extricate the vehicle was to clamber out, throw branches under the wheels and push.

The rain had not relented one bit and the three men were wet through by the time they had collected sufficient bark, small branches and palm leaves to give the jeep some hope of traction. Finally, Freddy and Bruce bent low and pushed with all their might; James pressed the accelerator and at last got some purchase. Yelling for Freddy and Bruce to get back in the jeep while he still had traction, James slithered drunkenly about but kept the vehicle moving. Opening the doors and clambering inside the erratically moving vehicle was no easy task. Bruce managed to get in safely, but Freddy somehow jammed a finger in the door in the process.

Jamming a finger in a door is a horribly painful experience. Freddy clutched the damaged digit tightly and as soon as they were safely back on the central track where driving conditions were better, he dared to inspect the damage. He didn't think it was broken but the flesh had been badly torn and the nail was only just hanging on. It probably needed a couple of stitches but there was no hope of that in Marsabit. Marsabit did not even boast a medical centre and there was probably nobody qualified to administer first aid. Since arriving in Marsabit, Eve had somehow become the 'go-to' person if anyone had something wrong with them. Eve never professed to have any medical training but could at least offer a sympathetic ear and happily dispensed what meagre medical supplies had been provided by the army.

Thomas had been complaining to Nairobi for months

about the lack of proper medical facilities at Marsabit. Years ago, it had been accepted by the army that a medical orderly should always be present for every KAR outpost and this had worked well enough. Medical orderlies had sufficient basic medical training to deal with most maladies and minor injuries. Anything more serious had to be sent to Nairobi where the army had a fully equipped hospital able to handle most situations. Marsabit, the first Battalion's headquarters, had missed out, however, because at any one time there were never more than thirty personnel living there. Most of the outposts, on the other hand, numbered at least a hundred men. Now that the army personnel at Marsabit, like everywhere else, was on the increase, Thomas felt entitled to at least a qualified medical orderly. Despite several requests, the army bureaucrats were still 'considering the matter'.

The rain eased somewhat as the three young officers made their torturous way slowly along the central track trying to avoid the largest of the pools of water. They had been out all day and James's arms were now aching from battling with the steering in such trying conditions. Freddy was holding his throbbing hand out in front of him and endeavouring to hang on with the other. Only Bruce seemed unperturbed; he bumped around in the back with his rifle still cocked and ready. He hadn't fired a shot all day, but had promised himself a trip back out into the bush sometime without his two colleagues when he would be free to shoot game to his heart's content.

It was nigh four o'clock when their mud-splattered jeep finally pulled up at the depot where the fleet of army vehicles was housed and serviced under Johnno's meticulous care. Johnno had mixed feelings about this Captain Freddy Drummond who had just been appointed the Battalion's first transport officer. Until now, Sergeant Johnno had managed the fleet quite successfully on his own, along with the mechanics and drivers he had trained. He had always answered directly to the colonel, but now there was to be an intermediary, this Captain Drummond. Johnno's fleet of vehicles was steadily expanding and the number of drivers and mechanics also. Clearly trouble was expected with the Italians. Reluctantly, Johnno accepted he would now have to have a commanding officer breathing down his neck.

Johnno wandered out to meet the jeep. He planned to have the vehicle inspected first by one of his mechanics and then washed and cleaned inside and out.

'Did you have a good day, sir?' he asked Captain James Hardcastle, as the officer lowered a dirty driver's window.

'Yes, thanks Sergeant. Where do you want her?'

'Shed four please, sir.'

'Before I park her, where's the medical centre?'

'Medical Centre, sir? We don't have one.'

'You're kidding me? No bloody medical centre? Captain Drummond here needs someone to fix his finger. What's he supposed to do? Put it up his arse?'

'Sorry sir. Mrs Dillon dispenses medicines and fixes up small wounds, but she ain't qualified.'

'Jesus Christ!' exclaimed James as he headed off towards shed four.

Freddy, listening to this brief exchange, smiled to himself. Now he had the perfect excuse to become reacquainted with Eve. Something good might come from smashing his finger after all.

* * *

At breakfast that morning, Eve had been surprised to learn that three of the newly appointed officers had already arrived and that Freddy was one of them. She found herself designing ways whereby she could 'accidentally' bump into him and then had to keep reminding herself that she wanted to have nothing to do with him. She felt conflicted. One side of her longed romance, a loving relationship, fulfillment; the other side admonished her for being disloyal to a faithful husband and possibly bringing shame to Thomas and the regiment.

She spent the day restlessly, unable to settle on any major tasks. The fact that Freddy was so close physically yet so far away emotionally disturbed her. Somehow, she knew, she must come to terms with this new situation. Even though she had decided she would not encourage another affair, she had warmed immediately to Freddy and still felt he was right for her. Eve had to admit that she was sitting on the fence still, unsure which way to go.

Tomasi had brought in a small tray of scones for afternoon tea, one of Mary's specialities. Local dates had been added to the mix which made the scones particularly palatable. Idly leafing through an old copy of Punch and with her feet up on a foot stool, Eve heard a jeep drive into the transport depot at the rear of the garden. She could hear voices. Five minutes later there was a polite knock at the front door.

'I'll attend to it, madam,' Tomasi assured her, as she quickly brushed some crumbs off her chest and instinctively tidied up her hair.

'Good afternoon sir, may I help you?'

'Yes, possibly. I have been informed that Mrs Dillon assists with first aid. If that is correct, I would like to see her please?'

Hearing this exchange, Eve jumped to her feet. It sounded as though it was Freddy and that he had come to see her on some pretext of needing first aid. She knew he was a mischievous character and this was no doubt just a clever way of inveigling his way back into her life.

'May I have your name please sir and I will see if Mrs Dillon is available?'

'It's Captain Drummond, and as you can see, I have an injured finger.'

'Yes indeed, sir, it looks very painful. Please wait here a moment and I will see if Mrs Dillon can see you directly.'

When Tomasi asked Eve what he should do, she had no hesitation in inviting Freddy in.

'Tomasi, please show the captain through to the dispensary.'

'Dispensary' was an overly grand name for the small spare bedroom where the meagre army medical supplies were housed. The room consisted of a single bed, a small white table with an angle poise lamp, two chairs and a couple of locked cupboards in which everything was neatly stored. Eve hurried down to the bathroom where she thoroughly washed her hands with soap and hot water. When she reached the dispensary, she found Freddy sitting comfortably on one of the chairs with the elbow of his injured finger resting on the table.

'Captain Drummond?'

'Call me Freddy, please.'

'And what have you been doing to yourself?'

'I had a disagreement with the door of a jeep.'

'Ooooo yes, and it looks as though the door won.'

'No, I won.'

'How come?'

'Because I get to come and see you.'

'Cheeky!'

'Can you do anything for this?'

'Captain, I mean Freddy, you do know that I have no medical qualifications? My sister's a nurse though.'

Freddy laughed. 'Well, it seems there's nobody else around here who is better qualified than you. Perhaps you can put on a bandage or something?'

'Let me have a look please.'

Eve sat on the edge of the table and positioned herself the better to inspect the damaged finger. Gently she took his hand and carefully perused the wound.

'Oh dear, you *have* made a bit of a mess of it. You're going to lose that fingernail for sure.'

'What about that flap of skin? Can you do stitches, Eve?'

'No, I can't. I think if I clean the wound well and then bandage it so the flap is back where it should be, it will heal okay. I have an excellent finger stall to protect it too.'

'Whatever you think.'

As Eve examined the injury, Freddy had a marvellous opportunity to study Eve up close, the first time this had been possible. He was not disappointed. Everything about her face and body was breathtakingly beautiful. The colonel was an extraordinarily fortunate man to be married to such a lovely woman. It was not just her looks that appealed to Freddy; she was intelligent, fun to be around but also a caring sort of person. Freddy had lost count of the number of girlfriends he had had over the years. They had all been attractive personalities and good-lookers, but Eve Dillon topped them all. Was she happily married, he wondered, was there a chance that he might have an affair with her?

'Ow!' he exclaimed as Eve gently washed the wound with TCP using a wad of cotton wool.

'Hold still Freddy, it's bound to sting a bit.'

He obliged, letting his eyes rove over her body as a distraction from the discomfort she was creating.

'There, I think that's clean now.' She smiled and their eyes met. 'I'll only put on a small bandage so there's room for the finger stall to go over it.'

He winced as she neatly tied off the bandage. Next, Eve moved over to the cupboard and looked about for the finger stall affording Freddy a pleasant view of her shapely legs.

'Have you ever had a finger stall before, Freddy?'

'No, I haven't.'

'Well, try to keep it clean and dry. It's made of soft leather but gives excellent protection if you look after it properly.'

'Eve, you're a real professional.' He smiled as she tied the two ribbons of the finger stall neatly in a double bow around his wrist. Her touch was soothing and he admired her well-manicured fingernails. The handsome wedding ring was impossible to miss.

Eve looked at Freddy directly and with a slight smile playing about her mouth, suggested he might like to return at the same time tomorrow for her to change the dressing and check everything was still looking good. Freddy could think of nothing he would like more. He thanked Eve for her attentions, perhaps rather more profusely than was necessary, and left the room positively glowing.

As Eve cleaned up in her small dispensary, she again pondered whether her decision to resist Freddy's advances was what she really wanted. As she had nursed his injured finger, she had felt a strong urge to get to know this man better but she suspected that if she lowered her defences, she might end up falling in love. But then, was that really such a bad thing?

CHAPTER TWENTY-SEVEN

Party Time

Freddy happily returned to the dispensary next day. Eve inspected the finger, pronounced it 'progressing nicely,' applied a clean dressing and complimented her patient on looking after the finger stall so well. Again, despite the two of them longing to develop a relationship, both ignored their natural inclinations and behaved politely and professionally. Freddy didn't try to flirt and Eve didn't encourage such behaviour. Eve suggested the dressing be changed one more time after another two days and encouraged Freddy to continue to protect the finger by wearing the finger stall day and night.

The six captains, appointed by the colonel to take responsibility for the six major areas of logistics, were now fully installed and work had started in earnest. Freddy reviewed the small fleet of vehicles currently at his disposal and checked their condition carefully with Johnno. New sheds were being erected to garage some of the troop transports expected to arrive next month. In a clever move, Freddy had persuaded the colonel to request a pay increase for Johnno and then give him the task of setting up and running a second transport hub at the foot of the plateau. Freddy had successfully argued that the forty minutes it took for a vehicle to climb up from the base of the plateau to the depot in Marsabit was a waste of time and precious petrol. If vehicles were to respond urgently to situations around the region it was necessary to have some, together with their drivers, stationed at the bottom of the hill. Placing Johnno in charge of this initiative, together with his salary increase, helped to bring Johnno on side.

Freddy's finger healed well and after a week he was able to dispense with the finger stall and keep only a plaster as protection. He complimented Eve on her medical skills. Nothing changed in their relationship until a few weeks later.

The colonel was due to set off on his next round of outpost inspections early in July. There had been a couple of minor incursions from the Italians based near Moyale that had been successfully countered without any loss of life. Additional troops had been stationed at several of the outposts already and Thomas was anxious to see how well this was working with first hand briefings from his company commanders. Thomas

Chapter Twenty-Seven   Party Time

was respected by his junior officers as a dedicated, thoughtful and considerate leader who kept his finger on the pulse and acted fairly and swiftly when the need arose.

'Freddy' (right) as the Transport Officer at Marsabit in 1939. (Photo donated by Army Personnel Centre)

Life had been so hectic that Thomas had not had time to hold a welcoming party for his six newly appointed logistics officers, so he arranged that this should happen a couple of days before he departed on his tour of duty. The date of the party coincided with the arrival home of young Michael for his six-week-long vacation, which was another reason to celebrate. The party was scheduled for eight o'clock on a Saturday night. Mary and Eve had been preparing finger foods most of the day and both Tomasi and Innocent had been dragooned into being the drinks waiters for the evening.

It was a large gathering by Marsabit standards: Colonel and Mrs Dillon, Major and Mrs Williamson, the six logistics officers, Johnno and three recently appointed additional sergeants. No children were allowed. Thomas had decreed that evening wear should be mufti which meant the party would be a more relaxed affair.

As with all army functions, liberal quantities of alcoholic drinks were readily available. As soon as somebody's glass looked in danger of being emptied, either Tomasi or Innocent would be alongside to offer another tempting cocktail, wine or beer. Not surprisingly, as the evening wore on, most of the gathering had consumed enough alcohol to loosen their tongues. Gradually, the noise level rose as any inhibitions declined. Colonel Dillon, as always, paced himself carefully and remained perfectly sober whereas most of his guests became mildly, or rather more than mildly, inebriated, Freddy included.

With only two women present and no music, dancing was out of the question. Most of the men sat about in small groups, joking and laughing, the sergeants together in one corner and the logistics officers in another. In the centre of the room were Colonel and Mrs Dillon, Major and Mrs Williamson and Freddy. The colonel had invited Freddy to join their group because he wanted to persuade the captain to spend some time with Michael coaching him in the finer arts of rugby union. Thomas expected to be away for almost the whole of Michael's six-week-long summer holidays and this was one way his son could spend his time usefully. Michael, now eleven years old, was playing scrum-half for the first XV at Kenton College in Nairobi and apparently showed considerable promise.

Freddy may have had a touch too much alcohol, but he immediately saw an opportunity too good to miss. Coming to the Dillon's home to take Michael out for rugger coaching on a regular basis whilst the colonel was away meant he could spend time with the gorgeous Eve. Nobody need suspect anything was amiss, as it was the unsuspecting colonel himself who had asked him to do this. Eve listened carefully to their conversation with increasing interest.

'So, what do you think, Freddy? I'm quite prepared to pay you a small fee for your services.'

'That's very good of you sir, but I don't think payment will be necessary.'

'Maybe not, but it does put everything on a professional footing. If you are receiving coaching fees, I know you will put your heart into it. I would also expect a full report at the end of the holidays outlining the activities and skills you have been developing and an assessment of progress.'

Freddy could hardly believe his luck. He stole a look at the gorgeous creature sitting next to the colonel and knew she was listening intently. Unexpectedly, Eve then entered the conversation.

'I wonder if we could go one step further Thomas, dear?'

'What's that my darling?'

'It would be most helpful if we settled on times and how often Captain Drummond will take Michael out for training.'

'Yes, I suppose that could be helpful,' Thomas agreed. 'What time would suit you Eve, dear?'

'Well, Captain Drummond is working during the week, so I guess it would need to be after work?'

Freddy was intrigued to see how cooperative Eve was being about the arrangements. Did she have an ulterior motive? Was it possible that Eve wanted to get to know *him* better after all?

'Yes, good thinking, Mrs Dillon. I'm usually finished by four o'clock so shall we make the sessions from a quarter past four until around five o'clock?'

'That would suit me fine, Captain.' Eve was looking at Freddy with her lovely eyes and Freddy wished he could take her in his arms there and then.

'And which days of the week would be most convenient, Mrs Dillon?'

'Let's start on Monday and make it a daily event from Monday right through to Friday? If that's too much we can always drop it back.'

'Good, so that's settled then,' chimed in the colonel, with a broad grin on his face. 'First session on Monday afternoon at four-fifteen and I'll make sure you receive some recompense for your expert tuition, Freddy. Michael is indeed fortunate to have such an accomplished rugby man as his personal coach.'

'Thank you, sir. I'm already looking forward to working with young Michael.'

'He has a football that we bought for his birthday in February, but it may need some air?' ventured Eve, looking at Freddy.

'I'll bring a pump on Monday. Could you see he's ready please in his rugger gear with clean boots?' Freddy requested, looking at Eve.

'I'll ask Tomasi to check his boots,' replied Eve.

The party broke up shortly before midnight. The Dillons left together and Freddy had no chance of spending time alone with Eve. The thought of what might transpire over the next few weeks, however, was exhilarating.

That night, as Eve undressed unhurriedly for bed, she wondered whether she would be able to resist Freddy's advances over the next six weeks. More to the point was whether she *wanted* to rebuff his intentions. The way Freddy looked at her might just be too much.

CHAPTER TWENTY-EIGHT

Rugby and More...

At 0700 hours Monday morning, the colonel's driver arrived at the front door of his bungalow. He saluted smartly as the colonel climbed into the passenger seat. Thomas had already said his goodbyes to Eve and Michael indoors and asked them not to come out. There was still a small group assembled to farewell the colonel in the dank early morning mist, namely his second-in-command, Major Williamson, Johnno and Freddy, his special officer in charge of transport. Johnno assured the colonel the vehicle was in tip-top condition having just had a full service and told him that at the bottom of the hill he would be joined by two escort vehicles conveying twenty well trained askaris.

Some of the plateau's wildlife had yet to settle down for the new day, or get moving, as the case may be. As the jeep began its steady descent there were fleeting glimpses of zebra, gazelle and camels and the occasional lone African fish eagle or falcon circling far above them. They passed the familiar strangler figs and miles of colourful acacia trees and nearly ran over a sleepy blue monkey who was enjoying an early morning warm patch of sun.

The colonel checked his watch; they had left in good time. At the foot of the plateau, they rendezvoused with the two escort vehicles as planned and set off to the west across the forbidding sand dunes of the Chalbi Desert. Thomas was pleased with what he had achieved so far with his troop reinforcements. It would be another six weeks before he returned to Marsabit, but Eve and the servants all managed to work together well enough and Michael would really enjoy Freddy's expert rugby tuition. He hoped Michael would continue his love of 'the game they play in heaven.' All in all, he felt he had left Eve and Michael in good hands and he didn't need to worry.

* * *

On the dot of four fifteen Freddy rang the Dillon's front doorbell and was promptly greeted by the ever-polite Tomasi.

'Good afternoon sir. We were expecting you. Please come in.'

'Thank you Tomasi. Is young Michael ready?'

Chapter Twenty-Eight Rugby and More...

'Yes, I am!' Michael came bounding out from somewhere unseen carrying his boots and a jumper should it get cool.

'Hello Michael. Good to see you looking so fit and keen. Tomasi, would you mind telling Mrs Dillon we will be back shortly after seventeen hundred hours... sorry, five o'clock?'

'Yes, of course sir. Mrs Dillon has asked that you stay and have afternoon tea with her after training.'

'Excellent, it will be my pleasure. Come on Michael, we'll run around the playground to warm up.'

Freddy had put considerable thought into the program he planned to run through with Michael over the ensuing six weeks but he wanted first to see what the lad was capable of doing. So, most of the initial session was taken up with running practice: swerving, tackling, running passes, special scrum-half passing from off the ground, drop kicking and even seeing how well Michael could convert. By the end of the first session Freddy was impressed with his young charge, but considered he might be better playing as a fly-half rather than a scrum-half.

Following training they removed their boots and headed back to the bungalow where Tomasi welcomed them back. Michael was despatched to have a hot bath and Freddy joined Eve in the drawing room. Immediately he noticed a marked change in her attitude towards him. She was flirtatious and seductive clad in a short dress that allowed her to reveal a bit of leg whenever she wished.

'Welcome Freddy. My, don't you look handsome in your rugby gear?'

'Well, I thought I should look the part if I'm going to tutor that gifted son of yours.'

'Gifted? In what way, Freddy?'

'Rugby, of course. I don't know enough about him to know if he's gifted in other things.'

'Of course, he is! He's my son, and a mother is never biased, is she?'

Tomasi entered with the tea trolley which he parked next to Eve for her to dispense. Everything was there; the teapot under its cosy, milk in a jug, a tea leaf strainer and its dish, three matching cups, and saucers and plates for when Michael joined them later. On the lower deck was a plate of what looked like cucumber sandwiches and another plate displaying chocolate biscuits and small colourful tea cakes.

Eve was conscious of retaining her exquisite figure and merely played with eating any food but enjoyed seeing Freddy quietly gorging himself. Encouraged by Eve's warm reception, Freddy decided to let his guard down too.

'Michael's a great lad. Is he your only child?'

'Yes, he's my only child.'

'Have you not wanted another child, Eve?' Freddy was aware he was possibly treading on dangerous ground by asking such a personal question. However, Eve seemed unconcerned and began to open up.

'Freddy, you might as well know now that our marriage is really only a marriage in name.'

She stopped there and looked directly at Freddy inviting him by her silence to probe further.

Chapter Twenty-Eight Rugby and More...

Freddy had a mouthful of cake and had to wait a moment before replying, 'I'm sorry to hear that.'

'I have never spoken about this to anyone else, except Jacko.'

'Jacko?'

'He was a friend I had in the past. So, I'm trusting you, Freddy, not to talk about our marriage to anyone else. Is that a deal?'

'Yes, of course, I promise that anything you want to tell me will stay with me.'

'We've been married for nearly thirteen years but it has never been a very happy life together. For a start, Thomas is sixteen years older than me and we don't share many interests. I've come from a working-class background and was desperate to marry up into a better, more comfortable, life. I think they call it being 'upwardly mobile'?'

'Yes, I've heard that term.'

'I guess I jumped at the first eligible gentleman that came along. At the time, Thomas seemed ideal. He was thirty-four but still a bachelor. He was decent, well off, going up the promotion ladder and he offered me a secure and sophisticated lifestyle. I was only eighteen, naive and impressionable and I thought I was in love.'

Freddy was a good listener and he sat quietly, looking intently at Eve, and willing her to continue.

'We got along well enough for a few years but gradually what little love there was seemed to just ebb away. Michael came along after a couple of years and that helped for a short time but then we drifted apart again. We are such different personalities, Freddy. I'm outgoing and like a bit of fun: parties, socialising.

Thomas is reserved, and to be honest, stuffy. He's also very religious which I'm not. So, you can see, we are not well suited.'

'If you forgive me saying it, Eve, I'm surprised you haven't separated or even divorced?'

'Thomas, being a strict Catholic, would never condone divorce. We did live apart for a time when I met Jacko. Jacko and I had a wonderful affair but that came to a tragic end.'

'What happened?'

Eve did not have to answer the question because at that moment Michael came bounding in looking for food.

'Can I join you, Mum?'

'Yes, of course, darling. Help yourself.'

Michael grabbed a couple of sandwiches and a handful of chocolate biscuits.

'Hey, what happened to a thing called a plate?'

'Sorry, Mum.'

'Well, I must be going, lots to do. Thank you for the afternoon tea, Mrs Dillon.' Freddy raised himself from the comfortable chair.

'Perhaps we can do the same again tomorrow afternoon, Captain?'

'Excellent idea, Mrs Dillon. Michael, I'll pick you up at four-fifteen and we'll concentrate on flinging out passes just in front of the receiver when he's running flat out, a really important skill.'

Michael nodded enthusiastically with his mouth full of chocolate biscuits.

* * *

Chapter Twenty-Eight Rugby and More...

That night Eve lay in bed thinking about her afternoon tea with Freddy. In retrospect she was surprised at how willingly she had opened up to Freddy and told him some very personal details about her married life. She felt she could trust this man, however, and it was almost cathartic to be able to talk to someone at last who seemed interested and empathetic. Apart from Jacko, she had not found anyone else to whom she could unburden. Her parents, and her siblings, Bell and George, had been supportive after her awful ending with Jacko, but she had never felt comfortable opening up to them about her failed marriage.

Emotionally, Eve sensed she was starting to see Freddy as something more than just a friend; perhaps a mentor, or a counsellor? She was attracted to him as a man. There was much to admire about Freddy, apart from his good looks. He was tough and confident and she liked that in a man. When she was around him, she felt safe, which was silly really, nevertheless it was a pleasant feeling. Eve was thrilled that he and Michael obviously enjoyed each other's company. She was sorely tempted to have a fling with Freddy whilst Thomas was away, it would be great fun, but she would like to find out a bit more about his background first. Eve was, understandably, rather more careful third time around. Tomorrow's afternoon tea would be the ideal time to delve deeper into Freddy's past before she committed herself to another affair.

Freddy's thoughts that evening also revolved around the engaging time he had spent with Eve at afternoon tea. He knew he was falling for this beautiful woman. He found it hard to believe that such a treasure was stranded out here in the middle of Kenya trapped in an unhappy marriage and clearly yearning for meaningful male company. In fact, he couldn't believe his luck. It was many months since he had had intimate relations with a woman and he was as sexually frustrated as hell. But he didn't want a relationship with Eve to be purely sexual, for he sensed that this relationship could be much more than basic sexual desire.

Freddy had enjoyed his way with many women over the years and had never had problems coaxing them to bed. But in all that time, there was only one woman he felt he might have wished to spend the rest of his life with. They had slept together a couple of times, and he thought he was falling in love, but then she had shocked him by casually announcing that she was going to get married in a couple of months to some lawyer he had never even met. She had been trifling with him all along, just using him to get some sexual experience. In hindsight, Freddy had found the whole affair rather hurtful and degrading. He now dared to dream that his commitment to Eve might become more than mere satisfaction of physical needs.

CHAPTER TWENTY-NINE

Second Thoughts

The rugby tuition the next day was another winner. Michael was quickly picking up on what Freddy was showing him and was keen to please. Michael seemed confident his school friend, who played fly-half, might be happy to change positions with him and play scrum-half. The friend had sometimes mentioned to Michael he would like to try out as a scrum-half. Freddy worked Michael hard for nearly an hour before they headed back to the bungalow.

All day Eve had been looking forward to seeing Freddy again for afternoon tea.

Michael already knew his after-rugby routine with a hot bath before any eats, and he ran off straight away. Freddy resisted the inclination to give Eve a kiss, instead launching into an enthusiastic description of how well Michael was doing, most of which fell on deaf ears, as Eve's knowledge of rugby was minimal and she didn't understand what he was talking about. Eve was just pleased that the two of them were enjoying exercising together.

Tomasi duly arrived with the tea trolley and Eve played hostess. Living in such a remote part of the world made it difficult to provide variety for afternoon tea. This time there were fish paste sandwiches and a slightly stale jam roll cake for afters.

Eve decided to pitch in straightaway before Michael returned with his tongue hanging out for sustenance.

'Freddy, yesterday I was very frank with you and told you about the problems in my marriage. I hope you didn't mind? I really felt the need to talk to someone and you seem to be such a good listener.'

'Eve, I was honoured you wanted to confide in me and I promise what you told me is safe and will not be repeated to anyone.'

'Thank you, Freddy, I do trust you. Now that you've heard my sad story, I would love to hear a bit about your background.' Eve passed the plate of fish paste sandwiches over to Freddy.

'Well, what would you like to know about?'

'Your love life for a start?' Eve smiled.

Freddy coloured, clearly embarrassed and uncertain how

to answer. He shoved a fish paste sandwich into his mouth to give him a moment longer to think how to respond, but Eve came to his rescue.

'For a start, have you ever been married, Freddy?'

'No.'

'So, you have never met the right girl?'

'No, although there was one woman, I think I was falling in love with, but it never worked out.'

'Oh, how sad, what happened?'

Freddy related the story of the woman who had used him to gain some sexual experience before then going off and marrying a lawyer.

'So, have you slept with any other women, Freddy?'

Freddy was somewhat taken aback by Eve's forthright questioning. Nobody had ever confronted him over his sexual exploits before.

'Yes, I have,' he admitted meekly, now feeling a little ashamed. Eve waited patiently, a ploy she used whenever she wanted a fuller answer from anyone.

When Freddy was not forthcoming, she tried again.

'Well?'

'Well, what?'

'Have there been any other women?'

'Of course, there have been. I've had heaps of girlfriends.'

'So, you have slept with many of these girlfriends?'

'Eve, you're embarrassing me.'

'Well, at least you are being honest with me. You're a bit of a Casanova, aren't you?'

Michael arrived, anxious to tell his mother what rugby moves he had been practising with Freddy. Much to Freddy's relief his conversation with Eve came to an abrupt end.

Freddy left that afternoon feeling deflated. He knew Eve was disgusted to hear about his promiscuous behaviour and that he had done himself no favours by being so brutally honest. Was this the death knell of their budding relationship? How would Eve respond to him now? Perhaps their afternoon teas together would be terminated? What a mess he had made of things!

That night it began raining and the inclement weather continued on and off for the next two days. Rugby training had to be cancelled which meant there were no afternoon teas to be shared afterwards. Eve and Freddy didn't see each other at all for the next two days.

Eve had been shocked to hear that Freddy had 'slept around'. In her view, a man who behaved this way would probably never settle down into a stable, happy marriage, content to live only with one wife. She believed such a man would always be looking elsewhere for sexual gratification. Whereas she respected Freddy for his honesty, she now saw him, not as a possible life partner, but only as someone with whom to have a fling. It would be an adventure, a distraction, to have a secret affair with Freddy but that was all it would be. Was this what she really wanted though?

Eve soon realised she was no better than Freddy if she was thinking this way. Here she was condemning him for *his* promiscuous activities yet *she* was seriously contemplating

Chapter Twenty-Nine Second Thoughts

a clandestine liaison. There was so much she adored about Freddy and there was no doubt in her mind that he had feelings of desire for her. The two of them had every opportunity to have an intimate relationship over the next five weeks with her husband away. Why not let it happen? Eve longed for the warmth and intimacy of sharing her body with an attentive man.

Friday morning dawned warm and sunny. There was an invigorating freshness in the air; everything was washed clean. The early morning chorus of birds was particularly cheerful. Eve woke and stretched, feeling refreshed herself, for overnight she had come to a decision: she would definitely encourage Freddy. She knew what she was letting herself in for; it was a sexy fling and nothing more. Why not enjoy themselves over the next few weeks and then drop the whole affair as soon as Thomas returned. If she was careful, her husband would never know. She and Freddy were adults both desperately in need of affection, so there would be no harm in it if they were sensible. Eve decided not to waste any more time: she would make her move today at afternoon tea time.

Freddy had no idea what to expect when he and young Michael were welcomed by Tomasi later that afternoon. He was much relieved to hear he had been invited to stay for afternoon tea again.

'Good afternoon Eve.'

'Oh, hello Freddy. Lovely to see you again. Please sit down.'

Freddy did as he was bid and looked across at his hostess who, he thought, was looking particularly attractive. Small talk ensued for a few minutes before Eve issued a surprising invitation.

'Freddy, would you like to come round for dinner tonight? It won't be anything special but we can share a bottle of wine and have a good old natter. I haven't invited anyone else.'

'Yes, I'd like that very much. What time would you like me to come?'

'About seven o'clock. I've given Tomasi and Mary the night off. Mary will leave us a nice salad and some desserts before she leaves. Michael has been invited to stay the night with the Williamsons.'

Freddy's heart was racing. The thought of having a private evening with Eve was instantly arousing.

'I'm afraid I don't have anything I can bring with me to contribute to the evening, Eve.'

'That's all right, Freddy, *you* are the most important thing,' and she gave him a knowing smile.

* * *

Eve and Freddy both knew what the evening was really about. They enjoyed their meal, accompanied by wine and followed by coffee and port before they retired to Eve's bedroom. Freddy returned to his officer's quarters in the early hours of the morning, and they both slept soundly for the remainder of the night in their own respective areas.

CHAPTER THIRTY

A Surprise

Eve and Freddy continued their clandestine affair for the remainder of the time Thomas was away. At about the same time that Thomas was expected to return from his tour of inspection, Michael was due to return to his boarding school in Nairobi. With Thomas's return, Eve and Freddy were obliged to cease their frequent liaisons and to seek more secretive ways of meeting.

When he arrived, Thomas was exhausted, having visited every one of his outposts and inspected his troops stationed right across the north of Kenya. He was well pleased with what he had seen, but deeply concerned at the constant reports of Italian troop movements. Air reconnaissance now estimated up to a quarter of a million enemies were currently positioned at various locations along the Kenyan-Ethiopian border. Mussolini continued to flex his muscles, and the great fear was that he would team up with Hitler if war broke out and his troops would come teeming across the border into Kenya. The KAR were constantly on high alert. A couple of minor skirmishes had occurred but without fatalities on either side. KAR officers considered the Italian forces to be less well trained than their own askaris. The Italians certainly had numerical supremacy, but the British forces were a superior fighting unit.

After all the grim news in August, Hitler invaded Poland on September 1st. Great Britain had signed a treaty with Poland whereby it promised to come to Poland's aid should it be attacked. Neville Chamberlain, the British Prime Minister, responded by declaring war on Germany two days later, and consequently, the many countries that made up the British Empire immediately declared their support. World War Two had begun.

On the same day war was declared, Chamberlain created a small war cabinet which included Winston Churchill as first Lord of the Admiralty. Men aged between 18 and 41 were declared eligible for national service or 'nasho' as it became known. At sea, the Steam Ship Athenia became the first casualty of the war when it was torpedoed by German submarine U-30 with the loss of 98 passengers and 19 crew.

Six days later, a massive troop movement began with the

crossing of the English Channel by close to 400,000 soldiers on September 9th. Known as the British Expeditionary Force these men were warmly welcomed by the French citizens and hastily deployed to assist in the defence of France.

News during the remainder of September continued to cause serious anxiety. On September the 17th the British Aircraft Carrier, HMS Courageous, was torpedoed and sunk by U-29 with the loss of 519 crew. It was the first warship lost. The very next day, Fascist propaganda broadcasts, in perfect English, began to be beamed into Britain from Berlin, as a result of the desertion of a Nazi fanatic known as 'Lord Haw-Haw'. The long-suffering British public had to learn to cope with petrol rationing from September 24th as Hitler relentlessly tightened his grip on essential sea lanes in and out of Britain. As if this wasn't enough, a special war tax was imposed on September 27th in the form of a substantial increase in income taxation.

For Colonel Thomas Dillon, however, and his ever-growing KAR forces dispersed across the remote North-West Frontier of Kenya, the escalating events in Europe barely registered. Life in the desert regions and in Marsabit continued virtually unchanged. Worrying news trickled through from time to time to the servicemen, but Mussolini and his substantial African troops remained inactive. It was a case of 'watch and wait'. Thomas, who was probably the only person fully cognisant of all that was happening in Europe, deliberately down-played events in an attempt to keep things calm within his household and out amongst his troops. He knew the British officers and NCOs serving with the KAR would naturally be concerned for their families back home, but he didn't want to exacerbate their worries. 'Stay calm' was his mantra.

With the outbreak of war, Michael's education at Kenton College Boys' Preparatory School was rudely disrupted. The KAR needed larger facilities for its second Battalion HQ and it took over the school's buildings and relocated the teachers and pupils to Westwood Park Hotel. Fortunately, rugby was not too seriously disrupted!

Mary, the Dillon's housekeeper, and her husband, Tomasi, the butler, were intelligent, observant souls. It wasn't long before they began to suspect that something untoward had been going on between their mistress and Captain Freddy Drummond. It all came to the fore when the colonel was away and Captain Drummond stayed for afternoon tea almost every afternoon for six weeks and then abruptly stopped coming when the colonel returned from his round of inspections. Mary, who had the responsibility for cleaning the Dillon's bedroom, told her husband on several occasions she smelt lavish use of Eve's perfume there and even the strong pungent smell of an aftershave. Two empty wine glasses, found in the bathroom one night, added to her suspicions. Another morning she discovered a man's handkerchief under the pillow.

Mary and Tomasi discussed several times what they should do about the suspected affair. Tomasi was of the opinion that he was the professional butler, and as such, he should never remark or comment on any of the doings within the house. It was not his place to do so and he might risk the sack if he was to voice an opinion or even raise the matter. Mary, however, had a different

Chapter Thirty   A Surprise

opinion. According to her strong Christian beliefs, the behaviour of her mistress was totally unacceptable as, indeed, was the captain's. This was adultery and clearly condemned by God. The couple were sinners, and by saying nothing, she, Mary, could be accused of condoning their disgraceful behaviour. Mary wanted Tomasi to tell the colonel what had been happening.

Tomasi stood his ground and refused. In the end he had to remind his wife that she had promised to obey him when they had taken their Christian vows of marriage. Very reluctantly, Mary accepted the situation and held her tongue.

Thomas never realised anything suspect had occurred during his six weeks away, indeed he was most grateful to Freddy for the coaching he had given Michael and invited him to return for more coaching during Michael's next two-week-long holiday at the end of October.

Ten days after the start of the new term, Eve and Thomas received a letter from Michael telling them he had been moved to fly-half in the school's first XV, the position he had craved.

* * *

Eve continued to lead a double life for the remainder of 1939; the respectful wife of the colonel and the secret lover of Freddy Drummond. Whereas Thomas remained blissfully unaware of her extra-marital activities, Eve suspected that Mary and Tomasi knew. They never mentioned it, but Eve sensed a subtle change in their attitude towards her. Sometimes she would catch Mary looking at her with an accusatory look on her face and the easy repartee they had previously enjoyed whenever Eve came to the kitchen had disappeared. Mary remained polite but more distant. Normally, Eve would ask her servants what was worrying them when they seemed upset, but she suspected the answer would only exacerbate the tensions between them, so she behaved as though nothing was wrong.

Michael came home to Marsabit mid-October and the rugby training resumed with Thomas's blessing. Every afternoon, unless it rained, Freddy would put Michael through his paces and they would practice their skills together. A few times Freddy persuaded a couple of his fellow officers to join them and they would accompany him to afternoon tea with Mrs Dillon afterwards. Michael returned to Kenton College at its new temporary location in the last week of October.

* * *

Freddy and Eve had always carefully taken the necessary precautions to avoid a pregnancy. It was, therefore, a nasty shock for Eve when her monthly period did not eventuate in November. She had not had intimate relations with her husband for many months, so if there was a baby on the way it was clearly Freddy's. She confided in Freddy and together they decided to wait another month to see what happened in December. Hopefully this was just some kind of an anomaly and everything would return to normal before Christmas. When Eve failed to have her monthly period again in December, she knew she was definitely pregnant.

Chapter Thirty A Surprise

Eve and Freddy were conflicted. They were thrilled to be having a child together but aghast at the situation they had created for themselves. In time, it would be obvious that Eve was expecting, and it would be equally obvious that it was not the colonel's baby. How best could they handle the awful predicament they were in? Contraceptive practices were never one hundred percent safe and now they had to manage the unexpected consequences. When should they break the awful news to Thomas and how would he react?

Eve remembered that when she was having Michael, twelve years ago, she remained unusually small until around the fifth month. If she followed the same pattern this time round, she would not have to tell Thomas until March next year. Since Thomas showed no interest in Eve sexually, she felt confident that he wouldn't notice anything before March. So, they resolved to wait and say nothing to Thomas until early March.

Christmas at the Dillon's came and went. Since the horrid events of Christmas Eve 1937, when Jacko had tragically died, Christmas for both Thomas and Eve was a time of sad reflection. Eve still harboured fond memories of Jacko, whereas Thomas regretted the whole sordid business of having to come to the rescue of his wife and the shame that ensued. Their private lives had been blown open for everyone to see, gloat and scandalise about and the whole nasty business had been acutely embarrassing. They did their best to celebrate this festive season for Michael's sake, but it was inevitably tinged with regrets about Christmas two years earlier.

CHAPTER THIRTY-ONE
September 1939 – March 1940

During the final months of 1939 and the start of 1940, the situation in Europe went from bad to worse. Hitler and Stalin signed a secret German-Soviet Nonaggression Pact whereby they agreed not to attack each other. This meant the Fuhrer could now be sure he was safe from attack from the USSR; in fact, the two countries even agreed on the carve up of Poland between them. Germany would occupy the western third of the country and the Soviets the remainder.

The Polish army had a million men under arms when the

Germans invaded in September 1939 but no tanks, their generals persisting in the totally outmoded view that horsed cavalry could repulse the invaders. The Polish were, of course, no match for the Germans whose Wehrmacht (army) was superior with regard to armaments, training and discipline and their troops were driven by their fervent belief in the Nazi doctrine. Under the leadership of General Heinz Guderian, a tank expert, the German Panzer Divisions swept all before them. It was soon obvious to European military observers that the firepower of the German Infantry Divisions far exceeded that of the Allies'. The speed and mobility of the German army had no equal in Europe.

In the air, the Luftwaffe quickly showed they were also superior. The Allies possessed more planes, but many were virtually obsolete. The only promising development during the latter part of 1939 was the erection of an additional fifteen RADAR stations across Britain. This was a great accomplishment given that the technology had only been invented late in 1938. Unbeknown to the Luftwaffe, Britain soon had a chain of RADAR stations in operation that could detect the number, position, altitude and speed of any approaching enemy aircraft. The German Airforce was at a loss to understand how it was that the British seemed to be able to anticipate their every movement.

In October, the USSR marched into Estonia, Latvia and Lithuania and started to garrison troops there. The Baltic countries offered little resistance. Finland, however, courageously resisted and repulsed the Soviet troops for months before finally collapsing in March 1940.

No less than 110 merchant vessels conveying food and

supplies to and from Britain were sunk by German U-boats between September 1939 and January 1940 with a shocking loss of life.

Throughout the entire period of September 1939 through to March 1940, events in Europe were becoming increasingly alarming for the Allies. Hitler appeared unstoppable and it seemed only a matter of time before he conquered, or occupied, the remainder of Europe and began the final invasion of Britain to establish his dream of total European dominance by the Aryan race.

In Africa, however, the war remained but a distant horror and the peace held. By March 1940 the KAR were at full strength with over 21,000 troops in place and ready for action. Thomas remained reasonably confident his superior armed forces could now resist a full-blown attack by the Italians even though the KAR was seriously outnumbered. The colonel had dedicated himself to his men and his responsibilities and had worked tirelessly to prepare for war.

* * *

Eve and Freddy continued to fret about how best to broach the subject of Eve's pregnancy with Thomas. When would be the best time? Should they both be present? How would Thomas react? Would Thomas perhaps be interested in adopting the child? To what extent might Freddy's career be impacted? Was there any chance of a divorce that might lead to Eve and Freddy parenting the newborn or even marrying?

At half term (mid-February) Eve had insisted on travelling down to Nairobi to see Michael at his new premises and taking him out for a couple of days to stay with her in a small hotel. The journey down to Nairobi had barely improved and she had found it horribly uncomfortable bouncing about in the truck like a cork in the water. She was certainly not going to mention the baby to Michael or disclose her other reason for coming to Nairobi, which was to visit a doctor. Thomas, as usual, was too busy to escort her, but seemed pleased she was making the effort to go and see Michael and gave her his blessing. He had arranged accommodation for her at Greystones, a small hotel close to Michael's school, where the truck dropped her off with her overnight bag late on Thursday evening. Eve was permitted to pick Michael up from his school at five o'clock the following day which gave her the remainder of Friday to find a doctor.

Mrs Brooks, who ran the hotel, was a kindly soul who had lived in Nairobi for many years. She was able to recommend two or three doctors to Eve and assisted her to arrange an urgent appointment. Early in the afternoon, Eve was comfortably thumbing through copies of *Punch* in the doctor's waiting room. Understandably, she was apprehensive, since this was the first time she had consulted a medical practitioner since the baby had been conceived, and the doctor was bound to be surprised by this failure to seek medical advice until so late. Eve was also in two minds about whether or not to admit that the baby was the result of an extra-marital affair or to try to pretend it was actually her husband's.

'Mrs Dillon?'

Chapter Thirty-One September 1939 — March 1940

Eve rose quickly, leaving her edition of *Punch* on her chair and followed the doctor into his surgery.

'How do you do, Mrs Dillon. My name is Doctor McHenry. Please take a seat.' The doctor held out a flabby, wet hand as his part of a handshake.

Eve studied this new doctor closely. Already, from his accent, she knew him to be Scottish but she liked the look of his face that oozed kindness and empathy. Instinctively, Eve felt she could trust this man. In five minutes, she had explained her awkward situation whilst the doctor listened and simply asked a couple of questions. Next, Doctor McHenry conducted a careful examination before announcing that, in his view, she was progressing well and that she could expect a baby late June or early July.

'Now Mrs Dillon, we should consider your health and the baby's health as we get close to the time for the birth. I don't imagine there is anyone who can assist you in little Marsabit?'

'Correct, doctor. My husband does not know about the baby yet and will be absolutely furious when I tell him. He may well insist on me leaving him altogether, in which case I'll need to come to Nairobi to give birth. Is it possible for me to have the baby here?'

'Of course, my dear. However, there is an added complication.'

'What's that doctor?'

'There is a war on! The best treatment you can possibly get is still back in the old country. If you have any complications, England is definitely the place to be. We can do a lot here, but are somewhat limited with our facilities and medical staff.'

'I see...'

'I'm not sure you do, my dear. According to my reckoning, you are five months into your pregnancy already. The longer you leave it, the more difficult it will be for you to travel. My advice is that you scamper back to England as soon as you can. That way you will be back in the UK if anything should go wrong. The longer you leave it, the more intense the war will become and then you could be putting your life and the baby in danger by trying to fly back into London. Flights to Gatwick are already being delayed or cancelled at short notice. Tell your husband about the baby and then fly home as soon as possible.'

Eve could see the logic in what Doctor McHenry was advocating. She thanked him gratefully, settled the bill and departed.

* * *

Shortly before four-thirty, Eve climbed into a rickety taxi with rusting paintwork and windows that wouldn't open and close properly. Her native driver was a cheerful soul with a cigarette that appeared to be permanently attached to his lip. He knew the way, however, and shortly before five fetched up at the main door of Michael's re-located school where Michael and a friend were waiting hugging their small suitcases. Eve was not aware until then that she was also taking out Michael's mate, Rodney, who, it transpired, now played as scrum-half in the first XV.

Bringing a friend with him turned out to be a smart move by Michael because the two twelve-year old lads kept each

Chapter Thirty-One September 1939 — March 1940

other entertained throughout the weekend. The weather was kind and there was a small but perfectly adequate swimming pool behind the hotel. The boys feasted on non-stop meals and snacks all day and well into the night which allowed Eve to do some serious thinking. By the time she had to return Michael and Rodney to Kenton College, her mind was made up. She and Michael would fly back to England as soon as a flight could be arranged and she would put Michael into a boarding school in England whilst she had the baby. If she was clever about it, Michael need never know she was expecting. She could explain their sudden departure to England as being necessary because of the war which was, she knew, at least partly true. Hopefully, she could persuade Thomas that this was the best plan and he would agree to pay for Michael's schooling in England and for somewhere for her to live.

When Eve put her mind to something, she could be decisive and proactive. She asked the taxi man to wait while she went in to speak with the headmaster. He was a little surprised that Michael would be leaving in the next week or two but admitted that a couple of his other pupils had already been whisked off to England by concerned parents. Eve swore Michael to secrecy, convincing him that the rugger back in England was far superior to what he was used to in Nairobi, and that sealed it for the budding rugby player. Satisfied that at least some things were being resolved, Eve bumped and groaned her way back to Marsabit.

* * *

On her return, Eve walked straight down to see Freddy in his small transport office and was relieved to find him sitting there writing up notes. Eve wanted to brief him about all that had happened in Nairobi and to explain her and Michael's imminent departure for England.

During the last few months, their feelings for each other had steadily intensified. Although they had not discussed it in so many words, both were thinking of a new life together once the war was over. Freddy could see the sense in what Eve was planning and he strongly supported her decision. He certainly didn't want to see Eve and Michael leave Marsabit, however, he would feel happier knowing she would have access to the top gynaecologists in London should this be necessary. As the officer in charge of transport, it was more than likely that he would be entrusted with the task of booking Eve and Michael's flights. Eve insisted she wanted to leave as soon as possible but one major barrier remained: Thomas had to be told everything!

That evening Eve did what she could to put Thomas in a reasonable mood. Mary had cooked a meal he particularly enjoyed, fish curry and rice, followed by stewed rhubarb from their own garden served with vanilla custard. As she looked at her husband, Eve felt a twinge of guilt that she was deserting him in his hour of need. He looked dog-tired and ready for a long relaxing holiday.

As was their custom, they moved to the lounge after the meal to have coffee and a few chocolates. Once they were settled and Tomasi had closed the door softly behind him, Eve

Chapter Thirty-One September 1939 — March 1940

took a deep breath and began what was perhaps to be the most difficult conversation of her life.

'Thomas, dear, I have an important matter to discuss with you.' Eve was sitting nervously on the edge of her chair and there was an element of tension in her voice.

Thomas looked over his coffee cup at his wife, 'Oh, and what's that, dear?'

He was constantly amazed at what a striking woman his wife was. She was looking at him now, intently, with those gorgeous eyes. After thirteen years of marriage, she still looked as beautiful as when he had first met her back in little Preston town.

'Thomas, I'm expecting.'

'Expecting? But you can't be? We haven't...'

'I'm terribly sorry, Thomas. It's not yours.'

There was a long silence as the shock of this disclosure began to sink in to Thomas's confused brain.

'Are you telling me, Eve, that you are having a child with another man?'

'Yes, Thomas, I am.' Eve could no longer look Thomas in the eye. She lowered her head and watched her fingers winding and unwinding in her lap.

'Good God woman! That's adultery! Adultery a second time!'

Eve couldn't see how she could usefully respond to Thomas's accurate accusation, so she said nothing and continued to sit with her head down intertwining her fingers.

Thomas's brain was leaping in several different directions all at once as he tried desperately to process this news and what the implications might be. Finally, he spoke.

'Who was it, Eve?'

'It was Freddy Drummond. I think we are in love.'

'Bah, you don't even know the meaning of the word!' he spat out. Unable to remain seated, he rose, and strode over to the large bay window and looked out over the darkening sky with hands clenched behind his back. The sky matched his mood.

'Have you checked you're pregnant?'

'Yes, I saw a doctor when I went to Nairobi for the weekend.'

'And when's it due?'

'End of June or first week of July.'

'Are you sure? There's nothing showing?'

'It's showing, it's just that you haven't noticed, Thomas.'

Thomas didn't reply. He was still standing with his back to Eve and occasionally shaking his head. Then he turned sharply, and for the first time in her life, Eve heard her husband swear.

'What a bloody mess! What a bloody, stupid mess!'

'Thomas, there's no going back now. I've spoken to the doctor and he has strongly advised me to return to England as soon as possible and to take Michael with me.'

'Aah, so you're both going to desert me now, are you?'

'Yes, Thomas. It's for everyone's good. Nobody will need to know this is not your child and I can have the baby far more safely in England. The facilities here in Nairobi are nowhere near so good as London's.'

'You're right. This is *not* my child! Furthermore, I want nothing to do with this child! Am I making myself clear, Eve? Go to England and have the child adopted. I don't care how you do it, that's up to you! You might as well stay there as well,

Chapter Thirty-One   September 1939 — March 1940

Eve. This is a hollow pretence of a marriage we have, but, as you know, I will never condone a divorce. The Roman Catholic Church will never agree to divorce. Like it or not, you will never be released from being my wife in the eyes of God.'

'You have made it quite clear where I stand, Thomas. I'll ask Freddy to book flights for Michael and me as soon as possible.'

Without another word, Eve left the room and ran back down to Freddy's office where she cried and vented to her partner for more than an hour.

CHAPTER THIRTY-TWO

Picking up the Pieces

Horrific scenes, such as the one that Eve and Thomas endured that night, often have unexpected ramifications. These began to emerge the next morning. Thomas had an almost sleepless night as he went over and over the conversation he had had with Eve. Immediately after breakfast he stormed off down to the office of his specially selected transport officer and confronted Freddy full on.

'Captain Drummond, I'm fully aware of your behaviour with my wife and the result of your liaisons. Today will be your last day as officer in charge of transport. Before you leave this position, you are to complete two tasks: the first is to prepare a handover document for your successor and the second is to book Eve and Michael onto the first flight to London that's available. I'm posting you back to Moyale with immediate effect under the command of Major Reynolds. You are to leave Marsabit tomorrow morning. Any questions?'

'No sir.' Freddy saluted smartly as the colonel left, slamming the door behind him.

So, Freddy's time sharing this little piece of paradise with Eve was at an end. He knew exactly what he must do next. He spent the day completing the two tasks Colonel Dillon had assigned to him, then waited in his office for Eve to come to see him for the very last time after work.

Eve arrived promptly at seventeen hundred hours in a distressed state. They held each other for a moment or two without speaking, just relieved to feel loving arms about them. Then Eve sat down and took out her handkerchief to wipe away her tears.

'Oh, Freddy, last night was just awful. I told Thomas everything and he was absolutely furious. I have never before seen him lose his cool, he even swore for the first time ever. He hasn't spoken to me at all today. He's sent me to Coventry.'

'I'm so sorry, Eve. It's a horrible situation to be in.'

'At least he agreed that Michael and I should leave for London as soon as a flight is available.'

'I know, your husband came to see me first thing this morning.'

'Oh God! What did he say to you Freddy?'

Chapter Thirty-Two Picking up the Pieces

'He's dismissed me from being the Battalion's transport officer and tomorrow morning I must return to Moyale.'

'Oh Freddy, how awful.' Eve stood and took Freddy in her arms. 'I'm so, so sorry,' she murmured softly into his ear. Freddy kissed her.

'But Eve we have to look at all this positively. Think about it. You'll be much better off having our baby in England and you have family there too. Michael can go to a top boarding school and get the best rugby he's ever had.'

'Yes, I know all that's good but what about us? When will we ever be together again?'

Freddy took Eve in his arms again. 'Eve, when this wretched war is over, I'll return to England and, if you would like it, we can live together as if we were husband and wife. Together we can raise our child.'

'Oh, Freddy, I so want to be with you, but Thomas will never allow me to divorce him so we will never be able to marry legally.'

'To be perfectly honest Eve, it doesn't worry me whether or not we are legally married. I want to live with you and be the father of our child.' Freddy hesitated, took hold of Eve's hands and continued. 'I guess this is as close as I'll ever get to proposing to you Eve. Will you live with me when I get back after the war?'

'Yes, yes, Freddy, I'd love to. If we go somewhere new, perhaps we could even pretend that we are man and wife?'

'Maybe so. I feel as though I should be placing a ring on your finger, Eve, but I haven't had any leave to get to Nairobi. I promise I'll buy you a beautiful ring when we're together again in England.'

Eve kissed him.

'I do have something for *you* though Freddy. I bought it last weekend when I was in Nairobi.' She opened her petite handbag and removed a small ultramarine leather box with gold rimming. 'With all my love and my dearest wishes for a life together in England after the war.'

Freddy had not expected a gift, but was delighted with what he discovered in the neat box: a pair of KAR cufflinks.

'Apparently they have only just come onto the market. Now that there are so many British officers and NCOs serving in the KAR some enterprising jeweller saw the potential. Do you like them?'

'They are great. Thank you, Eve. I will treasure them. When next you see me in England, I will make sure I am proudly wearing them.'

They embraced again.

'Eve, does Michael know we are having a baby?'

'Of course not.'

'Should we tell him? You can't hide it much longer?'

'I've been thinking about that Freddy. If he notices anything, he will assume he's going to have a baby brother or sister. It would never occur to him that *you* are the father and I don't think he is mature enough to be told about you and me having an affair. He's finding it difficult enough being moved to another school again. I certainly don't want to complicate his life any further by explaining that it's not his father's baby.

Chapter Thirty-Two   Picking up the Pieces

Michael is extremely fond of Thomas, you know, and he'd be very upset.'

'Well, Michael's fond of me too,' added Freddy.

'Yes, I know, after all your brilliant rugby training, he's got quite a crush on you!'

'He's going to have to find out sometime. You might be able to delay telling him for a bit longer but in a few weeks' time it will be so obvious you will have to break the news.'

'No, I've got a plan. We will be back home in a week or two just in time for the start of the new school term. That means Michael will be away boarding for almost all of April, May and June. When the school holidays start at the end of June, when I'm due, I'll arrange for him to go and stay for the summer holidays with my parents up in Preston. They have really missed him and would be thrilled to have him come and stay. I'll have the baby quietly without Michael even knowing.'

'What then?'

'Well, I guess I will have to tell him sometime after the birth, but he will be a few months older by then and hopefully happily settled into his new school. There's a much better chance that he could cope with this dramatic news in July rather than now. What do you think?'

'You may well be right. Which school will he be going to?'

'Chertsey. Thomas has told me in the past that when we return to England, he wants to enrol Michael at Chertsey. It's where Thomas went.'

'Umm, so Thomas can't complain about that!'

'True. Now have you been able to book our flights yet Freddy?'

'Yes, I have. It's going to be quite an adventure for you and Michael.'

Eve looked dubiously at her lover wondering what to expect. She was not disappointed.

'You are leaving next Sunday on a Short Empire S.30 medium range four engine monoplane flying boat.'

'Did you say, flying boat?'

'I did.'

'You're kidding me?'

'No, I'm not. The plane takes off from Lake Victoria at 0900 hours. I've arranged for you and Michael to travel there separately the day before and to stay the night at the flying boat terminal. Because the flying boat will be travelling all the way to England and will ditch just off the Isle of Wight, the Empire will be set up with sleeping bunks for a maximum of sixteen sleeping passengers. You can take a heap of luggage with you which will be roped down on the top deck. Passengers always stay on the lower deck.'

'How exciting. Do we fly direct to England?'

'Afraid not. The S.30 has to do hops so it can refuel. So, you will hit the water first at Alexandria in Egypt. The flying boat has a maximum range of about 2,300 miles which is why it can't be a non-stop flight.'

'Wow, Michael will just love this!'

'Imperial Airlines has been operating these flying boats at least once a week for a couple of years now. Your flying boat will have started its journey in Cape Town.'

'So, I had better get packing?'

Chapter Thirty-Two Picking up the Pieces

'Yes, ring Michael's headmaster tonight. Here are the details about where Michael has to go to catch the bus to Lake Victoria.' Freddy passed over an envelope.

'Oh gosh, I can't believe this is all happening so fast.'

'Everything is paid for. Your husband has authorised it today. Michael's tickets and yours will be taken to the terminal by the Nairobi Bus Service that Michael and most of the other passengers will be on. You will need to collect the tickets once you arrive at the reception desk at the Lake Victoria Terminal.'

'What's the road like out to Lake Victoria?'

'Surprisingly good. It's actually better than the road to Nairobi. Again, everything is organised. Johnno will drive you there. I wish it could be me.'

'Oh, Freddy, I feel so uncertain about the future. I wish you were coming with me.'

Again, they hugged and kissed passionately, reluctant to stop, for both knew this was the last time they would see each other until after the war. Finally, with tears falling freely down her cheeks, Eve released her hold and left the room. She sobbed the short way back to the bungalow where she stopped to recover her poise and blow her nose before going in to check with Mary about the evening's meal.

* * *

Everything moved at break-neck speed. The headmaster promised to have Michael packed and safely delivered to the assembly point for the Lake Victoria Terminal bus well on time on Saturday.

Freddy departed in the early hours of the morning for Moyale. Arriving there safely that evening, he reported to his commanding officer, Major Reynolds, who immediately appointed him to be his second-in-command.

Quietly, Eve spoke to the three faithful servants who had served them so loyally and handed each a handsome bonus. She made no mention of the baby, telling them that for safety reasons, the colonel believed it best if she and Michael returned to England. Mary and Tomasi saw through her story, but were professional enough to say nothing untoward, graciously and humbly accepting their bonuses.

With Mary's help, Eve washed, ironed and packed three large suitcases full of her and Michael's belongings hoping fervently that Freddy was right about carrying so much luggage on the flying boat.

Eve and Thomas barely spoke for the remainder of the week. On Eve's last night in Marsabit he put on a small farewell cocktail party for Eve and invited six of his officers, Major Williamson and Janet. There he made a well-deserved announcement. As from the first of April he had been promoted to the rank of a full colonel.

On Saturday morning, Eve climbed into the staff jeep, with Johnno at the wheel, and left Marsabit for the last time. Thomas didn't come out to wave her off.

* * *

Chapter Thirty-Two Picking up the Pieces

Eve's transport and Michael's bus-load of passengers arrived at the flying boat terminal almost simultaneously. It was already dark, so they were unable to see their flying boat moored approximately half a mile from the terminal. They had an enjoyable meal with their fellow passengers and the crew and retired early so they could be ready for a pre-dawn breakfast with departure shortly after first light.

Michael loved every moment of the flight. Despite the roar of the engines, he somehow managed to chat individually with all five crew members — the pilot, co-pilot, navigator, flight clerk and cabin steward — and pestered them with endless questions about their responsibilities. After he had been allowed in the cockpit a second time, he told his mother he might change his mind about becoming an army officer and study to be a flying boat pilot instead.

The plane was horribly noisy and rumbled and shook its way monotonously across the deserts of the Sudan and Egypt en route for the Mediterranean Sea where it splashed down just off Alexandria. With a cruising speed of only about 160 miles per hour this first stage took almost thirteen hours and it was dark by the time they were down safely on the water.

They dined in Alexandria that evening before re-boarding with a new crew, and took off in the dark bound for the Isle of Wight on England's south coast. It was another thirteen-hour trip and they were more than thankful they could sleep most of the way on the bunks provided. The captain made a surprise announcement just after take-off: this was to be the last Short Empire flight out of Africa until the cessation of hostilities.

Apparently, it was considered too dangerous to continue the service. The passengers congratulated each other on their good fortune, but then began to ponder how the loved ones they had left behind would be able to return to the United Kingdom.

Eve spent much of her waking time during the flight thinking about her situation. Thomas, clearly, was in no mood to forgive her a second time. He had agreed to continue paying Michael's private school fees, provided he attended Chertsey, and to pay her a retainer sufficient for her to rent a small flat in London or elsewhere. Their relationship was definitely over this time and there would be no going back. Naturally, Thomas wanted free access to his son at all times, although it was hard to see how this was going to happen in practice with the war on and Thomas based in Kenya as the commanding officer of the KAR's 1st Battalion.

Michael, she noticed, was still filled with excitement about this flying boat experience but Eve anticipated he would come down with a crash once they arrived in England and he had to face starting afresh at yet another boarding school. She realised she must give him all the love and attention she could muster in the few short days before term began. Michael loved his father dearly and was soon going to miss him. It could be months before Thomas was granted leave to return to England, so she would have to do her best to stand in for Thomas.

Her pregnancy was going well so far, but it was important she quickly find somewhere suitable to live and get registered with a family doctor she liked and trusted. She was carrying Freddy's and her special hopes for the future; she must do

Chapter Thirty-Two   Picking up the Pieces

everything in her power to make it work. Eve wondered how long this war would last? The Great War of 1914-1918 had dragged on for four terrible years with shocking loss of life. Surely this war wouldn't last that long and Freddy could come back to her soon? She was missing him dreadfully already.

It was a glorious spring day on the Solent as their Short Empire banked slowly and straightened up ready for a gentle splashdown on calm waters a couple of miles out of Southampton. After living in Marsabit for two years it would be interesting to see how things had changed in England.

After coming ashore with more than their fair share of luggage, they passed through passport control and customs and headed for the Southampton Railway Station to purchase tickets for Victoria Station. On arrival in London, Eve booked them into a small hotel where she planned to stay until it was time to take Michael to Chertsey. They had three days to kill and she wanted to spoil Michael with some of the exciting things that London offered. The first morning, however, had to be spent at Horne Brothers Boys and Men's Outfitters having Michael kitted out with his new school uniform and sports gear and then finding a seamstress who could sew 'Michael Dillon' nametags on every new item of clothing.

No buildings in London were damaged, but the place was not its usual vibrant self. Shops were still open but the large display windows were boarded up because of the curfew, thereby making the world-famous shopping streets look sadly drab. The pavements were full of people moving about purposely, with many now dressed in a wide variety of uniforms. Happy, excited faces of tourists and shoppers had been replaced by sterner more worried ones. The manager at their hotel warned them to be back before the curfew or they would be locked out. This was no longer the carefree party-filled capital Eve remembered. Despite the restrictions, they managed two wonderful days of fun; one at the London Zoo and the other at Madame Tussauds.

On the fourth day, Eve delivered Michael safely to his new school, Chertsey Boys College, in Surrey, some 31 miles south-west of London. Founded by the Salesian Roman Catholic Brothers, the school had established a fine reputation, which was why Thomas had insisted that Michael go there and follow in his father's footsteps. Eve liked the school motto, *'Enlightening Minds, Uplifting Hearts.'*

The headmaster, Father James, liked to meet the parents of the new boys and they had ten minutes alone with him. He seemed to take a liking to Michael and assured him they could use an excellent new fly-half in the under 13 team if he was good enough. Eve was surprised to hear that the whole school might soon have to be moved even further out of London to a temporary site deeper in the country where it would be safer. The headmaster explained that negotiations were at a delicate stage and he couldn't yet disclose just where this new location would be.

With Michael safely enrolled at Chertsey, Eve set about finding a small flat near a maternity hospital where she could complete her final three and a half months of confinement and prepare for the new arrival. She found what she was after in

Camberley, located only a mile from a hospital with a maternity wing, and was soon registered with a youngish family doctor who appeared to be knowledgeable about the latest thinking on childbirth. Camberley was where the Royal Military College, Sandhurst was located, a familiar area for Thomas, should he ever visit, since he had completed his officer's training at Sandhurst.

One evening Eve spoke at length to her mother in Preston and explained her whole predicament. Her mother took the news well and offered to come to Camberley to be with her when she came out of hospital and also promised that her husband George could take Michael for the long summer holidays if Eve still needed her in London.

Eve enjoyed an uncomplicated pregnancy. Thomas was paying all the bills and she had just enough money to get by. She made a few friends in the neighbourhood and spent much of her time reading or writing letters. Frequently she wrote to Michael. Chertsey School insisted that its boarders write a letter home every week, much to Eve's delight. Michael's letters varied according to his mood, but overall, she had the impression he had settled in well. He had made friends and was happy, and was doing well at athletics and cricket, the sports played during summer. Michael's one complaint was that the school was overly religious, with compulsory chapel every day and an extra-long mass on Sundays, feast days and saints' days as well. Michael moaned about how many saints there were!

Eve and Thomas exchanged letters a couple of times: Thomas wrote about business matters only, never anything personal. Eve sensed his anger in his letters and knew this time there was no chance of reconciliation, even if she had wanted it.

Eve received the greatest joy and comfort from corresponding with Freddy. They wrote love letters to each other like so many thousands of other couples separated by the horrors of war. Freddy was making the best of his transfer back to Moyale and was working well with his commanding officer, Major Reynolds, who had hinted that he would be prepared to put Freddy's name forward for promotion to Major at the end of the year. Freddy, understandably, given his association with Eve, wondered whether Colonel Dillon would ever be supportive of such a move. In her letters Eve described life in Camberley, plans for the baby and relayed the weekly news from Michael. Freddy spoke at length about what they might do when the war ended and he could finally come home. In the meantime, he had requested a month's leave over Christmas and, if granted, he planned to fly back to England.

CHAPTER THIRTY-THREE

War Intensifies

Now that Eve was back in England, she was able to keep abreast of what was happening in the war more easily than when living in Marsabit, although the British Government did its best to colour the reporting by their war correspondents to suit its own propaganda purposes.

Eve had barely moved into her flat in Camberley, and come to grips with the limitations of ration books that had been issued to everyone in Britain earlier in the year, when disturbing news of events in Europe started to be broadcast on the BBC News Service and appear in the daily newspapers.

In April, 1940 Germany invaded Denmark and Norway. Little Denmark surrendered immediately, but the Norwegians were made of sterner stuff, and fought back bravely with the aid of the British and French.

May 10th saw the replacement of the indecisive Prime Minister, Neville Chamberlain, with Winston Churchill, which was a popular move welcomed by most people. The very same day, Germany invaded France, Belgium and Holland in what became known as the 'Blitzkrieg' or 'lightning war'. Fast divisions of well-rehearsed Panzer tanks charged across the countryside destroying all before them while the planes of the Luftwaffe bombed and strafed the hastily retreating troops and panicked civilians. The Low Countries were no match for the combined might of the Wehrmacht and Luftwaffe, and by the end of May, Belgium and Holland both waved the white flag. It was like a row of dominoes as, one after another, the countries of western Europe capitulated.

The rapid advance of the German forces entrapped the remnants of the Belgian Army, the huge British Expeditionary Force and three French Field Armies in the north of France. In a desperate bid to rescue these men, Churchill ordered *'Operation Dynamo'* whereby some fifty destroyers and around 800 small craft of all kinds sailed to Dunkirk, a port in the North of France, to evacuate the troops. In the space of eight days between May 26th and June 4th no less than 338,000 men were successfully brought back to English shores to fight another day. Eve, along with her neighbours, was thrilled to learn of this daring retreat, only to hear Churchill's sobering comment afterwards on the

BBC, '...we must be very careful not to assign to this deliverance, the attributes of a victory. Wars are not won by evacuations.'

By early June, Eve was getting large and she wondered how she was going to last until the end of the month. The doctor, however, was unconcerned and assured her everything was progressing well. Eve had everything in readiness for the new arrival in her small flat and had arranged to give birth to the baby in the maternity ward of the nearby hospital. She had told Freddy she felt she was going to have another rugby boy, as this was a lively, active baby, that insisted on giving her violent kicks in the middle of the night.

With the war escalating in Europe, there was virtually no news reporting in Britain of what was happening far away in North East Africa. Essentially, according to the regular and very welcome letters Eve continued to receive from Freddy, Africa remained a waiting game. An estimated force of a quarter of a million Italian troops amassed along Kenya's northern border continued to be opposed by a far smaller British force of some 22,000 men. Freddy was still confident that if Italy decided to enter the war and invade Kenya, the British trained army could successfully repel them. The British were well dug in, heavily armed, fit and trained for action. Colonel Dillon continued to insist on the highest standards and was respected by his men for tough, but fair, treatment.

Eve was so proud of Freddy and read his letters over and over again. They continued to arrive regularly at least once a week and were full of humorous stories about life on the frontline, making light of the privations he endured and so, so romantic. Eve would take his letters to bed with her and read them out loud to the unborn baby. Sometimes she was sure the baby responded with a kick or a little nudge. Eve had no difficulty writing loving letters back full of amorous intentions and plans for their future together after the war.

June 10th marked a further serious deterioration on two war fronts. Paris surrendered and the French signed an armistice that permitted the establishment of the Vichy Government under the control of Marshall Petain whereby the unoccupied south and east of France remained nominally French while Germany controlled the remainder of the country. In essence, Marshall Petain was no more than a puppet of the Nazi regime. General Charles de Gaulle, as leader of the Free French, escaped to England to lead the French resistance.

The surrender of France on June 10th was the trigger for the Italian Prime Minister and dictator, Benito Mussolini, to enter the war. Anxious to share in the spoils of war, he could delay no longer, and the same day declared war on Great Britain and what remained of France and the French colonies. Mussolini had left it too late, however; Hitler had already conquered West Europe and viewed Mussolini very much as the junior partner of the Axis Alliance.

Mussolini, determined to be noticed, quickly persuaded King Emanuele III, Commander-in-chief of the Royal Italian Army, to permit him to start hostilities in North Africa. Italy had already colonised Libya (1934) and what was known as Italian East Africa (1936) and Mussolini wished to expand Italy's area of influence by attacking the British in Egypt, Kenya and

Chapter Thirty-Three War Intensifies

Sudan. Permission received, Mussolini ordered the Duke of Aosta, the commander of some 290,000 men across the Italian Army, Navy and Airforce to attack British positions.

On June 13th hostilities commenced with the Italian Airforce attacking the base of 237 Rhodesia Squadron of the Royal Airforce at Wajir, a small town in northern Kenya. Damage was minimal, but news of the attack spread quickly. Colonel Dillon immediately placed his troops on the highest alert level, anticipating further incursions at any moment.

Concerned about Freddy, Eve kept an ever-watchful eye on the newspapers and always listened to the BBC news broadcasts. The most comprehensive newspaper coverage of the war was inevitably in The Times so she made sure she had access to their daily publications and read them carefully. The Italian attack on the RAF Base at Wajir merited a brief mention in the paper because it was the first aggressive move by the Italians since entering the war. Eve didn't miss it!

About the same time as Eve read of the initial Italian attack on Wajir, she received two letters on the same day from Kenya, one from her husband and the other from Freddy. After reading both letters Eve reflected that it would be difficult to imagine receiving two letters so wildly contrasting in tone and warmth. Thomas's letter read more like an army directive, cold and dispassionate and was scribbled out hurriedly on a piece of official KAR letterhead paper.

Marsabit – June 10th, 1940.
Eve,

> *I have today sent a cheque for Michael's school fees for next term.*
>
> *Michael's end of term report should arrive in your letterbox shortly. Kindly ensure you forward the report onto me without delay. I am most anxious to see how well the boy has fared after his first term at Chertsey.*
>
> *I believe your illegitimate baby is due to be born very soon. I wish to reiterate that I want nothing to do with this child. I do not wish to see the child, or support the child financially or in any other way. Given the circumstances, you should take the necessary steps now to have the child adopted.*
>
> *I hope I have made myself clear.*
>
> *Your husband.*

Short, succinct and unfriendly. With a sigh of relief, Eve returned to Freddy's most recent letter, five pages long, newsy and full of loving thoughts and endearments. She re-read it carefully. It was dated June 9th, the day before Mussolini had declared war on Great Britain. Several times Freddy had mentioned in his previous letters that should the Italians decide to conduct a land invasion, as opposed to an aerial attack, it was highly likely they would advance on Moyale where Freddy was based. Eve was not convinced of the value of prayer, but if she was, she knew she would be praying for Freddy now.

Throughout June, the British and French intelligence were consistently reporting Hitler's plans and preparations for the invasion of Britain. The Luftwaffe had received orders to destroy British air power and coastal defences in readiness for the movement of troops into the country. Everyone was on edge. The final showdown was imminent but no date appeared to have been set. It was a deeply worrying time for Eve with the baby due anytime and her concerns increasing for Freddy back in Kenya.

Michael's school broke up on July 2nd and he travelled by train directly to Preston the same day to spend the long summer holidays with his grandparents. Arrangements had now been made for Michael to spend half of his holidays with his other grandparents, the Dillons of Bolton, in Lancashire. On July 4th Eve rang her mother to say she had been told to report to the maternity hospital the next day and could she please come to Camberley urgently.

Eve delivered a beautiful healthy boy in the early hours of the morning of July 7th. She and Freddy had discussed possible names for either a boy or a girl, so this new bundle of joy was simply named, David Dillon, with no other names. There were no complications and Eve immediately bonded with her little one. How she wished Freddy was there to share her happiness. Now, they had something precious to love and care for, which would enrich their future lives together. That evening, Eve wrote a short letter to Freddy informing him he was the proud father of a little boy and Eve's mother posted the letter next morning.

CHAPTER THIRTY-FOUR

Life at Moyale

Mussolini's eventual declaration of war on June 10th 1940 was actually welcomed with a sense of relief by the men of the Kings African Rifles stationed in outposts across Northern Kenya. They had trained so hard for many months in readiness for an Italian invasion and at last, it seemed, they might see some real live action!

Freddy had settled back easily into camp life at Moyale and was popular with his men. He had just finished writing another letter to Eve and had asked his batman to deliver the letter to the sergeant responsible for transporting mail to and from Nairobi. With any luck the letter should reach Eve around June 20th before the baby was due. Freddy lounged back on his chair and surveyed the familiar scene before him.

The rough scrub and 'wait-a-minute' thorn trees had been cleared many months ago for the erection of the long lines of new grass-thatched huts, each line with an extension tacked on the end being the African sergeant's quarters. On the edge of the dusty rammed earth parade ground stood the company offices with a flagpole in front. Set apart, and a little distance away from the askaris huts, were the British officers' 160-pound army flysheet tents pitched in a circle that was completed by a large open mess tent. In the centre of the circle, a log fire burned from sunset to sunrise to scare off the lions, hyaenas and jackals that prowled around menacingly during the night time hours.

Freddy pulled out his revolver, a point 38 Smith and Wesson. Only that morning, when walking around the campsite inspecting gear, he had encountered a Puff Adder, a viper found all over the African continent whose venom is a severe nerve poison. Startled by the snake, Freddy had instinctively drawn his revolver and blasted the unfortunate creature. Now, the revolver needed cleaning, a task he entrusted to nobody, not even his batman.

In his tent Freddy had amassed quite a bundle of letters from Eve, who, he had discovered, was an excellent correspondent. The letters were held together by a couple of large rubber bands. Freddy often wondered when he would finally be granted leave to return to England to be with Eve

Chapter Thirty-Four   Life at Moyale

and their baby. He suspected Colonel Dillon was still sitting on his leave application as a way of teaching him a lesson. As soon as he heard from Eve that the baby had been born, he would put in yet another leave application arguing that he was now a new father and, therefore, deserved to be considered for special leave.

Strict discipline was enforced at Moyale and the other KAR outposts and the soldiers knew all too well the penalties for failing to measure up. The very next morning, Freddy was carrying out a routine dawn inspection and was horrified to discover a sentry asleep at his post. Private Suhani was so dead to the world that he didn't even hear Freddy stop his vehicle, jump out, pick up his rifle and throw it in the back of the truck. Freddy then woke the unfortunate man and placed him under arrest. Later that morning Major Richardson held company 'Orders' at which defaulters were brought before him. Private Suhani was marched in under escort by Company Sergeant Major (CSM) Mulita and the charge read out. The company commander announced the punishment: twelve lashes of the kiboko, the rhino hide whip used throughout the KAR in cases of serious crime.

At noon, three platoons were marched on to the parade ground by their platoon sergeants to form three sides of a square. The platoon commanders then marched on and took up positions in a row five paces behind the company commander so that the officers completed the square. A heavy silence fell. The Union Flag hung limp from the flagpole; the regimental flag from a staff. A small dust devil formed and went twisting and swirling across the parade ground. CSM Mulita marched on, five paces ahead of two askaris carrying a triangular wooden frame with wrist and ankle straps hanging from it. The kiboko in his left hand, he barked out an order, and the escort marched forward with the prisoner already stripped to the waist.

Private Suhani was ordered to lie across a bulky grass-filled sack and the straps were fastened. The kiboko was passed to the corporal detailed to administer the flogging. Suhani's escort swiftly removed his trousers and laid a leather apron across his back to protect his vital organs. Major Richardson then read out the charge and the sentence.

In accordance with KAR custom, the CSM loudly called out each stroke in Arabic. The first lash sounded like a sharp pistol shot. Then a second, a third, a fourth, a long breath-catching pause between each one. All 120 men on parade, Britons and Africans, stared with fascination as Suhani's bottom broke into a mass of dark red, criss-crossing weals; it was as if all present were suffering with him and willing him to bear it. With each stroke he flinched but uttered no sound.

At last, the twelfth had fallen. In a moment the straps were unfastened and Suhani was on his feet. Again, in accordance with custom, he turned towards Major Richardson and gave a smart salute before being escorted off the parade ground by two medical dressers with their first aid panniers.

That evening, Freddy went to the lines to see that Private Suhani was as comfortable as possible and excused him from duty for two days. His stoic acceptance of the ordeal and his courage had won the admiration and sympathy of the company. Had the company at Moyale been actively engaged in war at the time, and a sentry fell asleep at his post, the penalty would have been death by firing squad!

10.11. KAR Askaris commanded by 'Freddy' in Kenya. (Photo donated by Army Personnel Centre)

The company at Moyale numbered 150. This comprised three full platoons, each with about 35 men, plus drivers, signallers, cooks, medical orderlies and staff assigned to the company's headquarters. Major Richardson always made sure his men were kept abreast of events likely to affect them, so they were fully cognisant of Mussolini's declaration of war on June 10th and the attack by the Italian air force on the squadron based at Wajir on June 13th.

With the company now on full battle footing, and expecting Italian incursions at any time, Major Richardson had ordered a number of night patrols to conduct reconnaissance work so that a clearer picture could be built up of the enemy's positions and movements. This was dangerous work. Apart from the risk of disturbing wild animals or snakes in the dark there was always the chance that the company's patrols might encounter enemy patrols doing the same thing. The patrols were small, seven or eight men, and always led by an experienced officer. Freddy found himself out on patrol every fifth night. He debated whether to mention night patrols in his letters to Eve, but in the end decided not to as it might alarm her. Quite possibly, the company censor would have blackened out any reference to night patrols anyway.

CHAPTER THIRTY-FIVE

Eve and David

Eve and her mother got along amazingly well considering the circumstances. Some mothers might not have been so forgiving of their daughters as Annie was. After all, in the space of three years, Eve had been up on a manslaughter charge and had now given birth to a baby conceived from an adulterous relationship. However, Annie was a practical person; what had happened, had happened. Her mantra was to get on with it and make the most of any situation. This is exactly what she did when she arrived in Camberley to help her daughter with the birth and the immediate care of the baby.

Annie remained non-judgemental, rolled up her sleeves and did whatever needed to be done.

Meanwhile, Michael was oblivious to the fact that he now had a half-brother and was enjoying himself on holidays in the north of England. The young lad had been surprised to fetch up at his grandparent's house in Preston to discover that his grandmother was not there. George, his grandfather, had explained the reason for her absence was having to look after a dear friend in Surrey who needed her help until she was stronger. Not really a lie!

Grandpa George was able to wrangle a few days leave from the stonemason business where he worked and took Michael camping in the Lake District. Thankfully, July 1940 was warm and sunny and not too cold at nights which meant fewer difficulties for George with his respiratory problems. In the Lake District George introduced Michael to the art of fly fishing, something the twelve-year-old took to with enthusiasm. George's respiratory problems had gradually worsened so that any walking was laboured and long walks were out of the question. They met up with some hikers camping nearby, however, and they were delighted to have Michael accompany them on their adventures. He came back with blisters each time, but full of pride at having climbed some of the famous peaks in the Lake District such as Scafell Pike, Old Man of Coniston, Walla Crag and Helvellyn.

Halfway through the long summer holidays, Michael was whisked off by his other grandparents to stay in Bolton. The Dillons, he discovered, were extremely wealthy and spoilt him silly. They were aware, of course, that Michael's mother was having a baby from an adulterous liaison but successfully shielded him from this news. At the end of the school holidays Michael returned to Chertsey none the wiser, a little peeved perhaps that he had not seen his mother or his grandmother during the long break, but happy nevertheless. Eve's plan to avoid telling Michael the truth about the baby had worked, at least for the time being.

Eve was considered well enough to leave hospital on July 13th, six days after David was born. She returned to her little flat with her gorgeous baby boy to find her mother had everything beautifully organised. Her recovery progressed easily and David thrived on the breast and slept well. Eve was missing Freddy desperately though, so increased her letter writing from once a week to three times a week. Normally, letters took seven to ten days to reach Moyale as did the letters coming from Moyale. Like Freddy, Eve was carefully keeping every one of his letters and would sometimes pull out one of her favourite ones that she had marked with a red lipstick kiss to read again. Freddy was quite the romantic, and she found it comforting to re-visit special parts of some of his letters.

On July 15th a particularly touching letter arrived from Freddy dated July 7th, coincidentally the day David came into the world. In this letter Freddy talked at some length about the kinds of activities he would like his son or daughter to be involved in as she/he grew up. He dreamed of a life in a stone cottage in a small village somewhere. There would be three bedrooms in case they were fortunate enough to have a second child together and a decent sized garden surrounding the cottage especially for Eve. Nearby, they would have a couple of ponies for the children to learn to ride. The back garden would be for chickens as well as Eve's vegetable garden. Freddy would be in charge of the front garden where there would be daffodils, crocuses, primroses and snowdrops in spring followed by gladioli, delphiniums, hollyhocks, climbing roses and geraniums in summer. The child or children would be encouraged to develop a love of gardening and to appreciate nature with walks in the woods and fun down at the babbling brook nearby. On reading this letter Eve realised that finally, at the age of thirty-two, Freddy was ready to settle down to a happy family life and she was determined to do everything in her power to provide her part of what they both yearned.

Freddy finished his letter by expressing his love for Eve and longing to hear news of the birth of their child. He made no mention of the increasing tension felt by the soldiers of the company stationed at Moyale with the constant threat of an Italian attack.

Eve's mother stayed for two weeks after David's birth. The short-term lease on the flat in Camberley was about to expire so Annie spent a couple of those days looking around for a suitable alternative. By now Eve realised that the allowance her husband was providing was barely sufficient for herself, let alone the additional expense of bringing up a child. From the outset, Thomas had made it abundantly clear he was not paying any of the costs of bringing up a child that was not his. The measly size of Eve's bank account was testament to that. However,

Eve was comforted by the knowledge that Freddy would be supplementing her finances as soon as he had word that their baby was born. This he had promised, and she had no doubt that he would honour his commitment. Once Freddy's money started flowing, she would be comfortable again financially.

Annie found another flat that was inexpensive and in reasonable condition not far away. The address was Flat 3, 'The Firs', Roman Road, Basingstoke, Surrey. The landlady was prepared to be accepting of a small baby provided Eve didn't allow the baby to scream; not something you can ever guarantee with such a young bairn! Eve and David moved in on July 21st exactly two weeks after wee David was born. Before Annie returned to Preston, she made arrangements for Eve's mail to be forwarded on to her new address.

July 21st was a Sunday and no mail was delivered on Sundays. Eve was, however, expecting to hear again from Freddy any day now. The letter her mother had posted early on July 8th bringing the good news to Freddy that he was a father, should have arrived in Moyale sometime between July 15th and July 18th. If the mail was running smoothly, and the connections were working efficiently, she could expect to hear back from Freddy any day now. Perhaps tomorrow, Monday July 22nd? But Eve's mail now had to be forwarded on from her previous address, so it was more realistic for Freddy's next letter to reach her by Tuesday, July 23rd. Eve longed to hear from Freddy and to know that the financial arrangements they had agreed on to support David were in place. With no letter on July 23rd, Eve despondently realised she would just have to be patient for another day or two.

CHAPTER THIRTY-SIX

The Battle of Moyale

Anticipating trouble particularly around Moyale, Colonel Dillon ordered an additional two companies to the area in early June. The full strength of British forces based at the village of Moyale was now three companies, approximately 480 personnel in total. Freddy's company, which had been based in Moyale for a couple of years was now referred to as 'A' company; the others became 'B' and 'C' companies.

The map (illustration 12) shows the village of Moyale located half a mile south of the Kenyan-Ethiopian border. The British had had a continuous military presence at the Moyale outpost since 1919 when the 3rd Battalion KAR had established Fort Harrington. The wooden fort and the British troops were situated inside the British Boma, an African stockade built as a protection against wild animals. The village of Moyale itself, consisting of some twenty houses and a small church, was outside the Boma to the south-east, with several water wells nearby. The KAR troops also had to draw their water from these wells. The road that passed through the middle of Moyale continued north to the border where a small customs house was situated. Half a mile further along the road was the Italian Boma.

Shortly after the Italians declared war, 'B' company was on detachment and was camped within the British Boma. In addition to the company there was a platoon of machine gunners and a group of sappers (mine disposal experts). The village had been secretly fortified with the houses on the perimeter being reinforced with concrete and the whole village surrounded with triple Dannert barbed wire. Trenches had been dug and several pill boxes erected. There was an underground command post and a field dressing station staffed by qualified medical orderlies. Located in the village were some antiquated Lewis guns but the British did have some more advanced Boyes anti-tank rifles, four-inch mortars and grenades.

Reconnaissance patrols soon confirmed that Italian troops were present in and around the custom house just over the border. The Italians fired some mortar bombs and in the skirmish that followed Private George was wounded, the first recorded casualty of what became known as the East African

Campaign. On June 11th the Italian defences were raided from the air, while 'B' company maintained intermittent fire to entice the enemy into revealing its position. On June 12th the Italians bombed Fort Harrington. Virtually no damage was done although one man was slightly wounded. After this initial show of force by both sides an uneasy ceasefire lasted until July 1st.

On June 23rd 'B' company had been relieved and replaced by 'A' company led by Captain F.C. Drummond (Freddy). Captain Drummond settled his men into their digs quietly and smoothly and some sort of normality was soon achieved. Regular small, well-trained patrols exited the British Boma every night to explore the environs, often crossing the Kenyan border to assess enemy strength and movements. The three patrols returning in the early hours of June 27th reported 2,000 Eritreans and more than 20 light tanks had joined the Italian garrison and a further 1000 troops were on the way. Before dawn on June 28th, Fort Harrington was bombarded for an hour by shells and small arms fire.

The first serious attack on British Moyale began at dawn on July 1st. Seventy shells fell upon the fort in the first ten minutes. This bombardment was followed by an Italian infantry assault involving about a thousand troops. 'A' company stood firm and by 8.15am the attack had petered out. At 10.30am the enemy infantry attacked again, creeping forward through the bush and standing maize under cover of mortar fire. Some of these troops got within 200 yards of the British wire before withdrawing. Gun fire, mortar bombs and small-arms fire continued at intervals throughout the day. Altogether about

350 shells fell upon the fort, though many of them failed to explode and damage was slight.

When news of this sustained attack reached Colonel Dillon, 'C' company was sent forward from Buna and by 7.00am on July 2nd had made good the Moyale aerodrome. Except for some irregular shelling on both sides, a lull in the fighting occurred over the next few days. Patrols from Moyale found thousands of expended cartridges and grenade caps outside the wire. Within the fort the troops dug trenches and improved their defences. They even found time to clean out the duck pond to enjoy a somewhat muddy bathe.

On July 8th, Freddy was thrilled to get the next long letter from Eve. He spent time that evening reading and re-reading her words. It lifted his spirits hugely to hear from Eve. She said she was well, but getting huge, and she expected their baby would be arriving any day now. She reiterated her belief that it was a boy but that the sex of the child didn't worry her. What mattered was that this was Freddy's child. Freddy kissed the letter fondly, and thought he could detect Eve's perfume, before carefully placing it with the growing bundle of epistles from Eve. Knowing sometime soon he could look forward to a future with Eve and the new baby gave Freddy the hope and comfort he needed to keep going.

On July 9th, 'C' company, under Captain Henderson, moved into the fort to relieve 'A' company who were to return to the village of Fannanyatta for a few days of well-deserved rest and recreation. That night Captain Drummond ordered his company to bivouac at the foot of the escarpment since it was

Chapter Thirty-Six The Battle of Moyale

too late to proceed on to Fannanyatta. At 5.40am next morning, the Italians attacked Moyale again with far greater intensity, first with artillery and then with rifles and automatic weapons. To support their besieged colleagues, 'A' company climbed back up the escarpment to occupy the area where the village wells were located, a vital resource to have control of if they were to hold Moyale. As they neared their objective they were pinned down by heavy enemy fire.

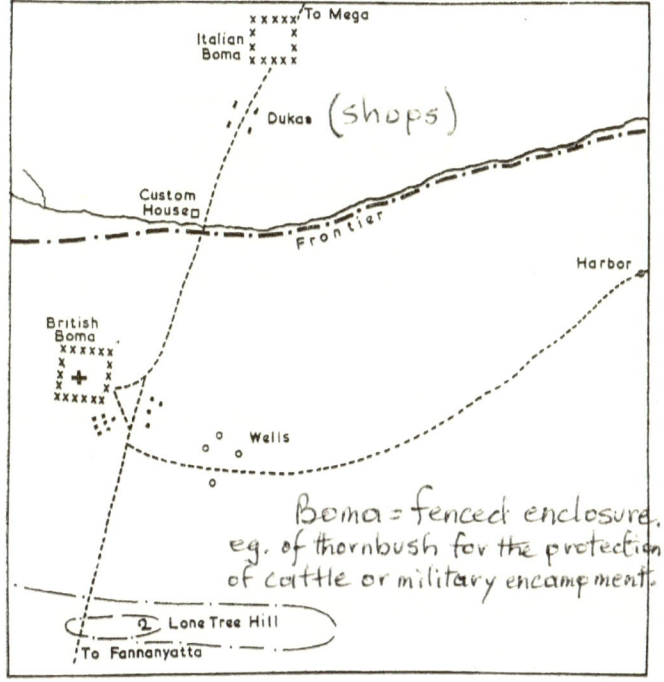

The environs of Moyale in July 1940. (Map taken from Colonel Moyse-Bartlett's book)

After about half an hour, Captain Drummond briefed his men about a proposed right flanking attack on the enemy who were still located near the village wells. As he led his men up the escarpment, Captain Drummond was wounded in the head. His colleagues were able to drag him back to relative safety where the extent of his injury was assessed. He was still alive but unconscious; the injury was horrific, a bullet having entered one side of his head and exited on the other side. There was no hope. Freddy Drummond died a few hours later and was buried in a temporary grave near where he fell. He never knew he was a father because Eve's letter bringing the news of David's birth didn't arrive until four days after he died of his wounds.

'Freddy's' temporary grave at Moyale July 10th, 1940.
(Photo taken from The Green Tiger*)*

Chapter Thirty-Six The Battle of Moyale

The loss of its commanding officer had a devastating effect on the remainder of the company. 'A' company tried again valiantly to dislodge the Italians occupying the village wells but their efforts were unsuccessful. The Italians held the high ground, had dug in and were well armed. Later in the day, 'A' company was ordered to retreat back to Fannanyatta.

The defence of Moyale lasted another six days by which time retreat was inevitable because the British forces no longer had sufficient drinking water as the Italians maintained control of the village wells and hadn't been dislodged. On July 15th an orderly night time retreat was staged and what remained of the badly damaged Fort Harrington abandoned. The British-led troops had fought bravely, but eventually succumbed to an Italian force many times larger. Since the first attack on Moyale the casualties amounted to ten killed, thirty-five wounded and nine missing in action, presumed dead.

The Italians eventually advanced into the Chalbi Desert of Kenya some 62 miles, reaching the small village of Buna where they halted. Morale, apparently, was not high, but the main constraint on any further advance was the failure to be able to guarantee and maintain efficient supply lines.

Captain Freddy Drummond's body was later recovered from Moyale and he was finally laid to rest in the Commonwealth War Graves Cemetery in Nairobi.

CHAPTER THIRTY-SEVEN

An Awful Dilemma

Wednesday, July 24th came and went and still no letter from Freddy. This was the longest time Eve had waited between letters and she was starting to worry. She had received several pieces of mail that had been forwarded from her previous address, so she knew that was not the problem. Eve was fully aware that Italy had declared war on Great Britain on July 10th and Freddy had told her it could mean trouble for the British forces defending their colonial interests in Africa. Had Italy now started a war in Africa? She had heard no mention of it on the BBC news or read anything in the papers.

The papers were full of the war in Europe which was much closer to home. If there *was* fighting in Africa it might not be considered important enough to be reported. She rang her mother in Preston who calmed her down and reassured her that a letter would probably arrive very soon.

Little David was a bundle of fun. He had lost all his birth wrinkles now and his cheeks were filling out beautifully. He was feeding well and starting to put on weight. The warm summer weather meant Eve did not have to put multiple layers of clothing on David so dressing and undressing him was not a difficult task. Her landlady was taking an interest in David too and popped in from time to time to have a cuppa and a chat and to 'goo-goo' over the baby. David responded delightfully to anyone who played with him and already had little games he liked. How she wished Freddy was with her to enjoy their baby at this magic age.

Financially, Eve was really struggling. Her allowance from Thomas barely covered the cost of the weekly rent and basic food. Rationing was in full swing and the cost of scarce food had risen frighteningly. The shortages of food meant Eve had to queue at the shops between David's feeds, a time-consuming business. Some people were understanding and encouraged her to move ahead of them in the queue. Others were not so kind! Fortunately, the shops were a short walking distance away and it was summer time. When it rained, she either had to postpone her shopping or go out and get wet. Financially, she kept telling herself, everything would improve enormously as soon as Freddy's letter arrived telling her what

Chapter Thirty-Seven An Awful Dilemma

arrangements he had made for them both and she could access the additional allowance.

The mailman came twice a day; once around ten o'clock in the morning, and then again near four in the afternoon. Finally, on July 25th the postman delivered a letter with the KAR postmark but, surprisingly, the writing on the envelope was not Freddy's. It was a letter from her husband with his distinctive, rather affected writing style. Unsure what to think, she raced back to her small flat where she sat down and tore open the envelope. David was still sleeping soundly. The letter was on official KAR writing paper and dated July 16th, 1940.

Dear Eve,

I am deeply sorry that I have some sad news to impart. Captain Frederic Drummond was killed in action on July 10th. At the time he was courageously leading his men in the defence of Moyale. He was hit by Italian sniper fire and died a few hours later.

Captain Drummond was a fine professional soldier and served the KAR with distinction.

I apologise for the delay in writing to you, however, protocol dictates that immediate family must be notified first and this I have done.

Kind regards,
Thomas Dillon (Colonel)

There is no way to describe the shock and horror that such a letter brings. Eve sat motionless for several minutes whilst the colour drained from her cheeks. Her first reaction was to refuse to believe it to be true. There must be some mistake, or perhaps, this letter was a ghastly, evil trick. She read it again. It looked like Thomas's writing and was the kind of succinct, matter-of-fact type of letter she would expect from him. Perhaps it was another soldier that had been killed or they had confused the names in some way?

David was stirring: it was nearly time for his next feed. This was the beautiful child that Freddy had given her, but now she must care for him by herself. Surely not! Freddy was going to come home and together they were going to find a lovely country cottage in a sweet little village somewhere. Freddy was so strong, so fit, so confident; he wouldn't get killed. This letter must be a hoax.

David began to whimper and, in a daze, Eve walked over and tenderly picked him up as if nothing had happened. She cuddled and kissed him, then bared her breast. As she felt David hungrily sucking, more dreadful thoughts clouded her mind. It was David's father who had died, now this poor child had only his mother left. How could she cope on her own? She had only the small allowance that Thomas was paying into her bank, scarcely enough for her to live on and certainly not enough for her and David. The extra allowance that Freddy planned to provide as soon as he heard the baby was born safely might now be in jeopardy. Hastily, Eve did the maths. David was born on July 7th and the next morning her mother had posted a letter with the wonderful news to the KAR in Marsabit where all mail went before being distributed to the outposts. But Freddy had told her several times that it took at least seven

Chapter Thirty-Seven   An Awful Dilemma

days for her letters to reach him and usually longer. If Freddy had died on July 10th there was no way he could have heard about David and arranged the finances for him.

As the awful situation she was in started to fully dawn on her, she began to softly cry. David stopped sucking and looked up at her with loving eyes as if asking what the matter was. Gently she moved him onto the other breast where he settled again happily. Eve had lost the man with whom she wished to spend the rest of her life, she had lost the remuneration he would have brought, and now she had to try to care for their baby with inadequate finances.

There was a gentle knock at the door, the knock of her landlady visiting to say 'hello' and to see little David. Eve remained seated, but called out for the kindly landlady to come in. It was obvious to the good lady, as soon as she entered, that Eve was very upset about something, so she made a cup of tea and sat down next to her. Eve needed to talk to someone and she spent the next fifteen minutes tearfully outpouring her problems to her sympathetic landlady. Eve was indeed fortunate to have such an understanding landlady who did her best to console her and offered two practical and unselfish suggestions. The first was that if she was a few days late paying her rent she would understand and the second was that living so close to London was too expensive for someone in Eve's position and a small place way out in the country would be far more appropriate.

That evening Eve rang the telephone operator to book a trunk line call to Preston asking her parents to reverse the charges. Her mother accepted the cost of the call and Eve cried through her tragic story again. Concerned for her daughter, Annie offered to come and stay, although she didn't know where she would find the money for the train fares again after exhausting their meagre savings coming to help after the birth of the baby. Bringing both Eve and David to Preston would be just as expensive, although babies in arms could travel free. Realising more train journeys were just too costly, Eve accepted she must try and manage on her own.

That night Eve eventually cried herself to sleep but not before she had thought through a few more things. Her landlady was right; there was no way she could afford to stay in her current premises. She must give her notice to the landlady and move into the country. But where would she go? She had no car and no money to catch trains or buses to look for a place to live. And who would look after David while she was trying to find somewhere?

Then there was Michael away at boarding school and totally unaware he now had a half-brother. Thomas had paid all his school fees at Chertsey until Christmas, but there were two weeks of school holidays coming up and she didn't know how she was going to collect him from school and feed a hungry twelve-year-old for a fortnight. Quite simply, there was insufficient money.

In the morning she rose feeling tired and depressed. Only a few months ago she was enjoying the kudos of being the wife of a full colonel in the King's African Rifles. She was the hostess at social occasions and regarded as an attractive and highly desirable woman by the many officers who visited. Marsabit left a lot to be desired as a location, but at least she enjoyed the services of three full-time servants and lived in relative comfort. Life now was but a shadow of what she had enjoyed in Kenya.

After giving David his early morning feed, she burped him and put him down for another sleep. Next, she found her fountain pen and some writing paper and penned a desperate pleading letter to Thomas.

Dear Thomas,

Thank you for your letter telling me of Freddy's tragic death. It goes without saying that I am heartbroken. Freddy and I had planned a life together after the war with our beautiful son, David. Freddy promised to open a generous account to cover all the additional expenses that David brings. Now, of course, that money will not be coming.

While I appreciate the allowance you have arranged for me, it's in no way sufficient to pay for the basic needs of David and myself. I am not coping financially and cannot pay my weekly rent. The landlady is being very kind and patient with me at the moment, but I must find a cheaper place in the country somewhere. Food and clothing are in short supply and now far more expensive.

Thomas, I am pleading with you to please increase my allowance so I can afford to feed and clothe David. I know you told me you were not prepared to take any interest in David, or to help pay for him, but you must realise that the situation has changed completely following Freddy's awful death.

> *I am still your wife. Please, please help me!*
>
> *Eve*
>
> *PS. Michael seems to be doing well at Chertsey. I have not yet told him about David. Sadly, I cannot afford to have him here for the school holidays. I don't know what to do.*

* * *

Eve struggled on for a few more weeks, at times missing meals in order to have money to help pay the rent. She was four weeks behind by now and the landlady was beginning to lose patience. She hadn't threatened eviction yet, but Eve sensed this might happen any day. The landlady seldom called in to see her anymore and Eve was trying to avoid meeting her in case she ordered her to leave.

Early in September the weather started to turn colder and it was harder to keep little David and herself warm. There was a coin-fed gas heater in the sitting room but she refused to use it until the weather worsened. Any spare money she used to buy another blanket for David or an extra jumper. He was growing so fast and would soon outgrow most of his garments.

When Eve went shopping, she was obliged to buy the cheapest fruit or vegetables from the greengrocer and could no longer afford to buy meat or fish. She would hurry past the butcher's window and cross the road to avoid the smell of fish emanating from the fishmongers. Fortunately, bread was still plentiful and she could buy yesterday's loaves at a reduced price. She gave up sugar and tea entirely and was able to trade these

Chapter Thirty-Seven   An Awful Dilemma

ration coupons for a bit of extra cheese or butter. Sometimes she worried that her restricted diet would affect the quality of her breast milk, but David was still thriving.

It was not uncommon for men to whistle at her when she was out shopping or taking David for a walk. She knew that some girls and women who were in a desperate plight turned to prostitution to help cover their expenses. Although not as smartly dressed, or turned out as she used to be, and devoid of any makeup, she still managed to turn heads. At thirty-two she was still attractive with her natural good looks and slim figure. With the recent shocking loss of Freddy, Eve was in no mood to start another serious relationship with a man, however.

The great joy in her life was sweet little David who gurgled and smiled happily whenever she played with him and responded delightfully to admiring strangers. Eve spent many pleasant hours entertaining him and loved him as only a mother can. David lifted her spirits when she felt down and made her feel life was worth living after all.

In the second week of September two things happened that offered some hope. First, she received an unexpected letter from her brother, George, now working as a senior engineer on Spitfires. George had done very well for himself. He had graduated with first class honours in Mechanical Engineering from the University of Manchester and was in high demand for his advanced skills and, consequently, received an attractive salary. Still single, and no girlfriend in sight, he was comfortably off. He had heard of Eve's plight and wanted to help. He enclosed a cheque, which, when banked, was sufficient to cover four weeks of Eve's back rent with a little bit left over. The landlady was delighted and the threat of eviction eased.

In the same week another letter arrived from Thomas.

Dear Eve,
I am in receipt of your letter of August 15th.

I have been granted four weeks annual leave and have timed my visit to England to coincide with Michael's school holidays. I will take care of him for the two weeks. I think it best that he doesn't meet you and David. I will refrain from telling him that you have had a baby out of wedlock! This will solve your problem about what to do for Michael.

An elderly aunt of mine died a couple of months ago and her cottage is now vacant. I will look into the possibility of you moving there temporarily, thereby saving some expenses. The cottage is in a small village near Newmarket. I'm unsure what condition the house is in but you will be able to stay there at a lower rental.

I'll be in touch again when I arrive in England. Am I able to contact you by phone?
Thomas

Thomas's letter was cold and unfriendly. There was no sign he had moderated his anger about Eve's affair and he remained aggrieved. Eve had to admit she had had two serious affairs in the space of just three years, and it would be an extraordinarily forgiving husband who would wish to remain married to such an unfaithful wife. Nevertheless, it takes two to tango,

Chapter Thirty-Seven   An Awful Dilemma

so, caught in a loveless marriage of Thomas's making, it was not surprising she had sought love elsewhere. Extraordinary, she reflected, that both men she had chosen to give herself to outside her marriage, had died from gunshot wounds.

Eve's small flat in Reigate was about thirty miles south of London. Early in September, Hitler ordered the Luftwaffe to start bombing Britain's major cities and sea ports. Night after night the German planes came over, wave after wave of them, relentlessly destroying buildings and killing thousands of civilians. Reigate, thank heavens, was too far south of London to be on the receiving end of these nights of terror, but often huge explosions could be heard and occasionally a plane in desperate trouble would come hurtling overhead before crashing nearby. Britain was throwing everything it had against the Luftwaffe for this was the Battle of Britain. Often Eve had sleepless nights listening to the sounds of war and fearing a plane would come smashing onto her flat. It was not good for Eve's nerves, and this, on top of her depression about Freddy's death and her anxiety about how she could keep going, was bringing Eve close to a complete nervous breakdown.

By late September, Eve was facing an awful dilemma: was she fit and capable enough to bring up David on her own, or should she give him up for adoption?

CHAPTER THIRTY-EIGHT

A Decision

Towards the end of September, the weather suddenly turned cold. Rain lashed against the windows of Eve's small flat and blustery northerlies kept the temperature low both day and night. Leaves quickly took on their autumnal hues and began to fall. Whenever Eve ventured out with David to do some shopping, they inevitably returned home cold and wet. Worried that David might catch a chill, Eve finally relented, putting a shilling in the gas heater's slot which was enough for one hour of warmth. In the mornings the ground was white from frost. Eve started bringing David into her bed at night so she could share her warmth with him.

Once again Eve had fallen behind with the rent, three weeks in arrears this time. By now the landlady was convinced that Eve was a deserted mother and that things would only go from bad to worse. She had not yet confronted Eve about her personal situation but had decided that if the rent was not paid by Monday, she would have to tell Eve to leave. Many people were leaving London to escape the blitz and were prepared to pay a high rental for a flat like the one Eve and David occupied. She had had a number of inquiries already.

Eve's mood was deteriorating further. Although she did everything for David, and made sure he was warm and well breast fed, she was sinking into a deeper depression. If she was to survive, she must find work of some kind, but how could she do that with David to care for? She had heard of a few mothers who took in ironing or sewing at home, but she didn't own an iron or a sewing machine. Increasingly, she found herself thinking of prostitution. The men could come to her flat and David would be none the wiser. But how could she promote herself, and if she did manage to hook a man, how would she be able to smuggle him in and out without the landlady knowing?

Her mood was not helped by Thomas's failure to materialise. He had arrived in England and he and Michael had gone off somewhere for the school holidays. He had written her another short letter.

Dear Eve.
I hope this finds you well?
Michael and I are having a most enjoyable time together and

I will get him back to Chertsey for the Christmas term on Sunday evening. He tells me he is doing well at school and sends you his love. When his school report arrives, I will send it on to you.

I have not told Michael about David. I am hoping that by the time you receive this letter you have had the boy adopted or are in the process of having this accomplished. This has been my position from the outset.

I'm afraid I will not be able to visit you in Reigate as I've been ordered to return to Marsabit early due to the deteriorating situation in Kenya. However, I have written to the Estate Agent in Newmarket who is looking after the cottage for me, and advised him not to allow any tenants in until November. If you are still interested in staying there, rent free, you will need to move there during October. I am prepared to allow you to stay there rent free until January 1st, 1941 after which date, I will expect you to start paying the full weekly rental.

The Estate Agent's address is:

John Davis Esq.

Davis, Thompson and Brooks Estate Agents,

48 The High Street,

Newmarket,

Suffolk

Hopefully, moving to the cottage in Suffolk will help alleviate your financial problems. Please notify me as soon as you have decided what you want to do.

Kind regards,

Thomas

Eve thought long and hard about Thomas's letter. A rent-free cottage in Suffolk for three months until the end of the year would be a huge help, but then from January, she would be back to paying full rental again when she had but a small allowance for an income. The rental for this cottage was probably higher than what she was currently paying for the flat. Moving to Suffolk would merely be delaying the inevitable. She simply *had* to find paid work and that was almost impossible when you have a small baby to care for.

There was a knock at the door. Eve climbed out of bed and scrambled into her dressing gown. It was ten o'clock in the morning, but recently Eve had been spending more and more time in bed trying to keep warm and because she had little incentive to get up anymore. She found she could feed and play with David in bed. Little David, sensing Eve's departure, began to whimper so Eve went back and picked him up. There was a second knock on the door. It had to be Mrs Agnew, the landlady; nobody else ever came to her door.

Eve couldn't find her slippers, so she padded over to the door in her bed socks. She opened the door a little way to find she was right; it was Mrs Agnew.

'Eve, I want to talk to you.'

Mrs Agnew didn't wait to be invited in, but exercised her right as the landlady to enter her own facility.

'You had better sit down, Eve, because I don't have good news for you.'

Eve knew what was coming. Without saying a word, she sat on the only easy chair in the flat still holding onto a

Chapter Thirty-Eight   A Decision

restless, wriggling David. Mrs Agnew remained standing, looking stern.

'Eve, I'm sorry to have to say this to you, but you are four weeks in arrears again, and I've had enough of your failure to pay the rent. Ever since you came here you have been a problem and I'm not prepared to put up with it any longer. I'll ask you one more time, do you have the money ready to pay me?'

Eve broke down. The tears and sobs coming uncontrollably. If she scrapped together what she had in her purse and the few shillings she had put aside for the heater, she might be able to pay off one week's rental but then there would be nothing left for food. Thomas's meagre allowance was simply not enough for both her and David.

Mrs Agnew was not normally a hard woman and what she was doing to Eve and David was hurting her. However, a couple of her other tenants had got wind of the fact that Eve was very slack in her rental payments and they were becoming careless too. Mrs Agnew knew she had to assert her authority and make an example of Eve. Besides, only yesterday, she had a nice elderly couple at her door pleading for a flat to rent. They said they couldn't stand the blitz any longer and even offered to pay twice the normal rent to escape the bombings. Other landladies were reporting the same phenomenon.

'Eve, I'll give you until the end of the week to move out. If you are still here on Saturday morning, I will be calling the police.'

'But I have nowhere to go. I can't live on the street, not with a baby!'

'Forgive me for being blunt, Eve, but if you have no money

you must find a job. There are lots of jobs available as a result of the war. There's an armaments factory just down the road crying out for workers.'

'Yes, I know, Mrs Agnew,' sobbed Eve, 'But I can't take a baby to work and there's nobody who can look after David for me.'

'Well dear,' said Mrs Agnew, softening a little, 'There are lots of women these days struggling with children on their own and many of them find that for the good of the child they must give them up for adoption. I know it's not my business, but have you thought of that?'

'Yes, I have,' blubbed Eve, 'I don't want to give up my beautiful boy. His father was killed and I'm on my own.' Eve broke down again. 'David is all I've got left.'

'But Eve, you can't go on like this. Something has to happen. My church is an official adoption agency. Would you like me to speak to the priest for you?'

Eve couldn't contain herself any longer and a few more minutes of sobs and moans ensued. When she had calmed down a little, she looked up at Mrs Agnew.

'Mrs Agnew, have you had children?'

'Indeed, I have, three actually,' replied Mrs Agnew, somewhat taken aback by the question.

'And did you have to give any of them up for adoption?'

'No dear.'

'Then you can have no idea what it is you are asking me to do!'

'I realise that, Eve. I just thought I'd mention it because there is a showing in ten days' time.'

'A showing?'

'Yes. There are so many babies being born out of wedlock these days, because of the war, that there is a showing once a month in the church hall. Everything is very sensitively done. If you agree to have David put up for adoption, then they will handle the official paper work for you and David will be placed in a comfortable cot along with all the other babies. Prospective parents, who have already been approved as being suitable, then come to view the little ones. If a couple selects David, they can then ask the officials for more confidential details about his background. You will need to provide this beforehand. The officials will want to interview you too.'

'Do I have to be there for the showing?'

'No, of course not. But you do need to be available nearby if further details are required. On a couple of occasions, I have been helping at a showing and I can promise you it's conducted most respectfully.'

David was becoming restless so Eve placed him gently on the floor to have a kick and a stretch.

'When do I have to make up my mind, Mrs Agnew?'

'You will need to let me know in the next couple of days so I can book David a place. If you do decide to go ahead with the adoption, I will allow you to stay an extra week rent-free. It's time we got you sorted out.' Mrs Agnew gave a sympathetic smile.

'Thank you,' mumbled Eve, 'I'll let you know.'

Mrs Agnew left quietly. Talking to Eve about adoption had not been easy, but she was sure adoption was really the only sensible option available to Eve. No income, no job and no husband made for a terrible and insurmountable trifecta.

That night, Eve rang her parents again by reversing the charges. She was surprised to hear matters at home were not good either. Her father had finally succumbed to the violent coughing which had been steadily worsening over the years and had just retired from his job as a stonemason. The doctor had said he had diseased lungs from the dust he had inhaled for many years at his workplace and declared George no longer fit for work. Her father was not bedridden, but apparently sat about all day, wheezing and essentially reliant on his wife for all his needs.

Once Eve had empathised with her mother about her father's condition, she poured out her own woes ending up by admitting that she was seriously thinking that David would be better off with a couple who had a home and the wherewithal to look after him properly. To Eve's amazement her mother instantly agreed and said she had been worrying about her ever since David came into this world three months ago. Her mother went on to say that Eve's siblings would not be able to help her. Bell and her husband were caring for four children and George was a confirmed bachelor with a top job designing war planes for the war office and had no time, or interest, in helping to look after a baby. Adoption, her mother urged, was definitely the right thing to do.

Next morning, Eve tapped lightly on Mrs Agnew's door and asked her to book David in for a showing.

CHAPTER THIRTY-NINE

The Showing

Eve felt a huge sense of relief after telling Mrs Agnew she wanted to proceed with David's adoption. Baby David would, hopefully, now find a loving home and his needs would be well cared for, which was by far the most important consideration for Eve. She was sure that if Freddy was watching from above, he would agree.

The mechanics of the adoption process, she discovered, were remarkably simple, eased by the fact that so many children were urgently in need of adoption nowadays. Courting couples faced with the distinct possibility that the man might not return from active war service, often threw caution to the wind and enjoyed sexual relations, in some cases without taking the necessary precautions. Thousands of married servicemen were dying in action and frequently left their wives with an extra baby to care for and insufficient means to do so. Then there were the children orphaned in the continuing blitz of London and other major cities. War had the effect of encouraging promiscuity amongst the unmarried and the abandonment of responsibility amongst those in wedlock. Towards the end of 1940 there was a massive surge in the number of babies up for adoption across the nation. They were sometimes referred to as 'the war babies.'

Eve was first asked to take David to visit the Catholic priest at Mrs Agnew's local church. At Eve's request, Mrs Agnew agreed to accompany her.

It was a miserable rainy day as the three of them hurried towards the church vestibule, crowding and jostling each other under Mrs Agnew's large dripping black umbrella. An icy wind was blowing and Eve snuggled David in as close to her body as possible. The wet pavements shone with the reflections of the lights of the passing cars, and despite taking care, they seemed to tread in far too many puddles. Eve had made an effort to look more presentable and had applied the last of her lipstick and taken extra trouble with her hair.

Once inside the church, they shook themselves out and deposited the dripping umbrella in the rack provided. The priest was waiting and ushered them into a small heated office that felt snug and welcoming after the inclement weather

Chapter Thirty-Nine The Showing

outside. After closing the door, the priest sat himself down behind a large wooden desk. Attached to the wall behind him was a modest cross and a coloured photograph of the pope. He gestured to the ladies to sit on the two straight-backed chairs available.

'Good morning ladies. A horrid day is it not?' he asked, looking from one to the other.

Rather than comment on the nasty weather, Mrs Agnew thought it best to introduce Eve.

'Father Cedric, may I introduce Mrs Dillon?' The priest stood again and extended a large warm hand to Eve who reciprocated.

'Welcome to St Francis of Assisi, Mrs Dillon. Mrs Agnew has long been a faithful parishioner here, indeed, she has sometimes assisted at our recent adoption showings.' Father Cedric beamed generously and appreciatively at his faithful parishioner.

Turning to look at Eve, the priest continued, 'Now, I understand from Mrs Agnew that you are considering giving this baby up for adoption? Is that correct?'

'Yes, Father.'

'Adoption is a very big step to take, Mrs Dillon. Please forgive me, but I need first to ask you some personal questions?'

'That's all right, Father.'

'Are you a member of the Roman Catholic faith, Mrs Dillon?'

'Yes, I am, but I'm afraid I don't attend mass very often.' This was news to Mrs Agnew, who, had she known this, would have tried to bring Eve and David along to mass on Sundays.

Father Cedric was not unduly disturbed to hear this;

increasingly he was encountering younger people these days who had strayed from their religious beliefs.

'Mrs Dillon, I need to ask what Mr Dillon would think about having this beautiful child adopted?' Father Cedric had chosen his words carefully for he was not sure whether there was actually a 'Mr Dillon'; so many young men were being killed or maimed in the war.

Eve was able to honestly reply, 'He is most anxious that David be adopted, Father.'

'Forgive me for asking, Mrs Dillon, but is your husband living with you?'

'No Father, he is serving with the King's African Rifles based in Kenya.'

Father Cedric raised a bushy eyebrow; something wasn't making complete sense here. He had to probe further.

'Mrs Dillon, is Mr Dillon the father of this child?'

Eve broke down and started fumbling for her handkerchief. 'No...' was all she managed.

The priest allowed Eve to recover a little before continuing.

'Before this child can be accepted for adoption, I have to know who the father is Mrs Dillon, and whether he also gives his approval?'

'He's dead,' Eve blurted out and buried her face in her handkerchief, 'David has no father. I've got no money and I can't get a job.' She looked up at the priest with teary eyes.

'I'm so sorry,' Father Cedric replied gently. It was clear to the priest that this woman needed help and that the adoption of her baby was possibly the best thing that could happen for

Chapter Thirty-Nine The Showing

her. He waited a moment or two for Mrs Dillon to recover her demeanour before resuming.

'I'm sorry,' he repeated and then went on, 'We will be having a showing of the little ones who are up for adoption next Saturday. Would you like David to be there?'

'No, I don't want to lose him,' Eve wailed, 'I love him so much.' Again, Eve lost control and sobbed. After a moment or two she gathered herself together and in a low, subdued voice said, 'Because I love him so much, I want him to go to a good home that I can't provide at present.'

'Then let me explain to you, Mrs Dillon, what we need to do.' He felt for this distressed woman and wished he could take her in his arms to comfort her.

'Yes, please,' Eve blurted out.

'I have the necessary forms here and we can fill them in now if you wish? Mrs Agnew might even be prepared to be your witness?' He looked inquiringly at the older lady who confirmed her willingness.

'We are an official adoption agency so you have no worries in that regard,' and he smiled kindly at Eve.

Eve nodded her assent.

'Before next Saturday it will be necessary for David to be assessed by a doctor as being fit and well. You will need to ask the doctor to give you a Medical Adoption Certificate that I will need to have before Saturday. David cannot be adopted without this certificate.'

'But I don't have the money to pay for a visit to a doctor,' pleaded Eve.

'That's all right. A visit to a doctor for a full medical examination for the adoption of a child is a free visit and so is the certificate he will give you,' Father Cedric assured her.

'I can book you an appointment with my doctor if you like?' Mrs Agnew intervened.

'The showing is for one hour only and takes place between 2.00pm and 3.00pm next Saturday. David will be placed in one of our cots along with the cots of the other babies to be adopted. At this stage, it looks as though there will be eight other children. Please have David here by ten minutes to two along with anything that he may like to play with. If he has had a feed just before arriving and is fast asleep that would be marvellous. You must also bring along a suitcase with his clothes, nappies, bunny rug and any toys you want him to take with him.'

Eve nodded again and Father Cedric continued. 'Only two pieces of information will be placed on his cot for the potential adopting parents to view, his name and the occupation of the father. May I ask what your husband's occupation is, please?'

'He's an army officer.'

'And the child's natural father?'

'He was an army officer also.'

'Thank you, Mrs Dillon. On Saturday you will be required to stay in another room and must on no account enter the room where the children are being viewed. Is that quite clear? There will be a policeman present to see that these strict instructions are complied with. If David is not selected this time, and that sometimes happens, you will be required to take David home

Chapter Thirty-Nine The Showing

and you may present him for the next showing in a month's time. Does that all make sense?'

'Yes, thank you, Father,' Eve whispered.

'Now, do you have any questions, Mrs Dillon?'

'One please, Father. Will I meet, or know, who has adopted David?'

'No, you will never know. It's against the law for you to know who has taken David, and it's against the law for you to ever try to find out who has him, or where he is living.'

'That seems terribly harsh, Father. It's only natural for me as his mother to want to know that David is being loved and cared for.'

'Yes, I realise that Mrs Dillon, but put yourself in the shoes of the adopting parents for a minute. David will become their son, legally and in every other way except that he is not naturally born to them. Understandably, you, as David's natural mother, will want to know how he's doing but you would only get in the way of a new relationship that is developing. Experience over many years tells us that allowing the natural parents access to their adopted child ends up in disaster for everyone concerned. On the form we are going to complete, you must promise *never* to even try to find out anything about David's future life. If you don't think you can do that, then you must not put David up for adoption. I cannot stress this too strongly, Mrs Dillon.'

Eve nodded again. 'I see,' was all she said.

'Now, how about a hot cup of tea?' Father Cedric asked, in an attempt to lighten the mood.

*   *   *

David played on the floor with a colourful rattle while the three adults completed the necessary paperwork.

It was just starting to get dark when they left and it felt cold enough for snow. On their way home they passed the surgery of Mrs Agnew's doctor so Mrs Agnew suggested they call in quickly to book David in for his medical the next day.

After a thorough examination, the doctor gave David an A1 for his health. He happily signed the all-important Adoption Certificate, and handed it to Eve.

Eve, Mrs Agnew, and little David, sallied forth just after one-thirty on Saturday and were at St Francis of Assisi in good time. It was October 7th, 1940 and David was exactly three months old.

Before they left, Eve had put David on the breast and he had fed well. He was ready for an afternoon sleep when she put him down, possibly for the last time, into cot number seven which had a simple notice at the end of the cot that read:

NAME: DAVID

FATHER'S OCCUPATION: ARMY OFFICER

Then, in the company of Mrs Agnew, Eve retired to the room assigned to them where there was a kindly lady with a large silver teapot dispensing cups of tea and encouraging the distressed visitors to try her homemade shortbreads.

The hour locked up in that room stretched on forever with Eve walking up and down and unable to sit. She barely noticed the others in the room, some quietly crying, others sitting silently looking blank.

Chapter Thirty-Nine The Showing

Eventually, the door opened and Father Cedric appeared together with another priest. The two priests started by calling for the mothers of the babies in cots one and two who then followed the priests out. Then the mothers of cots three and four left the room, next five and six until at last the mothers of cots seven and eight were called. Eve and Mrs Agnew returned to the same small office where they had met Father Cedric before.

The conversation was brief. Father Cedric was pleased to advise that David had gone to a new home. He disclosed one piece of information only: the adopting father was also an army officer. Then he asked Eve and Mrs Agnew if they would like to join him in a prayer for David and his new parents. They did.

Mrs Agnew invited Eve to join her and her husband for dinner that night.

* * *

Next day, Eve sat down and wrote to Thomas to tell him that David had been adopted and she wished to take up his offer to move into his aunt's cottage in Suffolk. She wrote also to her parents with the same news. A third letter went to Michael to give him her new address in Suffolk.

Michael still had no idea that his mother had had a baby and he didn't find out until sixty years later when, incredibly, out of the blue, his half-brother, David, made contact with him.

EPILOGUE

The little boy that Eve gave away on October 7th, 1940 is the author of this book. The adopting parents were Major and Mrs Roberts who loved and cared for me as their own. Brought up as an only child, I loved boarding school life, enjoyed a normal education and qualified as a teacher before migrating to Australia in September 1962.

Eve's brother, George, had a week's leave and drove down to Reigate on Monday to spend the week taking Eve to the cottage in Suffolk and getting her settled there. The cottage was somewhat neglected, as the elderly aunt had let things slip, nevertheless it was a godsend for Eve. She had a roof over her head and two months to find work to have enough money coming in to start paying rental that was first due to be paid from January 1st, 1941.

Naturally, Eve was depressed and angry about her and David's sorry situation. The grieving process lasted a long time and only slowly relented. Like any mother who surrenders a child, Eve must have wondered countless times what became of her little boy. She kept her promise, however, and never once tried to find me. I know this on good authority.

Rather than allow her depression to take over, Eve threw herself into working with the Women's Land Army. Most of the young women with the WLA were between the ages of 17 and 25 so Eve was considered a veteran. Nevertheless, she rolled up her sleeves and worked hard physically for the remainder of the war. By the end of hostilities in 1945 there were over 80,000 women providing around 70% of the nation's agricultural products and doing almost all the farm jobs that men normally did.

Eve was fortunate in that she was able to remain in her cottage, *'Oakhouse,'* in the small village of Lidgate, and spent the years until 1945 working on the same neighbouring farm that was but half a mile down the lane. The farmer was serving on a destroyer and his capable wife took charge of the operation. She and Eve hit it off and became trusted and lasting friends. The government paid members of the WLA a small salary and this, supplemented by Thomas's continuing allowance, was enough for her to manage.

After the war, the colonel eventually purchased *Oakhouse* for Eve for 685 pounds. She stayed there for many years until her son, Michael, purchased the house, modernised it, and sold it for a handsome profit. After the sale, Eve moved to number 1 Cropley Grove in the nearby village of Ousden. She died there in 1987 at the age of 79, seven years before I tried to find her.

The author conducted extensive family research in England in 1994. Speaking with villagers who knew Eve when she lived in Ousden provided a few interesting facts. Always 'the lady', Eve was well liked in the district and frequented the local pub where she was at one time the champion at dominoes. A staunch conservative throughout her life, she was a voluntary worker for the party at elections and fundraising events. She remained an enthusiastic gardener and sometimes entered exhibits at the local gardening and village shows. It seems she remained a nominal Catholic only.

There is no record of Eve having any more serious romantic attachments. She certainly never re-married. Those who knew Eve well were aware she had surrendered a child for adoption and that she had another son, Michael, who rarely visited his mother.

Colonel Thomas Dillon served the KAR with distinction for the remainder of the war and retired from the army in 1946 when he was 54 years old. He spent his retirement in the genteel town of Hove on the English south coast and never condoned a divorce from Eve.

Michael Dillon followed in his father's footsteps and entered the Royal Military College Sandhurst in 1946 and saw active service in the Korean War (1951-1953). He left the army as a captain and worked for Shell and then in Malaysia as a manager for Guthrie's Rubber. He returned a reasonably wealthy man and eventually retired with his wife to live in the Isle of Man (a tax haven). They had no children.

It was while I was in England in 1994 that I broke the news to Michael that I was his half-brother. Initially, he thought I was a fraudster after his money, but I was able to convince him otherwise. Eventually, he confided that he got along well with his father but didn't have a lot of time for his mother, Eve. He described her as 'flirtatious' and he was not surprised she had had a baby out of wedlock, although he never knew about it. It was Michael who identified a Captain Drummond, who taught him rugby, and always seemed to be hanging around his mother in Marsabit. DNA testing has since proved that Captain Drummond was indeed my father.

Interestingly, Kenton College Preparatory school for boys in Nairobi, where Michael was educated whilst living in Kenya, is still a thriving educational establishment today (2021). After the war, the KAR downsized and moved their headquarters out of the school. The school, founded in 1935, still occupies the original site consisting of 35 acres in the suburb of Kileleshwa, five kilometres from the city centre. Today the school is co-educational and rugby remains one of the sports on the curriculum.

ACKNOWLEDGEMENTS

I'd like to acknowledge a number of people and resources that were helpful in the writing of this historical novel.

A special thank you goes to Dorothy Livesey, a remarkable English lady, who voluntarily assisted me with my family research into Eve's background. It was she who unearthed the extraordinary incident that occurred at the Pull Woods boathouse on Christmas day 1937.

The reporting of Eve's manslaughter charge was well covered by numerous editions of *The Lancashire Daily Post* from December 1937 to January 1938.

A further acknowledgement goes to 'Ted' Knights for

information about Eve's later life in Lidgate and Ousden and the superb photograph that appears on the cover of this book.

Michael Dillon (half-brother) provided some of the photographs and valuable background information about Eve and Colonel Dillon. Crucially, Michael was also able to recall a captain (Freddy) who frequently visited his home in Kenya during 1939.

Fred Drummond (a first cousin) assisted with some valuable background information about the Drummond family and kindly agreed to undertake DNA testing, thereby proving that Captain Frederic (Freddy) Drummond was, in fact, my biological father. Interestingly, Fred Drummond had been so named in memory of Captain Freddy Drummond who had died of his wounds only six years earlier.

To better comprehend what it was like to serve as a British officer in the KAR during 1939-1940, I lent heavily on John Nunneley's excellent book entitled *Tales from the King's African Rifles* published in 1998.

The detailed description of the Battle of Moyale was taken from the scholarly work of Colonel Moyse-Bartlett, who in 1956, published *The King's African Rifles: A Study in the Military History of East and Central Africa, 1890-1945*.

A couple of the photographs and some helpful background reading about Captain Freddy Drummond were gleaned from many editions of *The Green Tiger 1928-1940*. *The Green Tiger* was the quarterly magazine of the Royal Leicestershire Regiment. Freddy was on secondment to the KAR from this regiment. My thanks to the staff at the Territorial Army Centre in Leicester who kindly allowed me to use their premises for a week as I laboured through many copies of *The Green Tiger*.

I am indebted to the Army Personnel Centre, Historic Disclosures, Glasgow, for supplying me with photographs of Freddy and full details of his military service record.

I am more than grateful for the help of my publisher, Sid Harta Publishers, my editor, Kristen Rohde, and Luke Harris, Working Type Studio. Together, they have successfully guided me through four books.

Finally, a huge 'thank you' to members of my family who have assisted along the way in too many ways to mention.

www.ingramcontent.com/pod-product-compliance
Lightning Source LLC
Chambersburg PA
CBHW021137080526
44588CB00008B/96